Oxford Studies in European Law

General Editors: Paul Craig and Gráinne de Búrca

JUDICIAL CONTROL IN THE EUROPEAN UNION

Judicial Control in the European Union:

Reforming Jurisdiction in the Intergovernmental Pillars

ALICIA HINAREJOS

OXFORD
UNIVERSITY PRESS

OXFORD
UNIVERSITY PRESS

Great Clarendon Street, Oxford OX2 6DP

Oxford University Press is a department of the University of Oxford.
It furthers the University's objective of excellence in research, scholarship,
and education by publishing worldwide in

Oxford New York

Auckland Cape Town Dar es Salaam Hong Kong Karachi
Kuala Lumpur Madrid Melbourne Mexico City Nairobi
New Delhi Shanghai Taipei Toronto

With offices in

Argentina Austria Brazil Chile Czech Republic France Greece
Guatemala Hungary Italy Japan Poland Portugal Singapore
South Korea Switzerland Thailand Turkey Ukraine Vietnam

Oxford is a registered trade mark of Oxford University Press
in the UK and in certain other countries

Published in the United States
by Oxford University Press Inc., New York

© Alicia Hinarejos, 2009

The moral rights of the author have been asserted
Database right Oxford University Press (maker)

Crown copyright material is reproduced under Class Licence
Number C01P0000148 with the permission of OPSI
and the Queen's Printer for Scotland

First published 2009

British Library Cataloguing in Publication Data

Data available

Library of Congress Cataloging in Publication Data

Hinarejos Parga, Alicia, 1979-
  Judicial control in the European Union: reforming jurisdiction in the intergovernmental pillars / Alicia
Hinarejos.
    p. cm.
  Includes bibliographical references and index.
  ISBN 978-0-19-956996-0
1. Constitutional courts—European Union countries. 2. Judicial power—European Union countries.
3. Political questions and judicial power—European Union countries. 4. Court of Justice of the European
Communities I. Title.
  KJE5461.H56 2009
  347.24'035—dc22
                                                                                                2009038350

Typeset by MPS Limited, A Macmillan Company
Printed in Great Britain
on acid-free paper by the
MPG Books Group, Bodmin and King's Lynn

ISBN 978-0-19-956996-0

1 3 5 7 9 10 8 6 4 2

ACKNOWLEDGMENTS

While preparing this monograph I was a British Academy Postdoctoral Fellow at the Faculty of Law, University of Oxford, and a research fellow of Brasenose College and the Institute of European and Comparative Law, also at Oxford. I am very grateful to these institutions for their support, as well as to the European University Institute, Florence, for welcoming me as a Max Weber visiting fellow.

This book is based on a thesis accepted for the degree of DPhil at the University of Oxford in 2008. I am grateful to my examiners, Anthony Arnull and Derrick Wyatt, for comments and advice that greatly improved the manuscript. I am especially indebted, however, to my mentor and supervisor Stephen Weatherill: his guidance, time, and kindness were essential in writing both the DPhil thesis and this monograph.

Others, too, have helped with discussion, written comments or suggestions. Among them, I would like to thank John Bell, Vernon Bogdanor, Damian Chalmers, Cathryn Costello, Paul Craig, Marise Cremona, Michael Dougan, Christina Eckes, Barbara Havelkova, Ester Herlin-Karnell, Jeff King, Jan Komárek, Adam Lazowski, Dorota Leczykiewicz, Vanessa Mak, Daniel Sarmiento, Takis Tridimas, Maria Tzanou, Bruno de Witte, Katja Ziegler, and two anonymous referees for OUP.

My greatest debt of gratitude, however, is to those who are closest to me. This book would not have seen the light without the loving support of my family and of my very patient husband Michael: it is only fair that it should be dedicated to them.

AHP

CONTENTS

TABLE OF CASES

EUROPEAN COURT OF JUSTICE

COURT OF FIRST INSTANCE

EUROPEAN COURT OF HUMAN RIGHTS

PERMANENT COURT OF INTERNATIONAL JUSTICE

NATIONAL JURISDICTIONS

Germany

France

USA

Italy

UK

Ireland

Denmark

Poland

Czech Republic

Cyprus

Introduction: The ECJ as a Federal Constitutional Court

This is a study of the jurisdiction of the European Court of Justice (ECJ) in two particular areas of activity of the European Union: the Area of Freedom, Security, and Justice (AFSJ) and the Common Foreign and Security Policy (CFSP). Before focusing on specific areas of its jurisdiction, however, it may be useful to reflect on the nature of the Court of Justice's role. Some of the Court's functions may be described as those of a national supreme court (ensuring the uniform application by lower courts of civil, criminal, or administrative law) and others as those of a constitutional court (building a coherent legal system, ensuring the vertical as well as horizontal division of powers, and protecting individual rights).[1] This monograph will focus on those aspects of the role of the Court that liken it to the constitutional court of a federal legal system.[2] Accordingly, any considerations on the Court's jurisdiction and its role within the legal system of the European Union are best placed in the context of the general discussion on constitutional adjudication and the problems it raises. With

---

[1] Although, as Lenaerts notes, there are also constitutional aspects to the Court's role as a supreme court, since divergent application of EC law would run counter to the objectives set out in the Treaties: K Lenaerts, 'The Rule of Law and the Coherence of the Judicial System of the European Union' (2007) 44 CML Rev 1625, 1651–2; see also V Skouris, 'The Position of the European Court of Justice in the EU Legal Order and its Relationship with National Constitutional Courts' (2005) 60 Zeitschrift für Öffentliches Recht 323. Finally, bear in mind that all functions may be fulfilled through a single channel, ie, the preliminary reference procedure, which makes the distinction difficult in practice.

[2] There is widespread agreement in the literature that the Court may be considered a constitutional court: A Dashwood and A Johnston, 'Synthesis of the Debate' in A Dashwood and A Johnston (eds), *The Future of the Judicial System of the European Union* (Hart: Oxford, 2001) 59. For a comprehensive review of the literature on this point, see M Claes, *The National Courts' Mandate in the European Constitution* (Hart: Oxford, 2006) 399 and ff.

this intention, the first section will provide a broad-brush overview of the different models of constitutional review, before focusing on the ECJ itself, its creation and posterior evolution into a constitutional adjudicator of sorts. The final section will shed light on the choice of two specific areas of the jurisdiction of the Court as the object of this study.

1.1 The Context: Models of Constitutional Review

Constitutional adjudication is a global phenomenon. In 1803, the US Supreme Court declared a statute unconstitutional in the case of *Marbury v Madison*, generally hailed in the literature as the beginning of judicial review;[3] since then, the principle of constitutional review has been accepted as a feature of most democratic legal systems. The US and European models of constitutional review do, however, differ substantially: while all US courts can carry out such review, this function is normally reserved in European legal systems for a special constitutional court (where it is allowed at all).[4] A distinction has therefore been drawn in the literature between a centralized and a decentralized model of constitutional review.[5]

In the classic European model, the judiciary can be divided into two main branches: ordinary courts, on the one hand, and a constitutional court, on the other. Whereas ordinary courts are entrusted with the 'ordinary judicial function', or applying the law to decide specific cases, the constitutional court is entrusted with the 'constitutional function', or reviewing the compatibility of legislation with the constitution. The decentralized nature of the American model means that a single judicial branch is entrusted with both functions.[6] Furthermore, review in the American model is concrete, in

[3] *Marbury v Madison* 5 US 137 (1803). But see also WM Treanor, 'Judicial Review before Marbury' (2005) 58 Stanford L Rev 455.
[4] M Shapiro and A Stone, 'Introduction: The New Constitutional Politics' (1994) 26 Comparative Political Studies 397, 400; L Favoreu, 'Le Droit Constitutionnel, Droit de la Constitution et Constitution du Droit' (1990) 1 Revue Française de Droit Constitutionnel 71. But see eg the 'conventionality control' exercised by ordinary courts in France: O Beaud, 'Reframing a Debate Among Americans: Contextualizing a Moral Philosophy of Law' (2009) 7 I-CON 53, 60.
[5] V Ferreres Comella, 'The Consequences of Centralizing Constitutional Review in a Special Court: Some Thoughts on Judicial Activism' (2004) 82 Texas L Rev 1705. Ferreres Comella has also distinguished between more and less rigid centralized models: the less rigid a centralized model is, the more it approaches the American or decentralized model: ibid, 1706–11.
[6] Ibid, 1706.

the sense that courts only decide on the constitutionality of a law as it applies to the specific facts of an actual controversy, whereas review is to a large extent abstract in the classic European model: the constitutional court does not decide on the substance of specific cases, in accordance with the separation of competences already outlined.[7]

The protection of constitutional rights was one of the aims of judicial review in the US model since its origins.[8] Yet the same cannot be said of the European model of constitutional review, the roots of which can be found in the constitutional court of the First Austrian Republic,[9] the brainchild of Hans Kelsen. The Kelsenian model of constitutional review sought to avoid the creation of a Government of judges by clearly distinguishing between positive and negative legislating: while Parliament could legislate freely, in a creative manner (positive legislating), the constitutional court could only apply the constitution and strike down legislation which did not comply with it (negative legislating).[10] Kelsen argued forcefully that the principle of separation of powers could only be respected if constitutional courts were not allowed to become positive legislators. To this end, the constitution must be a positive body of higher norms that merely lay down how the legal system is organized, but cannot include a list of constitutional rights. The reason for this is that rights provisions are vague, open to interpretation, and value-laden: if a constitutional court has to interpret rights provisions, it is likely to become politicized and to start legislating in a positive manner, thereby usurping a task that belongs rightfully to Parliament.[11]

---

[7] For a comparison, M Rosenfeld, 'Constitutional Adjudication in Europe and the United States: Paradoxes and Contrasts' (2004) 2 I-CON 633; J Ferejohn and P Pasquino, 'Constitutional Adjudication: Lessons from Europe' (2004) 82 Texas L Rev 1671.

[8] Since the main corpus of individual rights was included in the Constitution early on in the form of the Bill of Rights. For a brief overview: AT von Mehren and PL Murray, *Law in the United States* (2nd edn, Cambridge University Press: Cambridge, 2007) 146–9.

[9] 1920–34. A Stone-Sweet, *Governing with Judges* (OUP: Oxford, 2000) 34.

[10] For a more encompassing historical introduction, see M Shapiro and A Stone, 'Introduction: The New Constitutional Politics' (1994) 26 Comparative Political Studies 397, 400–3.

[11] For a more general overview: H Kelsen, 'Judicial Review of Legislation: A Comparative Study of the Austrian and American Constitution' (1942) 4 The Journal of Politics 183; H Kelsen, 'La Garantie juridictionnelle de la Constitution' (1928) 44 Revue du Droit Public 197. It can be argued that this is not the only way in which a constitutional court may usurp the legislator's legitimate role: even if the constitution contains no 'dangerous' rights provisions, the constitutional court may not act only as a negative legislator—by merely saying no to the legislator—but may amend legislation, commanding the legislator to behave in a certain way: A Stone-Sweet, *Governing with Judges* (OUP: Oxford, 2000) 135.

Later developments, however, set a very different trend. There have been two waves in Europe whereby appreciation of the damaging effect of arbitrary and poorly controlled state power generated a strong momentum for rights protection: firstly, post-1945, in Western Europe; and secondly, post-1989, in Central and Eastern Europe. Fundamental rights were thus embedded in national constitutions, and powerful constitutional courts emerged with the mandate to protect those rights and, in general, supervise state power. The protection of constitutional rights is, nowadays, an integral part of constitutional adjudication across the globe.

It is in this context that the role of the European Court of Justice is better understood: the European Union has a federal judicial system with a mixed model of constitutional adjudication (partly centralized and partly decentralized, as will be explained below). At the apex of this federal judicial network sits the ECJ, a court that may be comparable to a young US Supreme Court in some respects,[12] but that has unavoidably acquired the most prominent features of a European constitutional court. The how and why of this evolution will be explored in the following section.

1.2 The ECJ as a Federal Constitutional Court

One of the premises of this book is that the European Court of Justice acts as a federal constitutional court of sorts: there is a Constitutional Charter of the European Union,[13] and the European Court of Justice can be considered its ultimate interpreter and guarantor,[14] ultimately able to declare legislation unconstitutional if necessary. Furthermore, given the federal features of the judicial system of the EU, the Court's tasks best resemble those of the highest court in a federal system. The aim of this section is to briefly describe how this evolution has taken place.

[12] For a general comparison, see eg M Rosenfeld, 'Comparing Constitutional Review by the European Court of Justice and the US Supreme Court' (2006) 4 I-CON 618.

[13] See eg Opinion 1/91 *Draft agreement between the Community, on the one hand, and the countries of the European Free Trade Association, on the other, relating to the creation of the European Economic Area* [1991] ECR I-6079 [1]. The Court itself uses the language of a Constitutional Charter, and so by implication labels itself a constitutional court.

[14] Art 220 EC, first para: 'The Court of Justice and the Court of First Instance, each within its jurisdiction, shall ensure that in the interpretation and application of this Treaty the law is observed.' In the Court's own words, it 'carries out tasks which, in the legal systems of the Member States are those of the constitutional courts, the courts of general jurisdiction or the administrative tribunals as the case may be': CJEC Annual Report, 'Report of the Court of Justice on Certain Aspects of the Application of the Treaty on European Union' (1995).

The ECJ was created as a supranational court, integral to the European Community project. The establishment of this sort of court at a supranational level follows a similar logic to that of any other court: individuals rely on an impartial third party to solve controversies and ensure compliance with a pre-agreed set of rules.[15] In this particular case, Member States decided to establish a third-party institution that would ensure that the other parties to the agreement would comply with it, even if it meant that they themselves would be held to comply with it too;[16] this was necessary for the long-term commitments undertaken pursuant to the Treaties to be credible. Because of the characteristics of the Treaty system it was supposed to guard—a polity with an areal division of powers between the central government and a number of constituent governments—the first and foremost function of the European Court would be to ensure the correct balance of powers between the central power and the peripheral ones.[17] Following the dynamics that have affected all European systems of constitutional review, and which have been described above, the European Court of Justice slowly transformed, however, into not only a decider of boundary conflicts between powers, but also a guarantor of constitutional rights.

Consider first the way in which the ECJ comes to see the protection of fundamental rights as part of its remit. Fundamental rights were not mentioned in the founding Treaties and, initially, the Court resisted attempts to be transformed into a guarantor of fundamental rights.[18] Finally, though, the necessities of collaboration with national judiciaries proved too much: the European Court of Justice had to adjust its position to what national constitutional courts expected of it, that is, to the European model of a constitutional court. We must not forget that the judicial system of the Community rests upon the respect that national courts are willing to grant to the Court of Justice and this, in turn, rests upon their conception of what the proper role of the Court of Justice as a constitutional court should be. In this case, the ECJ was conditioned by the willingness of national constitutional courts to step in to secure protection of

---

[15] See generally M Shapiro, *Courts. A Comparative and Political Analysis* (University of Chicago Press: Chicago, 1981) ch 1; A Stone-Sweet, *Governing with Judges* (OUP: Oxford, 2000) 13–17.

[16] This is the second-best strategic possibility: the best one would be making everyone else comply without having to comply oneself: M Shapiro, 'The European Court of Justice' in P Craig and G De Búrca (eds), *The Evolution of EU Law* (OUP: Oxford, 1999) 321–2.

[17] Ibid, 321.

[18] See eg Case 1/58 *Stork v High Authority* [1959] ECR 17; Case 40/64 *Sgarlata and others v Commission EEC* [1965] ECR 279.

fundamental rights, should they conclude that the ECJ's approach is wanting.[19] This distinctive dialogue coined the development of the role of the Court of Justice within the EC judicial system. As a result, the Court had to execute a double twist by introducing human rights into the Constitutional Charter of the Community, first, and by declaring itself competent to review the compatibility of legislation with these constitutional rights, second.[20] To the extent that it was the Court itself that had to introduce rights into the constitution, this double manoeuvre was decidedly remarkable.

The protection of classic fundamental rights, although an extremely important milestone in the development of the ECJ as a constitutional court, is by far not the only function that has allowed it to grow into its current role. The Court has further used the language of individual rights to legitimize and provide a basis for the developing federal legal system in place,[21] only this time referring to EC rights, or rights contained in binding EC legislation, be it primary or secondary.[22] By using the language of rights to develop the legal system of the EC, the Court managed to intertwine its two main functions (to protect rights and to develop a coherent base for a young legal system) even further.

It has been recognized as a common pattern that constitutional courts tend to empower the central level of government while federal systems are still young.[23] The ECJ has not been an exception to this rule. And, as Ward convincingly shows, the notion of 'individual rights' (together with that of

---

[19] Such willingness was, for instance, expressed by the German and Italian Constitutional Courts in: BVerfGE 37, 271 *Internationale Handelsgesellschaft v Einfuhr und Vorratsstelle für Getreide und Futtermittel (Solange I)* [1974] 2 CMLR 540; BVerfGE 73, 339 *re the application of Wünsche Handelsgesellschaft (Solange II)* [1987] 3 CMLR 225; *Frontini v Ministero delle Finanze (Case 183)* [1974] 2 CMLR 372; *Corte Constituzionale, 21 Aprile 1989 n. 232 - Pres. Conso; red. Ferri - S.p.a. Fragd c. Amministrazione delle finanze dello Stato* [1989] 72 Rivista di Diritto Internazionale 104.

[20] Case 20/69 *Stauder v Stadt Ulm* [1969] ECR 419; Case 11/70 *Internationale Handelsgesellschaft mbH v Einfuhr- und Vorratstelle für Getreide und Futtermittel* [1970] ECR 1125; Case 44/79 *Liselotte Hauer v Land Rheinland-Pfalz* [1979] ECR 3727. On this evolution, see also M Claes, *The National Courts' Mandate in the European Constitution* (Hart: Oxford, 2006) 417–22.

[21] A Ward, *Judicial Review and the Rights of Private Parties in EU Law* (OUP: Oxford, 2007) 1, 14–15.

[22] C Hilson and T Downes, 'Making Sense of Rights: Community Rights in EC Law' (2009) 24 ELR 121. There is of course a degree of overlap between EC Rights as defined in the main text and fundamental rights as principles of Community law (ibid, 121–2).

[23] RD Kelemen, *The Rules of Federalism: Institutions and Regulatory Politics in the EU and Beyond* (Cambridge University Press: Cambridge, 2004) 13–14; D Halberstam, 'Comparative Federalism and the Role of the Judiciary' in KE Wittington, RD Kelemen, and GA Caldeira (eds), *The Oxford Handbook of Law and Politics* (OUP: Oxford, 2008) 151.

effet utile) has been the justification underpinning all major interferences with national regulation.[24] The most flagrant cases are the direct effect of Treaty provisions,[25] the direct applicability of regulations and decisions,[26] and the principle of Member State liability for breach of EC law,[27] among others. Indeed, it can be said that the notion of individual rights has prompted the Court of Justice to introduce the elements of a federal judicial architecture;[28] but not only that. It has also used the 'individual rights argument' to win national courts over, to make them collaborate and accept said elements.

It has already been discussed in the previous section how giving constitutional courts the capacity and the obligation to protect individuals' rights is widely considered to be the reason for the transformation of modern European constitutional courts into positive legislators, or courts which have to take political—or at least, 'creative'—decisions in their function as controllers of political decision-making.[29] The European Court of Justice was set up, originally, as a supranational court that would decide on boundary conflicts in a polity with an areal distribution of powers. Slowly, however, the Court developed into much more. It has been argued here that this came partly as a result of the need for the ECJ to conform to the expectations of national constitutional courts, and also of the duty placed on the Court to enforce a constitutional bargain that was necessarily incomplete at its inception.[30] The Court managed to unite both

---

[24] A Ward, *Judicial Review and the Rights of Private Parties in EU Law* (OUP, Oxford 2007) 2. For a fuller discussion of the examples that follow, see ibid, 2–9. For an illustration of the affinity between the principle of effectiveness and fundamental rights (in this case, the right to judicial protection), see Case 222/84 *Johnston v Chief Constable of the Royal Ulster Constabulary* [1986] ECR 1651; also T Tridimas, *The General Principles of EU Law* (2nd, edn, OUP: Oxford, 2006) 443–4.

[25] See for instance Case 43/75 *Defrenne v Sabena* [1976] ECR 455 [24] or Case 36/74 *Walrave and Koch* [1974] ECR 1405 [34].

[26] On the direct applicability of regulations (justified because they 'confer rights on private parties'), see for example Case 34/73 *Variola* [1973] ECR 981, 990. On the direct applicability of decisions, see Case 9/70 *Grad v Finanzamt Traunstein* [1970] ECR 825 [5].

[27] Joined Cases C-6/90 and C-9/90 *Francovich and Bonifaci v Italy* [1991] ECR I-5357.

[28] A Ward, *Judicial Review and the Rights of Private Parties in EU Law* (OUP, Oxford 2007) 9.

[29] Some authors accept it as a necessary condition for this transformation, although not a sufficient one. Hirschl, for example, argues that there are other causes at play, related to the balance of power in a society: R Hirschl, *Towards Juristocracy: The Origins and Consequences of the New Constitutionalism* (Harvard University Press: Cambridge, 2004) 212 and ff.

[30] The precise contents of the federal bargain are always incomplete: D Halberstam, 'Comparative Federalism and the Role of the Judiciary' in KE Wittington, RD Kelemen, and GA Caldeira (eds), *The Oxford Handbook of Law and Politics* (OUP: Oxford, 2008) 143. On incomplete agreements more generally, C Sunstein, 'Incompletely Theorized Agreements' (1995) 108 Harvard LR 1733, 1739–40.

aims by using the language of individual rights to appeal to national courts in their role as protectors of rights,[31] while at the same time using these individual rights to build a new legal system.

The role played by national courts in this process should come as no surprise. The legal system of the European Community placed an area of decision-making outside the realm of control of national constitutional courts and within the realm of control of the European Court of Justice. National constitutional courts were not able to discharge what they considered their duty and a requirement of the rule of law; but saw that the European Court of Justice was in a position to do so. The famous inter-court dialogue that took place during this time had as a result a change in the role of the ECJ,[32] which had to take to itself the role of guarantor of rights. In order to make the legal system of the EC acceptable to national constitutional courts, such legal systems had to have a modern European constitutional court.[33]

With the benefit of hindsight, this seems to be a natural evolution since the moment the Member States created a legal system with a last interpreter that was in a position of authority in relation to national constitutional courts in matters pertaining to that system. It was natural for national constitutional courts to expect this court to have an ethos similar to theirs, and that this would be a requirement if they were to accept relinquishing some of their control in favour of this court. Further, the need for collaboration and inter-court dialogue in the system was also likely to lead to an accommodation between the national courts'

[31] A Burley and W Mattley, 'Europe before the Court: A Political Theory of Legal Integration' (1993) 47 International Organizations 41, 64.

[32] A-M Slaughter, AS Sweet and JHH Weiler (eds), *The European Courts and National Courts: Doctrine and Jurisprudence* (Hart: Oxford, 1998); J Schwarze (ed), *The Birth of a European Constitutional Order: The Interaction of National and European Constitutional Law* (Nomos: Baden-Baden, 2000); S Weatherill, 'Activism and Restraint in the European Court of Justice' in P Capps, M Evans, and S Konstadinidis (eds), *Asserting Jurisdiction: International and European Legal Perspectives* (Hart: Oxford, 2003).

[33] F Jacobs describes the constitutional role of the Court as 'inescapable': F Jacobs, 'Is the Court of Justice of the European Communities a Constitutional Court?' in D Curtin and D O'Keeffe (eds), *Constitutional Adjudication in European Community and National Law* (Butterworths: Dublin, 1992), 32. On how this position may be reinforced in the future, see T Tridimas, 'The European Court of Justice and the Draft Constitution: A Supreme Court for the Union?' in T Tridimas and P Nebbia (eds), *European Union Law for the Twenty-First Century: Rethinking the New Legal Order* (Hart: Oxford, 2004).

expectations and the role of the European Court of Justice. The fact that the ECJ's legitimacy is more contested because it operates in a transnational context makes the collaboration and support of national constitutional courts even more necessary.

Kelsen argued that giving the role of guardian of rights to a constitutional court meant it would become politicized, because rights provisions are typically vague and admit several, value-laden interpretations. He was certainly right in the case of the European Community, a legal system where, firstly, human rights provisions were not even at hand and had to be created, to some extent, by the constitutional court itself—or, at least, borrowed and reshaped from other sources, mainly the ECHR and national constitutional traditions. The ECJ was creating this role for itself, if not from scratch, then at least without having a proper starting point in the Treaty; the Court did not only have to deal with vague and ambiguous concepts, it also had to cherry-pick them from external sources and adapt them to the EC legal system. Secondly, the same argument applies to the role of the Court in building a legal basis for the Community using the language of EC rights. The Court had to build a complex legal system on the basis of a very ambiguous corpus of Treaties and, as a consequence, its development into a positive legislator was inescapable.

The upshot, then, is that the legal structure of the European judicial system and its characteristics—mainly, the existence of the European Court of Justice at its apex and the need for it to secure the respect and collaboration of national constitutional courts—meant that the ECJ had to present itself as a guarantor of individuals' rights. At the same time, the Court had to develop an incomplete constitutional bargain and it used the language of rights to do so. Both aspects of the role of the Court are closely intertwined and they both contributed decisively to the evolution of the Court into a federal constitutional court of sorts and, clearly, a positive legislator. The result is well known: for years now, the ECJ has been 'deciding issues of political governance, defining democracy at European and national level, and contributing through the process of judicial harmonization to the creation of a European demos'.[34]

---

[34] T Tridimas, 'The European Court of Justice and the Draft Constitution: A Supreme Court for the Union?' in T Tridimas and P Nebbia (eds), *European Union Law for the Twenty-First Century. Rethinking the New Legal Order* (Hart: Oxford, 2004) 113.

Of course, the Court's bold approach has been met with criticism and its role is decisively problematic in terms of democratic legitimacy.[35] This will be further explored in the conclusion to this monograph. For now, let us bear in mind that the European Court of Justice considered itself legitimized to create judge-made law from the beginning.[36] The foremost argument, made always explicit, is that the Treaty itself gives the Court of Justice jurisdiction to ensure that in the interpretation and application of its text, the law is observed (Article 220 EC). We have, then, a constitutional provision which foresees constitutional review, and which has been interpreted to include the development of the law, when needed, to provide a 'firm legal base' for the Community.[37]

Further than the formal legitimation granted by the Treaty, the Court obtains its practical legitimacy from its position in the legal system of the Community, from its standing as an established and objectively acting institution, and from 'its manner of decision-making in formal and strictly regulated judicial procedures, with the independence, impartiality and professional qualification of its members'.[38] These elements of legitimation are hardly unique to the European Court of Justice, and can be

---

[35] For some of the best-known early criticisms, see: H Rasmussen, *On Law and Policy in the European Court of Justice* (Martinus Nijhoff: Dordrecht, 1986); H Rasmussen, *The European Court of Justice* (GadJura: Copenhagen, 1993); P Neill, *The European Court of Justice: A Case Study in Judicial Activism* (European Policy Forum: London, 1995); T Hartley, 'The European Court, Judicial Objectivity and the Constitution of the European Union' (1996) 112 LQR 95. Some authors who have defended the constitutional role of the Court are, among others: M Cappelletti, *The Judicial Process in Comparative Perspective* (Clarendon Press: Oxford, 1989); F Jacobs, 'Is the Court of Justice of the European Communities a Constitutional Court?' in D Curtin and D O'Keeffe (eds), *Constitutional Adjudication in European Community and National Law* (Butterworths: Dublin, 1992); T Tridimas, 'The Court of Justice and Judicial Activism' (1997) 2 ELR 199; A Arnull, 'The European Court of Justice and Judicial Objectivity: A Reply to Professor Hartley' (1996) 112 LQR 95; A Arnull, *The European Union and its Court of Justice* (2nd edn, OUP: Oxford, 2006) 620–1. For the most recent controversy, see R Herzog and L Gerken, 'Stop the European Court of Justice' http://www.cep.eu/678.html?&L=1 (accessed January 2009) and a reply in 'Editorial' (2008) 48 CML Rev 1571

[36] U Everling, 'On the Judge-Made Law of the European Community's Courts' in D O'Keeffe (ed), *Judicial Review in European Union Law* (Kluwer, The Hague 2000) 35; A Arnull, 'Does the Court of Justice Have Inherent Jurisdiction?' (1991) 28 CML Rev 669; J Ukrow, *Richterliche Rechtsfortbildung durch den EuGH* (Nomos: Baden-Baden, 1995).

[37] U Everling, 'On the Judge-Made Law of the European Community's Courts' in D O'Keeffe (ed), *Judicial Review in European Union* Law (Kluwer, The Hague 2000) 36; I Pernice, 'Die Dritte Gewalt im europäischen Verfassungsverbund' (1996) 31 Europarecht 27; J Ukrow, *Richterliche Rechtsfortbildung durch den EuGH* (Nomos: Baden-Baden, 1995) 90 and ff.

[38] U Everling, 'On the Judge-Made Law of the European Community's Courts' in D O'Keeffe (ed), *Judicial Review in European Union Law: Liber Amicorum in Honour of Lord Slynn of Hadley* 36.

The ECJ as a Federal Constitutional Court 11

extrapolated to any European constitutional court; they all are formally legitimized by a constitutional provision, and their social legitimacy can be said to come as a consequence of their position in the constitutional system (constitutional politics, over time, reinforce their stability and authority)[39] and of their perception as qualified, independent, and impartial organs.

Although the ECJ and national constitutional courts share similar mechanisms to justify their role, the legitimacy of the ECJ is, needless to say, far more contested than that of its national counterparts. Any modern constitutional court has to take politically-charged decisions that affect the shape of the legal order. At the national level, this may seem less outrageous because there is a stable, traditional polity with an established constitution. There is likely to be a consensus on constitutional values among the population, what has been termed a commitment to 'constitutional patriotism' in the literature.[40] The greater this consensus is concerning the fundamental values behind the constitution, the less polemic the guidance of the constitutional adjudicator will seem.[41] At the European level, the level of consensus is much lower. When exercising its role as constitutional adjudicator, the ECJ is developing a constitutional bargain that is more incomplete than a standard national constitution, and it is operating in the absence of a pan-European consensus on the values that should underlie the new system and how these values should be articulated.[42] Consequently, the crisis in legitimacy of constitutional adjudication will always be greater at the EU level.

It is not my intention to argue that there is no difference between what national constitutional courts, on the one hand, and the ECJ, on the other, do. Rather, my point is that both sides of this comparison are, in essence, behaving like the positive legislators that constitutional courts are. Differences, of course, occur because of the different contexts in which they

[39] A Stone-Sweet, *Governing with Judges* (OUP: Oxford, 2000) 151–2.

[40] A term coined in the German literature (*Verfassungspatriotismus*) and originally used in: D Sternberger, *Verfassungspatriotismus* (Insel: Frankfurt am Main, 1990) and famously taken up by Habermas in: J Habermas, *Faktizität und Geltung: Beiträge zur Diskurstheorie des Rechts und des demokratischen Rechtsstaates* (Suhrkamp: Frankfurt am Main, 1992). Since then, it has been widely used in the political debate. A recent overview can be found in: JW Mueller, *Constitutional Patriotism* (Princeton University Press: Princeton, 2008).

[41] M Rosenfeld, 'Constitutional Adjudication in Europe and the United States: Paradoxes and Contrasts' (2004) 2 I-CON 633, 666.

[42] Kumm believes, in fact, that constitutional patriotism is not possible in the EU, at least under the current political conditions: M Kumm, 'Why Europeans Will Not Embrace Constitutional Patriotism' (2008) 6 I-CON 117.

operate. The ECJ stands on far shakier ground when exercising its role as a constitutional adjudicator and one may foresee that the Court will be likely to adopt a degree of pragmatic and/or principled caution in its rulings for this very reason.[43] Albeit taking into account these distinctions, the ECJ may be studied as the constitutional court of a vertical federal system, where the central government and the constituent states share a significant range of powers.[44] This vertical federal system has opted for a mixed system of judicial review, in the sense that only the ECJ may review EC law for compliance with the 'constitutional charter' (centralized model) while all courts review national law for compliance with the same standard (decentralized model).[45]

Once the ECJ has been placed in the more general context of constitutional adjudicators across the globe, the aim of this monograph is to study the evolution in the jurisdiction of this Court in two specific areas, namely the second and third pillars of the European Union.

1.3 The ECJ as a Constitutional Court in the Second and Third Pillars

The second and third pillars of the European Union will be the focus of this monograph for several reasons. These are the areas of the European Union that are evolving fastest, from mere intergovernmental cooperation to more 'constitutionalized' parts of the legal system. As a consequence, they offer a valuable insight into how new areas of EU activity come to the fore, with all institutional actors having to decide how such activity will

[43] The classic example is Grogan: Case C-159/90 *The Society for the Protection of Unborn Children Ireland Ltd v Stephen Grogan and others* [1990] ECR I-04685; see also Cases C-36/02 *Omega Spielhallen- und Automatenaufstellungs-GmbH v Oberbürgermeisterin der Bundesstadt Bonn* [2004] ECR I-9609; C-91/91 *Paula Faccini Dori v Recreb Srl* [1994] ECR I-3325; Opinion 2/94 of 28 March 1996 *Accession by the Community to the European Convention for the Protection of Human Rights and Fundamental Freedoms* [1996] ECR I-01759.

[44] As opposed to a horizontal federal system, where 'central and constituent governments are organizationally distinct, each with a full complement of legislative, executive and fiscal powers': D Halberstam, 'Comparative Federalism and the Role of the Judiciary' in KE Wittington, RD Kelemen, and GA Caldeira (eds), *The Oxford Handbook of Law and Politics* (OUP: Oxford, 2008) 142.

[45] V Ferreres Comella, 'The European Model of Constitutional Review of Legislation: Toward Decentralization?' (2004) 2 I-CON 461, 481. In the case of the ECJ, the review of national legislation may be direct (through infringement proceedings) or indirect (through the preliminary ruling procedure). Although the review of national law is decentralized, in case of controversy national courts may turn to the ECJ, shifting the burden of decision to the centre.

come to be controlled. In this process, the ECJ has had to lead the way in the face of legislative forestalling, as in the case of the Commission's proposals to extend the jurisdiction of the Court by Council decision,[46] or demise, as in the case of the failed Constitutional Treaty.

The fact that the ECJ has had to lead the way means that these areas offer a fascinating example of a constitutional court coming to grips with new parts of the legal system that need 'building'.[47] Just like the Court had to do with the first pillar, it now has to shape new areas of the legal system of the EU, providing a coherent legal basis for them and ensuring that the rights of individuals are properly protected. In order to do so, it has had to push the boundaries of its own jurisdiction, to the extent that this was possible. Further changes are nevertheless afoot; the nature of the law created in the intergovernmental pillars as well as the competence of the Court to control its constitutionality are part of the wide-ranging changes proposed in the Lisbon Treaty (LT).[48] The Union is, it seems, deciding how and to what extent governmental activity in these areas should be subject to judicial control.

It is for all these reasons that these particular areas of the European Union have been chosen for this study, the aim of which should be considered twofold: to map out the evolution of judicial control in two specific fields of Union activity, but also to study this process as a further step in the development of the ECJ as the constitutional court of the EU.

---

[46] Communication from the Commission to the European Council. A Citizens' Agenda: Delivering Results for Europe. Brussels, 10.5.2006. COM(2006) 211 final, 10; Communication from the Commission to the European Parliament, the Council, the European Economic and Social Committee, the Committee of the regions and the Court of Justice of the European Communities: Adaptation of the Provisions of Title IV of the Treaty establishing the European Community relating to the jurisdiction of the Court of Justice with a view to ensuring more effective judicial protection. Brussels, 28.6.2006. COM(2006) 346 final.

[47] This study focuses on the role of the ECJ as part of a wider process; it does not assume that the Court alone is regularly responsible for major changes in wider policy, but that it has initiated them in some cases. See in this respect L Conant, *Justice Contained* (Cornell University Press: Ithaca, NY, 2002).

[48] Treaty of Lisbon amending the Treaty on European Union and the Treaty establishing the European Community, *OJ* (2007) C 306/1, 17 December 2007. The consolidated version will be used throughout this paper: Consolidated versions of the Treaty on European Union and the Treaty on the Functioning of the European Union, *OJ* (2008) C 115/1, 9 May 2008. The Lisbon Treaty is not a substantive Treaty: it reforms—without turning them into a single document—the TEU and the EC Treaty, renaming the latter Treaty on the Functioning of the European Union or TFEU. For that reason, references to the Lisbon Treaty will appear as 'Article X TEU (after LT)' or 'Article X TFEU'. On the process leading up to the signature of the Lisbon Treaty and its current status, see Section 2.4.3.

Judicial Control in the Area of Freedom, Security and Justice

2.1 Introduction

Only after a long time was the European integration project ready to tackle issues as sensitive as immigration, asylum, policing, or criminal law. That is no wonder: not many issues are as close to the core of a state's sovereignty; nor indeed were such issues of pressing concern in the immediate post-war period as Europe was frozen into its East/West fragmentation. Cooperation in these fields started tentatively and was slowly unfolding when a combination of factors catapulted it very high up in the list of Union priorities: for one, terrorism suddenly commanded the attention and anxieties of the citizens of the Union in a way it had never done before.

Member States know that cooperation in these areas is indispensable in today's world: the nature of the threats is such that a state alone cannot expect to counter them effectively by acting on its own. The European integration process has also played a part in this respect: the internal open frontiers of the Union are not only open to well-behaved citizens. A joint effort, in sum, was deemed to be required.

Informal cooperation on justice and home affairs matters among the Member States took place as early as in the 1960s.[1] Institutionalized cooperation, however, started officially with the Maastricht Treaty, which created the so-called third pillar of the Union ('justice and home affairs'—JHA): an area of intergovernmental cooperation within the general, supranational framework of the European Union, different from the first or Community

---

[1] For a historical overview of this evolution, S Peers, *EU Justice and Home Affairs Law* (OUP: Oxford, 2006) 5–10.

pillar. Cooperation is regulated in Title VI TEU, which foresees special decision-making processes and where the Community method is not applied.[2] Not all justice and home affairs were included in this inter-governmental pillar: some, very specific, areas (certain aspects of visa policy) were included in the EC Treaty or first pillar, where the Community method does apply, albeit with some unorthodox features.

At Amsterdam, things changed slightly; new, substantial aspects of the third pillar were included in the first one, Title IV EC (immigration, asylum, and civil law issues), and some aspects of the Community method—albeit in a *sui generis* mode—were extended to the matters left in the third pillar. All of these areas together, Title IV EC and the third pillar or Title VI TEU ('police and judicial cooperation in criminal matters'), became what is now termed the 'Area of Freedom, Security and Justice' (AFSJ).

This is the institutional framework in which the third pillar and the AFSJ, more generally, are included nowadays.[3] As regards the level of activity undertaken, it should not come as a surprise that it has grown exponentially in the last years. It was perhaps the moment to move on to further challenges, having achieved so much in terms of economic integration; an integration that seemed to push the Union to new endeavours in other fields of competence. Notably, the need to somehow counter the terrorist threat in a globalized world has given rise to a multitude of measures adopted in this area. This evolution in the activities undertaken by the Union has prompted concerns related to the nature of the Area of Freedom, Security and Justice: an evolution in the way the Union exercises power should come coupled with an equivalent evolution in the way this power is to be controlled. The AFSJ, however, lacks transparency and accountability, problems that will be further addressed in the next chapter.

The evolution of the third pillar is still an ongoing process: one that seems to be leading to further integration and the progressive adoption of the Community method. The failed Constitutional Treaty crystallized political intentions in this regard. Even in the wake of its failure, the

---

[2] For some critical comments on the Maastricht third pillar, M Spencer, *States of Injustice: A Guide to Human Rights and Civil Liberties in the European Union* (Pluto: London, 1995); E Guild, 'The Constitutional Consequences of Lawmaking in the Third Pillar of the European Union' in P Craig and C Harlow (eds), *Lawmaking in the European Union* (Kluwer: London, 1998); D O'Keeffe 'Recasting the Third Pillar' (1995) 32 CML Rev 893.

[3] The Nice Treaty did not make substantial changes to the Area of Freedom, Security and Justice.

European Court of Justice has transposed some of the Community pillar principles to the third one, and the Commission has made it plain that it wants the whole third pillar to be included in the Community one, with the Community method applying across the board. A second political agreement was reached in the form of the Lisbon Treaty, set to unify first and third pillars. The third pillar of the European Union is a fast-changing area, and the matters it deals with are highly sensitive and touch upon personal freedom, fundamental rights in general, and the core of state autonomy: it is fair to say that the future questions of EU constitutional law are already being discussed, to some extent, in the third pillar.

This chapter deals with a primordial aspect of the evolution of the AFSJ: judicial control. It maps out what the present situation is and what the future is likely to be—and should be. The study of judicial control in this area presupposes, however, a previous analysis of the nature of the measures that are produced in it. From an organizational point of view, therefore, the chapter will firstly deal with the current and future legal effects of the measures adopted in the AFSJ. Secondly, the current and future jurisdiction of the Court will be scrutinized, distinguishing between the following aspects: direct and indirect review of measures, policing the borders, infringement proceedings, damages and action for failure to act. The section on the future jurisdiction of the Court will examine the changes envisaged in the Lisbon Treaty. And finally, the last section will deal with different 'cherry-picking' proposals—put forward by different institutions in the interim between the Constitutional Treaty and the Lisbon Treaty—to change the jurisdiction of the Court in this area.

2.2 The Nature of AFSJ Measures

As has already been explained, part of the AFSJ provisions are contained in the EC Treaty and are therefore part of the first pillar. The majority of the AFSJ, however, consists of the third pillar. Since only third pillar measures are set to undergo a major transformation in terms of their legal effects, they will be the focus of this section as well as the following one.

At the moment, the law adopted in the first pillar (EC law), on the one hand, and the law adopted in the second and third pillars (EU law), on the other, have different legal effects. There is disagreement in the literature as to whether EC law is a special kind of public international law, or

something completely different from it.[4] It is not necessary, for the purposes of this chapter, to dwell on this discussion: what is important is that
EC law has developed stronger effects than those of classic international
law. 'EC law' will be used throughout this piece, then, to denote something
different from 'public international law'. Note that the latter label refers to
classic public international law; all arguments put forward in this chapter are
compatible with considering EC law as a particular and distinct branch of
international law that has developed stronger features.

EU law is adopted outside the framework of the Community, by means
other than the Community method. Consequently, it is different from
EC law and has traditionally been considered public international law of
sorts.[5] This means not only that EU measures, in theory, do not have the
effects of EC law measures (direct effect, primacy, etc),[6] but also that
national courts—depending on national law—may be in a position to
review these measures according to national standards and disapply them.[7]
This is not possible with measures of EC law because, firstly, they have
primacy over all national law and thus cannot be reviewed against national
law standards and,[8] secondly, because of the *Foto-Frost* principle: only the
ECJ can review and leave an EC law measure without effect.[9]

What has been described is the orthodox view of EU law, applicable to
both second and third pillars of the Union. In the case of the third pillar,
however, the situation is slightly more complex. Whereas the effects of the
measures adopted under the second pillar can still be fully explained using

---

[4] The majority of the doctrine considers EC law and public international law two separate
systems: JHH Weiler and UR Haltern, 'Constitutional or International? The Foundations of the
Community Legal Order and the Question of Judicial Kompetenz-Kompetenz' in A-M
Slaughter, A Sweet, and JHH Weiler (eds), *The European Courts and National Courts: Doctrine and
Jurisprudence* (Hart: Oxford, 1998). De Witte, on the other hand, argues very convincingly that
EC law is international law that has developed innovative features: B de Witte 'The European
Union as an International Legal Experiment' forthcoming EUI Working Paper, on file with the
author.

[5] For an in-depth analysis of the distinction between EU and EC law and the unity of the legal
order, C Hermann, 'The Unity of the Legal Order Revisited' in M Cremona and B de Witte
(eds), *EU Foreign Relations Law: Constitutional Fundamentals* (Hart: Oxford, 2008).

[6] As a matter of EU law (ie not because such features are accorded to public international law
as a matter of national law).

[7] P Eeckhout, 'The European Court of Justice and the "Area of Freedom, Security and Justice": Challenges and Problems' in D O'Keeffe (ed), *Judicial Review in European Union Law: Liber
Amicorum in Honour of Lord Slynn of Hadley* (Kluwer: London, 2000) 160.

[8] *Inter alia*, Case 11/70 *Internationale Handelsgesellschaft mbH v Einfuhr- und Vorratstelle für
Getreide und Futtermittel* [1970] ECR 1125.

[9] Case 314/85 *Foto-Frost v Hauptzollamt Lübeck-Ost* [1987] ECR 04199.

classic international law terminology, this is not so easy in the case of the third pillar. The latter offers a wider range of possible measures, some of which are comparable to some extent to EC measures (framework decisions and decisions on the one hand, directives and regulations on the other).[10] More importantly, although direct effect is explicitly excluded in the TEU, the ECJ has extended other features of EC law to third pillar measures in its case-law,[11] creating the impression that the line between EC and EU (third pillar) law is fuzzier than ever;[12] as a consequence, it has been argued that the most distinct feature of EC law, primacy, should also be recognized as a feature of the law adopted in the third pillar.[13] I do not share this view, though it is clear that the nature of third pillar measures is more complex than that of the second one, and that brings this area closer, in any case, to the EC pillar. The pragmatics of European integration has pushed this area further, resulting in something other (or 'more') than orthodox public international law. This was to be expected: after all, the whole of EU law should be regarded from the start as a public international law 'of sorts'. It is still the case, however, that third pillar measures are closer to classic international law than they are to EC law: even features such as indirect effect can be explained in terms of classic international law—allowing of course for special alterations due to the fact that these particular measures of international law are adopted within the very special setting of the EU.

[10] Their descriptions are identical, except for the fact that direct effect is excluded for framework decisions and decisions (Art 34 TEU).

[11] C-105/03 *Criminal Proceedings against Maria Pupino* [2005] ECR I-5285, where the ECJ stated that the duty of conform interpretation applies in the third pillar. For a general overview of the case, M Fletcher, 'Extending "Indirect Effect" to the Third Pillar: The Significance of Pupino' (2005) 30 ELR 862; J Spencer, 'Child Witnesses and the European Union' (2005) 64 CLJ 569; E Spaventa, 'Opening Pandora's Box: Some Reflections on the Constitutional Effects of the Decision in Pupino' (2007) 3 EuConst 5; E Spaventa, 'Remembrance of Principles Lost: On Fundamental Rights, the Third Pillar and the Scope of Union Law' (2006) 25 YEL 153; S Peers, 'Salvation outside the Church: Judicial Protection in the Third Pillar after the Pupino and Segi Judgments' (2007) 44 CML Rev 885. For further discussion, see also S Prechal, 'Direct Effect, Indirect Effect, Supremacy and the Evolving Constitution of the European Union' in Barnard C (ed), *The Fundamentals of EU Law Revisited* (OUP: Oxford, 2007).

[12] Note the ambiguous remark of the ECJ in *Kadi* that the EU and the EC are 'integrated but separate legal orders': Case C-402/05 P *Kadi* [2008] ECR I-6351 [202].

[13] This view presupposes that only 'narrow' direct effect is excluded by Art 34 TEU, and thus that the so-called exclusionary effect is a manifestation of primacy and not of direct effect. Accordingly, the primacy of third pillar measures would have consequences that would not be barred by the exclusion of direct effect in this area. A recent and polemic contribution in this respect has been Lenaerts and Corthaut's compelling submission that the principle of primacy applies already both in the second and in the third pillar: K Lenaerts and T Corthaut, 'Of Birds and Hedges: The Role of Primacy in Invoking Norms of EU Law' (2006) 31 ELR 287.

Although there is a trend of approximation between first and third pillar, the distinction between both types of law is still valid and, what is more important, should remain in place as long as other institutional arrangements remain untouched. This will be argued in detail later on in this chapter; for the moment, suffice it to say that the situation will change once all institutional arrangements—most importantly, judicial oversight—are reformed at once to unify first and third pillar. In such a scenario, the unification of EC and EU law would be, to a great extent, unproblematic.

This reform, first proposed in the Constitutional Treaty and now taken up in the Lisbon Treaty, would mean that the third pillar would be included in the institutional and legal system of the EC (to be called the EU). Generally, the Lisbon Treaty seeks to do away with the three-pillar structure and the distinction between the EC and the EU. As a result, there would also be no distinction between the law adopted under the second and third pillars and EC law; all measures may have the current 'stronger' effects of EC law, and they would all be termed EU law. This is a very significant reform: the change in the nature of EU law would have important consequences in terms of the effects these measures may have on individuals and on the way they can be controlled by the courts.

2.2.1 Legal Effects of Third Pillar Measures: Terminology[14]

Before appraising the legal effects of third pillar measures, it may be useful to clarify the criteria that will be applied to them. This section seeks to clarify the meaning of, and relationship between, five labels concerning the effects of legal measures—'directly applicable', 'directly effective', 'indirectly effective', 'self-executing', and 'supreme'—to find out whether or to what extent they can be applied to third pillar measures, both before and after the entry into force of the Lisbon Treaty. The meaning and scope of these labels is often unclear or disputed, mainly because they have been used with different meanings in the public international law and EU law literature. It is not the aim of this section to put an end to such disputes, but merely to draw attention to the fact that the way in which we define one of these labels prejudges the role played by the rest in the third pillar: especially significant is the definition of direct effect, given that it is explicitly banned for framework decisions and decisions by Article 34(2) TEU.

---

[14] An earlier version of this and the following section have appeared in A Hinarejos, 'On the Legal Effects of Third Pillar Measures: Directly Applicable, Directly Effective, Self-Executing, Supreme?' (2008) 14 ELJ 620.

This will be a general discussion of what these concepts mean in the abstract. The following section, then, will focus on whether or which of these labels can be applied to current third pillar measures. In matching these measures to their labels, it will become clear that the definition of 'directly effective' and related labels presupposes an underlying policy choice on the future of the third pillar.

2.2.1.1 Defining Questions and Labels

Firstly, specifying what questions can be asked about the legal effects or features of an international law measure is helpful in order to clarify to which feature each of these labels refers.

There are four such questions: (1) whether the international measure is, and how it becomes, the 'law of the land'. This is a purely formal question that concerns the validity of the measure within the national legal order; its answer depends, traditionally, on national rules; (2) whether the national courts can take cognizance of such rule, generally speaking. The answer to this question seems to be quite straightforward, once the law of international law has become the 'law of the land';[15] (3) whether the norm can be invoked by an individual as a standard of review of a national measure; (4) whether the norm can be invoked by an individual with the result that the court applies this norm as the rule which governs the substance of the matter before it.

2.2.1.1.1 Direct Applicability. The first label, 'directly applicable', is one of those expressions the meaning of which has changed when exported from public international law to Community law. In the former, the 'direct applicability' of a measure concerns its capacity to be applied directly by a court due to its sufficient clarity and precision: it is therefore an answer to questions 3 and 4 above, concerned with the application of a rule to a particular case, and it purely depends on the substance of the measure. In this public international law sense, 'directly applicable' is synonymous with 'self-executing', and independent from the answer to the first question—how international law becomes the law of the land, depending on whether the state is monist or dualist. Since 'direct applicability' depends on the substance of the measure, this will remain a feature of the measure whether the state is monist or dualist. A dualist legal system will merely prevent a directly applicable measure from being directly applied.[16]

---

[15] M Claes, *The National Courts' Mandate in the European Constitution* (Hart: Oxford, 2006) 72.

[16] J Winter, 'Direct Applicability and Direct Effect: Two Distinct and Different Concepts in Community Law' (1972) 9 CML Rev 425, 428.

When imported into Community law, though, this label was 'emptied' of its public international law meaning.

Several (though by no means all) commentators have used the expression 'directly applicable' as a synonym for 'directly effective'.[17] I will, however, distinguish between these two concepts. Direct applicability, as used in Article 249 EC, designates a special feature of EC regulations: the Treaty uses this label to clarify that Member States cannot decide anymore how or whether these measures become the law of the land: they shall do so in their original form. The monist/dualist choice is out of the question: 'Direct applicability' is therefore used in the EC Treaty as an answer to the first question (how does a measure penetrate a legal order?). Better still, the Treaty makes it clear that this question is no longer for the Member States to answer.[18]

This cannot mean that all regulations have direct effect, regardless of whether they fulfil the *Van Gend en Loos* criteria[19]—since we know that that is not the case.[20] It simply means that regulations, in their original form, are automatically law of the land in the Member States and do not need any sort of incorporation to be so. This feature is understandably absent from the description of directives given in the same article of the EC Treaty. Direct applicability—when used in this 'EC law sense'—relates to the form of the legal instrument and not to its substance, and is something different from direct effect. This distinction between direct applicability and direct effect has been backed by the ECJ in its case-law.[21]

---

[17] For instance S Prechal, 'Does Direct Effect Still Matter?' (2000) 37 CML Rev 1047; S Prechal, *Directives in EC Law* (2nd edn, OUP: Oxford, 2005) 226–9; P Eleftheriadis, 'The Direct Effect of Community Law: Conceptual Issues' (1996) 16 YEL 205. In disagreement, J Winter, 'Direct Applicability and Direct Effect: Two Distinct and Different Concepts in Community Law' (1972) 9 CML Rev 425; Opinion of AG Warner in Case 131/79 *Santillo* [1980] ECR 1585; S Weatherill, *Cases and Materials on EU Law* (8th edn, OUP: Oxford, 2007) 129; K Lenaerts and P Van Nuffel, *Constitutional Law of the European Union* (2nd edn, Sweet & Maxwell: London, 2005) 702–3; D Wyatt and A Dashwood (eds), *European Union Law* (5th edn, Sweet & Maxwell: London, 2006) 128; A Arnull, *The European Union and its Court of Justice* (2nd edn, OUP: Oxford, 2006) 185–7.

[18] See Case 39/72 *Commission v Italy* [1973] ECR 101 [17]; Case 94/77 *Zerbone v Amministrazione delle Finanze dello Stato* [1978] ECR 99 [23].

[19] The provision must be sufficiently clear; it must be unconditional; and it must confer a specific right on the individual. Case 26/62 *Van Gend & Loos* [1963] ECR 1.

[20] See for example Case C-403/98 *Azienda Agricola Monte Arcosu Srl v Regione Autonoma della Sardegna, Organismo Comprensoriale No 24 della Sardegna and Ente Regionale per l'Assistenza Tecnica in Agricoltura (ERSAT)* [2001] ECR I-00103.

[21] Case 9/70 *Grad v Finanzamt Traunstein* [1970] ECR 825; Case 41/74 *Van Duyn v Home Office* [1974] ECR 1337. Further proof of this distinction is that even directly effective directives have to be implemented (ie they are not directly applicable): Case 104/86 *Commission v Italy* [1988] ECR 1799 [12]; Case 102/79 *Commission v Belgium* [1980] ECR 1473 [12].

2.2.1.1.2 Direct Effect. There is an ongoing disagreement on the exact definition of 'direct effect', the cornerstone of this analysis. The loose use of the concept made by the ECJ has not helped settle the matter.[22] For the purposes of this section, I will roughly distinguish between a wider interpretation (direct effect is the mere capacity of a norm to be invoked by an individual before a national court to his or her advantage) and a narrow one (direct effect is the capacity of a norm to confer rights on individuals—rights which can be enforced in the national courts. This can equally be described as the capacity of the norm to govern an individual's legal position).[23]

In the first case, direct effect concerns both questions 3 and 4: the important feature is that the measure can be relied upon by the individual, independently of whether the rule deploys an exclusionary or a substitutionary effect—that is, whether the measure will merely be used as a standard of legality and thus preclude the application of a conflicting measure of national law or whether it will be governing the substance of the matter. On the contrary, the narrow conception of direct effect relates only to question 4. For the supporters of this narrow conception, the exclusionary effect of an EC measure—precluding the application of another, contrary measure—is not strictly speaking direct effect, but a consequence of the fact that the EC measure is binding and supreme.[24]

The consequences of choosing one notion over the other within the first pillar have arguably been overplayed. To use a well-known example: our

---

[22] The ECJ has equally described direct effect as creating enforceable rights (Cases 12/81 *Garland v British Rail* [1982] ECR 359; C-236/92 *Comitato di coordinamento per la difesa della Cava and others* [1994] ECR I-483) and as the capacity to be relied upon before the courts (Case 8/81 *Becker v Finanyamt Münster-Innenstadt* [1982] ECR 53).

[23] For a general overview of the discussion, S Prechal, *Directives in EC Law* (2nd edn, OUP: Oxford, 2005) 231–41.

[24] It is generally directives that deploy exclusionary effects: this can only be the case once the deadline for their implementation has passed, because they become binding at that point. 'Binding' here means that, by the time the transposition period is over, the national implementing measures should be in place; this cannot be demanded before. Of course, directives are binding in a more loose sense on states even before the deadline for implementation has passed (Case C-129/96 *Inter Environnement Wallonie* [1997] ECR I-7411 [41]: 'a directive has legal effect with respect to the Member State to which it is addressed from the moment of its notification'). These early legal effects only mean that, before the deadline has passed, states cannot adopt measures which will seriously compromise the achievement of the objective of the directive (an obligation based on Articles 10 and 249 EC: *Inter-Environnement Wallonie* [45]). Before the deadline for implementation has passed, however, it is not possible for a directive to deploy exclusionary effect: in *Mangold*, the Court had to shift away from a directive in this situation and resort to a general principle of Community law (non-discrimination on grounds of age) in order to instruct the national court to discharge the *Simmenthal* duty to disapply a conflicting national rule: Case C-144/04 *Mangold* [2005] ECR I-9981.

conception of direct effect will determine whether we believe that Directive 83/189 could be invoked and could develop an exclusionary effect[25] in cases like *CIA Security*[26] and *Unilever*[27] because it is not proper direct effect that we are talking about, but the consequences of the principle of supremacy (thus creating no conflict with the prohibition on the horizontal direct effect of directives),[28] or whether we believe these cases to be instances of direct effect that can be singled out as exceptions to the mentioned prohibition. The result, in both cases, is the same: the individual will be able to invoke a directive in order to preclude the application of a conflicting national measure. The exclusionary effect is a fact. Considering this a logical conclusion from one general rule (invocability as a consequence of the fact that the directive has become binding and is part of the law of the land once the deadline for implementation has passed, coupled with the principle of supremacy) or an exception to another general rule (directives can have no horizontal direct effect) does not change the result. It does seem more intuitive, however, to consider these cases as the application of a general rule rather than continuous exceptions to another one. The fact that continuous exceptions cannot be accounted for by a general rule is generally an indication of the fact that a new, more satisfactory one should be found.

In any case, the practical consequences of choosing one conception of direct effect over the other do not seem terribly important—as long as we remain within the first pillar of the European Union. As soon as we consider the legal effects of the measures adopted within the third one, the consequences of the adopted choice are far greater. This is, it is submitted, one of the very few occasions on which the choice of scope of 'direct effect' changes the outlook of the field totally. I shall return to this later.

---

[25] For a discussion of the so-called exclusionary effect: Opinion of AG Saggio in Joined Cases C-240/98 and 244/98 *Oceano Grupo Editorial* [2000] ECR I-4941; P Figueroa Regueiro, 'Invocability of Substitution and Invocability of Exclusion: Bringing Legal Realism to the Current Development of the Case-Law of Horizontal Direct Effect of Directives' (2002) Jean Monnet Working Paper 7/02 www.jeanmonnetprogram.org/papers/02/020701.pdf (accessed January 2007). [26] Case C-194/94 *CIA Security International* [1996] ECR I-2201.
[27] Case C-443/98 *Unilever Italia* [2000] ECR I-7535.
[28] M Lenz, D Sif Tynes, and L Young, 'Horizontal What? Back to Basics' (2000) 25 ELR 509; T Tridimas, 'Black, White and Shades of Grey: Horizontality of Directives Revisited' (2002) 21 YEL 327; K Lenaerts and T Corthaut, 'Of Birds and Hedges: The Role of Primacy in Invoking Norms of EU Law' (2006) 31 ELR 287; D Wyatt and A Dashwood (eds), *European Union Law* (5th edn, Sweet & Maxwell: London, 2006) 183–5. For a very rigorous analysis of the discussion, see M Dougan, 'When Worlds Collide: Relationship between Direct Effect and Supremacy' (2007) 44 CML Rev 931, which finds irreconcilable features in the case-law.

2.2.1.1.3 Indirect Effect. National courts are under obligation to interpret the whole of national law, as far as possible, in the light and spirit of EC law. This includes Treaty provisions, fundamental rights, general principles of EC law, and rules of international law that are applicable in Community law.[29] This obligation is referred to as a duty of consistent or conform interpretation; it is also said that the EC law measures in question deploy 'indirect effect'.

This obligation has sparked the most litigation in relation with directives.[30] The Court has clarified that it extends to the whole of national law, including case-law, and not only to legislation passed to implement the directive in question.[31] The indirect effect of directives somewhat mitigates situations in which directives cannot deploy direct effect; understandably, this effect can be described as 'weaker' than direct effect, given that it is, strictly speaking, national law that is being applied to the substance of the case. The duty of conform interpretation of directives can apply in both vertical and horizontal situations (ie between individuals) and it arises once the deadline for implementation of the directive has passed.[32] There are clear limits to the indirect effect of EC law: the caveat 'as far as possible' forbids a *contra legem* reading of the national measure; the general principles of law (particularly legal certainty and non-retroactivity) impose a substantive restriction. It has been clarified in the case-law that this substantial limitation prevents this duty alone from leading to the determination or aggravation of an individual's criminal liability.[33]

In *Pupino*,[34] the ECJ considered that the duty of loyal cooperation (Article 10 EC) applied also to Title VI TEU and consequently extended the duty of conform interpretation to the third pillar, with the same limitations as in the first one. As a result, framework decisions can have indirect effect in the same circumstances as directives.

2.2.1.1.4 Self-Executing. The third label is not one traditionally used by the Court of Justice or the literature in this field. Once the scope of this label has been discussed, I will argue the case for using this public international law label within the context of EU law.

---

[29] K Lenaerts and P Van Nuffel, *Constitutional Law of the European Union* (2nd edn, Sweet & Maxwell: London, 2005) 667–8.

[30] Case 14/83 *Von Colson and Kamann v Land Nordrhein-Westfalen* [1983] ECR 1891.

[31] Case C-106/89 *Marleasing* [1990] ECR I-4135.

[32] The first example of indirect effect in a horizontal situation was *Marleasing*, above.

[33] Case 80/86 *Criminal Proceedings against Kolpinghuis Nijmegen BV* [1987] ECR 03969.

[34] Case C-105/03 *Criminal Proceedings against Maria Pupino* [2005] ECR I-5285.

'Self-executing' is synonymous with 'directly applicable' as understood within public international law. As opposed to the EC meaning of direct applicability, this feature refers to the substance of the legal instrument: whether the measure in question needs further legislative development to be properly enforced or applied, or whether its contents are detailed enough to make any further legislative implementation unnecessary.

This feature may be explained in terms of judicial application: the norm is legally perfect enough to be applied by a national court (this is equivalent to justiciability), but also in terms of efficacy—the norm is legally perfect enough to achieve its aim. As mentioned above, this is independent of how the measure penetrates the national legal system: a self-executing measure is such because of its substance, and the fact that it may have to face incorporation in a dualist state does not change its character.[35] This would merely mean that the measure would not be applied by the courts, or that it would not achieve its aim directly; whether the measure is clear and detailed enough to be self-executing is a different matter.

As regards the relationship between 'self-executing' and 'directly effective', note that a measure will be self-executing independently of whether it confers rights on individuals, although most of them probably do: accordingly, if we adopt a narrow reading of direct effect—that is, conferral of rights on individuals—the self-executing character of a measure in terms of judicial application is a precondition for, but something different from, its direct effect. Alternatively, if we adopt a wide reading of direct effect— that is, invocability before national courts—the self-executing character of a measure for the purposes of judicial application means exactly the same as its direct effect.

'Self-executing', then, is a useful label if we adopt a narrow reading of 'directly effective', in that it allows us to define a feature which is not encompassed by the latter: the fact that such measure is detailed enough to be applied by the courts, without necessarily conferring enforceable rights on individuals. On the other hand, if we adopt a wider reading of 'directly effective', the label 'self-executing'—in terms of judicial application—is almost totally pre-empted because both labels cover almost the same area of the spectrum, with the exception of those occasions in which a court may apply a rule of its own accord, given that even the wider reading of direct effect requires an individual's reliance on the rule. On the other hand, there is always use for the label 'self-executing' in terms of efficiency

[35] J Winter, 'Direct Applicability and Direct Effect: Two Distinct and Different Concepts in Community Law' (1972) 9 CML Rev 425, 428.

of a rule—meaning that it is detailed enough to achieve its objective—independently of the scope we afford to the concept of direct effect.

In general, then, it is submitted that the term 'self-executing', in its two different variants—as regards judicial application, on the one hand, and efficiency, on the other—can be a useful label in EU law. This is especially the case if we adopt a narrow reading of direct effect, because the label 'self-executing' covers a vast area of the spectrum that is not covered by the narrow conception of 'directly effective' (rules which are detailed enough to be applied by the courts, but do not confer rights on individuals). This label can help us analyse exhaustively the legal effects of framework decisions and decisions in particular situations. At the same time, and although they are synonyms, it is better to import this term rather than 'directly applicable' from public international law (relating to substance) to avoid confusion between the latter and the 'directly applicable' Community label (relating to validity).

This understanding of self-executing measures in a judicial context corresponds loosely to the theory of self-executing treaties in the United States, first handed down by Chief Justice Marshall.[36] It differs from the European conception of self-executing treaties, which places its emphasis on whether a treaty can create direct rights and obligations for individuals.[37] Most treaties qualified as self-executing by the American doctrine will in fact give rise to individual rights in practice, but that must not necessarily be the case.[38]

In EC law, 'self-executing' can be understood as a non-rigid benchmark. The fact that a measure is self-executing means that it is clear and detailed enough *for the particular purpose at stake*. Thus in the context of judicial application, if we wish to use a Community measure as a standard of legality against a national rule, it may only be necessary to be able to construe the EC measure as imposing an obligation on the state. The measure may not need to be very detailed in the way this obligation is to be discharged, for instance, but it is enough to be able to extract a clear obligation from it.[39] On the other hand, if we want the Community rule to substitute the national one, the standard of clarity is understandably higher. As mentioned

---

[36] *Foster and Elam v Neilson* 27 US 253 (1829) (US Supreme Court).

[37] And which can be traced back to the *Danzig Railway Case* (1928) PCIJ, Series B, 15 (Permanent Court of International Justice).

[38] The distinction between both conceptions was pointed out in J Winter, 'Direct Applicability and Direct Effect: Two Distinct and Different Concepts in Community Law' (1972) 9 CML Rev 425, 428–9.

[39] Case C-431/92 *Commission v Germany (Grosskrotzenburg)* [1995] ECR I-2189.

before, the term may also be used in a non-judicial context, to convey that the measure is detailed enough to achieve its aim and hence needs no further development before doing so: in that case, the standard of required legal perfection will be determined by the objective of the measure.

2.2.1.1.5 Primacy. We finally come to our last label, 'supreme'. Although 'Primacy' is the normal word in English, 'Supremacy', of French origin, has come to be used in the same terms. Both expressions will be used interchangeably throughout this book.

Much has been written about primacy; for the purposes of this discussion, I will only give a brief account of this long-standing principle of Community law.[40]

Whenever there is interaction between different legal systems, a rule of conflict is needed. The European Court of Justice defined this rule in the landmark cases of *Costa v ENEL* and *Simmenthal*:[41] when faced with a conflict between a national rule and any Community rule, national courts must disapply the first one in favour of the latter. The Court further clarified in *Internationale Handelsgesellschaft* that this rule also applies when it is the national constitution that conflicts with EC law.[42] This label, then, concerns form rather than substance: any Community law, regardless of its rank or content, is superior to (at least in the Court's definition of primacy) any national rule, equally regardless of its rank or content. Primacy has long been accepted as one of the defining features of the Community legal order and, perhaps until recently, as one of the most important differences between the EC and the intergovernmental pillars.

Primacy and direct effect have been inextricably linked in the case-law of the Court of Justice: all the benchmark decisions cited above involved directly effective provisions. In fact, the Court has never explicitly said that the duty to disapply conflicting national norms, the strongest manifestation of primacy, applies also in the absence of direct effect.[43] Some

---

[40] For an overview of the concept and its evolution, B De Witte, 'Direct Effect, Supremacy and the Nature of the Legal Order' in P Craig and G De Búrca (eds), *The Evolution of EU Law* (OUP: Oxford, 1999).

[41] Cases 6/64 *Costa v ENEL* [1964] ECR 585; 106/77 *Amministrazione delle Finanze dello Stato v Simmenthal* [1978] ECR 629.

[42] Case 11/70 *Internationale Handelsgesellschaft mbH v Einfuhr- und Vorratstelle für Getreide und Futtermittel* [1970] ECR 1125.

[43] M Claes, *The National Courts' Mandate in the European Constitution* (Hart: Oxford, 2006) 115; L Besselink, 'Curing a "Childhood Sickness"? On Direct Effect, Internal Effect, Primacy and Derogation from Civil Rights: The Netherlands Council of State Judgment in the Metten Case' (1996) 3 Maastricht J of Eur and Comparative L 165, 171.

commentators interpret this to mean that there can be no duty to disapply (the '*Simmenthal* duty') in the absence of direct effect; in such situations, supremacy can nevertheless have other, weaker, manifestations—such as conform interpretation.[44] This means that the duty to disapply a national measure, be it with a view to applying an EC measure in its place or not, comes always coupled with direct effect; in turn, this means that the exclusionary effect *is* direct effect. This seems an unhappy conclusion for the advocates of the narrow reading of direct effect, who draw a distinction between the substitutionary effect (where there is primacy and direct effect) and the exclusionary effect (where there is only primacy, but no direct effect, strictly speaking). Interpreting the Court's case-law as saying that there is no duty of disapplication—of whatever type—of national law without direct effect means accepting that the exclusionary effect is a consequence of direct effect too—not only of primacy—and that, therefore, direct effect is wider than they would have us believe.

On the other hand, one may argue that it is not possible to draw satisfactory conclusions from the Court's case-law because it has avoided until now giving a clear answer to the key issue here: whether using an EC norm as a standard of legality against national rules (the exclusionary effect) is necessarily linked to direct effect.[45] The Court has never said that the duty to disapply applies in the absence of direct effect, but it has also never expressly said that it does not; its case-law in the matter is unreliable.[46] This may

[44] M Claes, *The National Courts' Mandate in the European Constitution* (Hart: Oxford, 2006) 115–7; on the relationship between what he calls 'the primacy model' and the duty of conform interpretation, see M Dougan, 'When Worlds Collide: Relationship between Direct Effect and Supremacy' (2007) 44 CML Rev 931, 945–7.

[45] The perfect occasion came with Case C-287/98 *Linster* [2000] ECR I-6917. AG Léger did not dodge the question and concluded in his Opinion that EC measures could deploy an exclusionary effect in absence of direct effect ([81]–[82]). The ECJ did not address the AG's arguments, although it did conclude that the measure should be allowed to deploy an exclusionary effect without examining the question of whether it was directly effective.

[46] In several cases the Court seems to agree implicitly with the idea of exclusionary effect in absence of direct effect: C-287/98 *Linster* [2000] ECR I-6917; C-365/98 *Brinkmann* [2000] ECR I-4619; C-457/02 *Niselli* [2004] ECR I-10853. There are also instances where the Court can be said to have implicitly rejected the distinction: Joined Cases C-397/01 to C-403/01 *Pfeiffer and Others v Deutsches Rotes Kreuz* [2004] ECR I-8835; Joined Cases C-387/02, C-391/02, and C-403/02 *Berlusconi and Others* [2005] ECR I-3565. The latest addition to the case-law is *Palacios de la Villa*, where it could be argued that the Court opts for the narrow definition of direct effect (presenting invocability as a result of primacy). It could be considered too hasty, however, to read too much into this case for the moment: C-411/05 *Palacios de la Villa* [2007] ECR I-8531. For an extensive analysis of the case-law of the Court in this matter, see A Arnull, *The European Union and its Court of Justice* (2nd edn, OUP: Oxford, 2006) 239–52; M Dougan, 'When Worlds Collide: Relationship between Direct Effect and Supremacy' (2007) 44 CML Rev 931, 948–63.

reflect internal judicial disagreement or it may simply reflect a cautious preference to avoid deciding major issues before they *have* to be decided.

To summarize: it is possible to support the opinion that the most important manifestation of primacy, the duty to disapply or '*Simmenthal* duty', is a feature of directly effective measures only: from this point of view, direct effect and primacy appear inextricably linked. It is also possible, on the other hand, to deny a necessary link between these two concepts, with the result that the *Simmenthal* duty can apply independently of whether a measure is directly effective. This disagreement is more apparent than real, and a consequence of the disagreement on the scope of direct effect, not of primacy itself: a wide concept of direct effect is presupposed in the first case, a narrow one in the second. The crucial difference is whether we believe that direct effect covers the so-called exclusionary effect: if yes, then the *Simmenthal* duty and direct effect are always coupled. If not, there is an area of the spectrum that is covered by the *Simmenthal* duty but that is not covered by direct effect; an area where the most important manifestation of primacy appears independently of direct effect.

Again, it can also be said that whether we believe in practice that the exclusionary effect of a directive—for example—is a consequence of direct effect plus supremacy or whether we believe it to be a consequence of the fact that the directive has become binding, can be constructed to impose an obligation on the state, and is supreme (without the measure having direct effect as understood in the narrow sense) makes, in practice, little difference. The scope of primacy itself is not contested within the first pillar: what is contested is whether primacy, in its manifestation as the duty to disapply conflicting rules, and direct effect appear always together, which happens if direct effect is given a wide reading, or whether primacy can appear without direct effect, which happens if direct effect is given a narrow reading.

2.2.2 *Legal Effects of AFSJ Measures before the Lisbon Treaty*

Let us now consider the range of measures that is currently available within the AFSJ. Again, this section will focus on third pillar measures: as mentioned above, some matters that formally pertained to the third pillar were transferred to the first one in Amsterdam: the provisions on visas, asylum, and immigration policies, located in Title IV EC. The Community method applies to these provisions, if with some exceptions. The choice of legal instruments, however, is not subject to any of these 'anomalies', and thus the range of measures that can be adopted in this area is identical to all other areas of the EC treaty and need not be examined here.

The third pillar proper is, of course, a different matter. Still an inter-governmental area, the range of measures that can be adopted here differs from the classical EC range of measures, and is detailed in Article 34(2) TEU. According to this provision, the Council may adopt common positions, framework decisions, decisions and conventions:

- Common positions are instruments binding on the Member States that define 'the approach of the Union to a particular matter'.[47]
- Framework decisions are comparable to directives in some aspects; these legal instruments aim at 'approximating the laws and regulations of the Member States' and 'shall be binding upon the Member States as to the result to be achieved but shall leave to the national authorities the choice of form and methods'.[48] They 'shall not entail direct effect'. It is in this latter feature that Framework decisions differ from directives—the definition of which, contained in Article 249 EC, does not contain an explicit exclusion of direct effect.
- Decisions can serve 'any other purpose consistent with the objectives of this Title, excluding any approximation of the laws and regulations of the Member States' (which should be done by framework decisions). Like the latter, they are binding but direct effect is precluded.
- And finally, the legal effect of conventions is not properly defined in Article 34(2) TEU. It may be nevertheless presumed that, as an established instrument of public international law, a convention is binding and its legal effects are to be determined by national law.[49]

Now that all labels have been discussed, in what terms—if at all—is it possible to apply them to the current range of measures that can be adopted within the third pillar?

---

[47] The ECJ has clarified that these measures are generally not supposed to produce legal effects in relation to third parties; if they do, they are reviewable under Article 35 TEU: C-355/04 P *Segi* [2007] ECR I-1657 [52]–[56]. It was in the same case that the Court confirmed that common positions are binding on the Member States by virtue of the duty of loyal cooperation, [52].

[48] The Commission has stated that in order to assess whether national implementation of framework decisions has taken place correctly, it will apply the same criteria used in the case of directives: 'Report from the Commission based on Article 9 of the Council Framework Decision of 28 November 2002 on the strengthening of the penal framework to prevent the facilitation of unauthorised entry, transit and residence' COM(2006) 770 final, 6 December 2006, 4–5. See generally on the implementation of framework decisions MJ Borgers, 'Implementing Framework Decisions' (2007) 44 CML Rev 1361.

[49] S Peers, *EU Justice and Home Affairs Law* (OUP: Oxford, 2006) 33. In practice, conventions have been phased out since the Treaty of Amsterdam entered into force: ibid, 33–5.

2.2.2.1 *Direct applicability of third pillar measures?*

As defined above, 'direct applicability' is a feature of some Community rules: in the instances where this label is applied, the Member States have no say in how the measure in question penetrates the legal order; it does so in its original form. Article 34(2) TEU makes no mention of direct applicability: this should lead us to believe that the Union has no claim as to how these measures penetrate the legal order. In theory, then, there is no corresponding obligation on the part of the Member States to consider any of these measures as law of the land directly after their adoption and in their original form. The way and the shape in which they penetrate the national legal system may differ among the Member States, depending on their national rules on the matter.[50]

2.2.2.2 *Direct effect of third pillar measures?*

Common positions and conventions are not depicted in the Treaty as able to deploy direct effect as a matter of EU law: presumably, in the first case, because they are general declarations, intended to define the Union's approach to a particular matter; in the second one, because they will have the effects accorded to them by national law.

But what of framework decisions and decisions, roughly equivalent to directives and regulations in their likely content and level of detail? Article 34(2) TEU expressly excludes direct effect for both types of measures. The question, then, is which meaning of direct effect we should adopt. If the narrow one, Article 34(2) TEU only excludes the possibility that framework decisions and decisions may confer enforceable rights on individuals. It would still be possible, though, to argue that these measures can be invoked before the national courts—as long as it is not in order to enforce a right contained in them: they could be used as a standard of review of national measures, to exclude the application of a conflicting national rule (according to the principle of supremacy); or the individual could just urge the court to take these measures into account when interpreting national law.

If we adopt the wider meaning of direct effect, however, the legal effects of these third pillar measures are dramatically curtailed: they cannot be invoked before a national court—with the exception of the case where an individual urges the court to interpret national law in the light of a

---

[50] K Lenaerts and P Van Nuffel, *Constitutional Law of the European Union* (2nd edn, Sweet & Maxwell: London, 2005) 804–7.

framework decision or a decision.[51] It is submitted that this choice is not neutral: the choice of the more narrow scope may allow these measures to develop other effects linked to primacy (if primacy is accepted as a potential feature of third pillar measures), since the invocability of these measures would remain intact, as long as it is only with an exclusionary effect and not with a view to enforcing new 'Union rights'. On the contrary, if we adopt the wider meaning of direct effect, the prohibition of Article 34(2) TEU has a wider scope and encompasses any situation in which a framework decision or decision may be invoked before national courts. This leaves no room for the principle of primacy to develop any effects: so even if we accepted primacy as a potential feature of third pillar law, there would be no occasion for it to be applied. Accordingly, an important policy choice underlies the definition of direct effect within the third pillar.[52]

Until now, it has been assumed that our choice of scope of direct effect within the first pillar would determine the scope of direct effect within the third one. This is, of course, debatable. Some may suggest defining direct effect within the third pillar as a new concept, independently of its meaning within the first one. This would acknowledge the fact that wider policy issues seem to underlie the definition of the concept within the inter-governmental area, as opposed to the less problematic Community pillar. Consistency within the pillars seems to nevertheless advise against this; even more so when there is no agreement on the definition of the concept within the first pillar—a more general discussion will not upset long-standing and unproblematic choices.

Coming down to specific arguments which may favour a particular definition of direct effect, it is necessary to note that the ECJ is competent to give preliminary rulings on the validity and interpretation of framework decisions and decisions, with some limitations. This seems to entail that these measures can be invoked before national courts; otherwise, there would be no use for a preliminary ruling mechanism.[53] One could argue that the spirit of the

---

[51] Since national courts are under a duty of conform interpretation within the third pillar also: C-105/03 *Criminal Proceedings against Maria Pupino* [2005] ECR I-5285. We may safely infer from this that it must always be possible for an individual to invoke an EU measure before a national court in order to make the latter aware of its duty of conform interpretation and perform it, regardless of the scope we attribute to the prohibition of direct effect.

[52] To a similar conclusion comes S Prechal, 'Direct Effect, Indirect Effect, Supremacy and the Evolving Constitution of the European Union' in C Barnard (ed), *The Fundamentals of EU Law Revisited* (OUP: Oxford, 2007) 44–7.

[53] K Lenaerts and P Van Nuffel, *Constitutional Law of the European Union* (2nd edn, Sweet & Maxwell: London, 2005) 807; M Claes, *The National Courts' Mandate in the European Constitution* (Hart: Oxford, 2006) 95.

Treaty, then, seems to favour a restrictive reading of the prohibition on direct effect (that is, a narrow reading of direct effect itself): if invocability is presupposed, then direct effect—within the meaning of Article 34(2) TEU—may be taken to mean only the conferral of enforceable rights.[54]

2.2.2.3 Indirect effect of third pillar measures?

We have seen that Article 34(2) TEU describes framework decisions in very similar terms to those used in Article 249 EC to describe directives (apart from the fact that the former cannot have direct effect). A different matter is whether they can have indirect effect. Traditionally, there is an obligation in dualist countries to interpret the implementing law in accordance with the original international instrument; an obligation which arises from public international law.[55]

The ECJ went further than this in *Pupino*,[56] applying the 'fortified' EC version of this obligation to framework decisions. The Court declared that the obligation to interpret national law in the light of directives (indirect effect of directives, or duty of conform interpretation) applies also within the third pillar: there is an obligation to interpret all national law in the light of framework decisions adopted in the context of Title VI of the Treaty on European Union.[57] The ECJ based this obligation on the fact that the duty of loyal cooperation (Article 10 EC) was deemed—for the first time—to apply in the third pillar:

When applying national law, the national court that is called upon to interpret it must do so as far as possible in the light of the wording and purpose of the framework decision in order to attain the result which it pursues and thus comply with Article 34(2)(b) EU.[58]

---

[54] Further, Claes has argued that the exclusion of direct effect in Article 34(2) TEU amounts to an exception in Union law, and should therefore be interpreted narrowly: Claes, ibid, 96. It is, of course, arguable that direct effect is no general rule of Union law but, rather, only of Community law. [55] Ibid.

[56] C-105/03 *Criminal Proceedings against Maria Pupino* [2005] ECR I-5285.

[57] For a more exhaustive comment on the constitutional significance of *Pupino*, see M Fletcher, 'Extending "Indirect Effect" to the Third Pillar: The Significance of Pupino' (2005) 30 ELR 862; J Spencer, 'Child Witnesses and the European Union' (2005) 64 CLJ 569; E Spaventa, 'Opening Pandora's Box: Some Reflections on the Constitutional Effects of the Decision in Pupino' (2007) 3 EuConst 5; E Spaventa, 'Remembrance of Principles Lost: On Fundamental Rights, the Third Pillar and the Scope of Union Law' (2006) 25 YEL 153; S Peers 'Salvation Outside the Church: Judicial Protection in the Third Pillar after the Pupino and Segi Judgments' (2007) 44 CML Rev 885. For further discussion, see also S Prechal, 'Direct Effect, Indirect Effect, Supremacy and the Evolving Constitution of the European Union' in C Barnard (ed), *The Fundamentals of EU Law Revisited* (OUP: Oxford, 2007). [58] *Pupino* [43].

This challenges the well-settled conception we had until now of third pillar measures as measures of public international law, which cannot display any effects until implemented through national instruments. The analogy drawn between the first and the third pillar also holds in the sense that the same—sometimes fuzzy—limits which apply to the indirect effect of directives apply as well to that of framework decisions. Thus the ECJ repeats the caveat 'as far as possible', which is taken to mean that the principle does not require a *contra legem* reading of the national measure. Further, the substantive limitation imposed by the general principles of law (particularly legal certainty and non-retroactivity) is also to be taken into account. And just as it was, too, outlined in the case-law relating to the indirect effect of directives,[59] this substantial limitation prevents this obligation from 'leading to the criminal liability of persons who contravene the provisions of a framework decision from being determined or aggravated on the basis of such a decision alone, independently of an implementing law'.[60]

Finally, it is arguable that other third pillar acts may also deploy indirect effect in the right circumstances, once it is accepted that the duty of loyal cooperation applies in the third pillar.

2.2.2.4 Self-executing third pillar measures?

The question of whether framework decisions can be self-executing prompts two reflections: on the one hand, and as regards efficiency or achievement of the measure's aims, the definition given by the Treaty seems to answer this question—implicitly—in the negative. These measures are supposed to be roughly equivalent to directives, in that they indicate a goal but leave to the Member States the election of means to achieve it. This type of framework legal instrument seems to exclude the necessary detail that a self-executing measure needs, at least in terms of achievement of the measure's aim, without further legislative implementation.

On the other hand, we can consider the concept from the perspective of judicial application: if the benchmark is that the norm could be applied by the courts to regulate the substance of a dispute before them, then this seems to be ruled out by the same reasons exposed above—the very nature of framework decisions. And even if such a framework decision came into being, it would not be applied by the courts in this manner as a result of the

---

[59] Case 80/86 *Criminal proceedings against Kolpinghuis Nijmegen BV* [1987] ECR 03969.
[60] *Pupino* [45].

prohibition of direct effect. It is not that unlikely, however, to think that a framework decision which imposes a clear obligation on the state is self-executing enough, in theory, to be applied by a national court as a standard of legality. Of course, for this to happen in practice, we would have to pre-suppose the following: (a) that we believe the use of a Union measure as a standard of legality against a national rule is not encompassed by the concept of direct effect and therefore prohibited; and (b) that we believe that the principle of supremacy applies within the third pillar, given that otherwise it is not possible to justify the use of a Union measure as a standard of legality.

The very same reflections apply to Common Positions and, to a great extent, to Conventions.[61] It is easy to imagine, however, decisions being self-executing. They are binding in their totality and there is no formal limit to how detailed they may be; it is possible, at least in theory, to pass decisions which are detailed enough to achieve their objectives without further implementation.[62] This can be significant because, hypothetically, it is possible to envisage national police acting directly under a self-executing decision—that is, without any sort of national rule between the EU decision and the police action. How this would accord with the limited jurisdiction of the Court in such situations is debatable—but, arguably, problematic.[63] There is equally no theoretical obstacle to the

---

[61] Although it could be possible to encounter a very detailed convention—in that case, the reflections on whether decisions can be self-executing would apply. This is, of course, in relation to the substance of the convention only; its effects in practice would be determined by national law.

[62] For the use that decisions are being given in practice, see S Peers, *EU Justice and Home Affairs Law* (OUP: Oxford, 2006) 36. For an example of fairly detailed instructions given to national authorities in third pillar decisions, see for example Council Decision 2005/876/JHA of 21 November 2005 on exchange of information extracted from the criminal record, or Council Decision 2005/671/JHA of 20 September 2005 on exchange of information and cooperation concerning terrorist offences.

[63] According to Art 35(5) TEU, the Court 'shall have no jurisdiction to review the validity or proportionality of operations carried out by the police or other law enforcement services of a Member State or the exercise of the responsibilities incumbent upon Member States with regard to the maintenance of law and order and the safeguarding of internal security'. Thus the Court would have jurisdiction to review the third pillar decision, but not its national enforcement. On the one hand, this may pose no problem, since the Court, in theory, never reviews national action. On the other hand, it is arguable that the Court may adopt a more-cautious-than-normal approach in reviewing the third pillar decision if there is no national law between the EU measure and the action of a national law-enforcement body. Depending on how a preliminary question is framed by the national court, the ECJ may feel it should decline to answer, or may not be able to give a very useful reply (so as not to overstep the boundary of Art 35(5) TUE). Further, see Section 2.3.1.1.2.

creation of self-executing decisions in terms of their application by the courts, be it as a standard of legality or as a rule to govern the substance of the matter. This relates only, of course, to the substance of the decision and the fact that it *could* be applied by a Court; in reality, the prohibition of direct effect would, again, prevent this.[64]

2.2.2.5 Supreme third pillar measures?

It has been argued in the literature that third pillar measures, just like EC law measures, have primacy over national law.[65] This section will argue that, in the absence of a treaty reform, the extension of the principle of primacy to the third pillar is not desirable due to the absence of guarantees that are present in the first one. The lack of a comprehensive system of judicial control at EU level in the third pillar is only excusable as long as third pillar measures are treated as measures of public international law that can be checked by national courts for their compliance with national standards, and disapplied if necessary.[66] If national courts start doubting their competence (as a matter of EU law) to do this, third pillar measures may be allowed to affect individuals in a much stronger fashion that they were ever supposed to; national law may not be able to offer any guarantees. The problem is, of course, that an EC measure that has supremacy over national law can be controlled at the EC level in a number of ways, whereas an EU measure cannot. Under the first pillar, control has been taken out of the hands of national courts and given to the ECJ. On the contrary, if third pillar measures are treated as supreme under the current judicial arrangements, control is taken away from the national level (at least from the point of view of EU law) without being taken up at the EU level.

---

[64] At least as regards application of the decision as the rule that governs the matter; whether we think that the decision could be applied as a standard of legality in practice depends on our conception of direct effect.

[65] K Lenaerts and T Corthaut, 'Of Birds and Hedges: The Role of Primacy in Invoking Norms of EU Law' (2006) 31 ELR 287, 289–91. Other authors have restricted their primacy claims to principles as fundamental rights in the third pillar: E Spaventa, 'Remembrance of Principles Lost: On Fundamental Rights, the Third Pillar and the Scope of Union Law' (2006) 25 YEL 153, 170–2. AG Bot has argued in his Opinion in *Kozlowski* that the principle of primacy applies, in theory, in the third pillar, but that there are no mechanisms to enforce it apart from indirect effect or the duty of conform interpretation: Opinion of AG Bot in Case C-66/08 *Kozlowski* [2008] ECR I-6041 [115] and ff. The Court did not address the issue.

[66] Of course, the extent of the national court's powers depends on national law.

An EC measure can be reviewed directly by the ECJ at the instance of an individual, something that is lacking in the third pillar,[67] as we shall see later. But more importantly, an EC measure can be reviewed indirectly when any national court has doubts as to its interpretation or validity and uses the preliminary reference procedure. In the third pillar, the ECJ may give preliminary rulings in relation to the validity and interpretation of framework decisions and decisions and in relation to the interpretation of conventions.[68] The Court's jurisdiction is nevertheless voluntary and varies across the Member States,[69] since the latter decide which national courts may ask for a preliminary ruling and whether the national court of last resort has an obligation to do so.[70] Finally, there is no infringement action against a disobedient state,[71] nor is there a damages action against the Union institutions for third pillar acts.[72]

[67] Art 35(6) TEU: direct actions challenging the validity of framework decisions and decisions can only be brought by the Commission and the Member States. Since *Segi*, this is to be interpreted to apply to common positions that have legal effects on third parties: Case C-355/04 P *Segi and others v Council* [2004] ECR I-1657 [52]–[56]. For an analysis of the case: S Peers, 'Salvation outside the Church: Judicial Protection in the Third Pillar after the Pupino and Segi Judgments' (2007) 44 CML Rev 885, 885–902; A Hinarejos, 'Recent Human Rights Developments in the EU Courts: The Charter of Fundamental Rights, the European Arrest Warrant and Terror Lists' (2007) 7 HRL Rev 793, 809–11.   [68] Art 35(1) TEU.

[69] For a critical view of the judicial arrangements in the third pillar, see: A Albors-Llorens, 'Changes in the Jurisdiction of the European Court of Justice under the Treaty of Amsterdam' (1998) 35 CML Rev 1273, 1278; S Peers, 'Salvation outside the Church: Judicial Protection in the Third Pillar after the Pupino and Segi Judgments' (2007) 44 CML Rev 885; S Douglas-Scott, 'The Rule of Law in the European Union: Putting the Security into the EU's Area of Freedom Security and Justice' (2004) 29 ELR 219.

[70] At the time of writing, all Member States of the Union of 15 have accepted the jurisdiction of the Court with the exception of Denmark, Ireland, and the UK ([1999] OJ C120/24). Of the Member States that have acceded since 2004, the Czech Republic and Hungary accepted in 2005 ([2005] OJ L327/19) and Latvia, Lithuania, and Slovenia in 2008 (in that year, Hungary also extended its acceptance from only courts of last resort to all national courts): [2008] OJ C69/1. Of the 17 Member States that have accepted, only Spain currently restricts its acceptance to courts of last resort, and 10 Member States have reserved the right to make provision in their national law to oblige their courts of last resort to refer (the exceptions are Finland, Greece, Portugal, Sweden, Hungary, Latvia, and Lithuania). The Court published a scorecard in March 2008 that indicates which of these 10 Member States have made use of that right and have imposed the duty to refer through national legislation: http://curia.europa.eu/en/instit/txtdocfr/txtsenvigueur/art35.pdf (accessed April 2009).

[71] There is no equivalent provision to Articles 226–8 EC in the TEU: only a mechanism of inter-state and Commission-state dispute settlement, typical of a public international law setting (Art 35(7) TEU).

[72] Confirmed by the CFI and the ECJ in Case T-338/02 *Segi and others v Council* [2004] ECR II-1647 [40] and Case C-355/04 P *Segi and others v Council* [2004] ECR I-1657 [46]–[48], respectively.

In *Costa v ENEL*, the ECJ famously stated that 'the executive force of Community law cannot vary from one state to another in deference to subsequent domestic laws, without jeopardizing the attainment of the objectives of the Treaty set out in Article 5(2) and giving rise to the discrimination prohibited by Article 7'.[73] Consistency across the Union was, therefore, one of the main reasons behind primacy in the first pillar. It could perhaps be argued that the same reason—achieving consistency—would speak in favour of extending primacy to the current third pillar as well. It is, however, submitted that doing so would not achieve the desired effect because the competence of the Court to review measures indirectly through the preliminary ruling procedure varies across the Member States. Accordingly, the Court would be able to offer guidance on the proper interpretation of third pillar measures to some national courts, but not to others. The latter would then have to deal with allegedly supreme measures of EU law without being clear as to their correct meaning and, therefore, as to whether there is a conflict with national law and what its consequences should be. As a result, the interpretation and effect given to these measures would vary across the Union. The results are even more worrying when we consider the assessment of validity of a third pillar measure, rather than just its interpretation. When faced with a potentially invalid EU measure—for example, because of a breach of fundamental rights—and if we assume that the *Foto-Frost* principle would also apply within the third pillar,[74] a national court which is not allowed to ask the ECJ for guidance would have to enforce the 'suspicious' measure or else disapply it, in breach of *Foto-Frost*. The first option is undesirable for obvious reasons;[75] the second one would be a further source of inconsistency and inequality across the Union. In fact, it has been argued that *Foto-Frost* should not apply in the current third pillar in

---

[73] Case 6/64 *Costa v ENEL* [1964] ECR 585, 589.

[74] Only the ECJ is competent to assess the validity of an EU measure and annul it: Case 314/85 *Foto-Frost v Hauptzollamt Lübeck-Ost* [1987] ECR 04199.

[75] This would be a grave flaw in the system of judicial protection of the EU. The European Court of Human Rights, for one, would be likely to consider that the EU does not offer equivalent protection to that of the ECHR. On the equivalent protection doctrine and the EC, see Case *Bosphorus Hava Yollari Turizm ve Ticaret Anonim Sirketi v Ireland* (2006) 42 EHRR 1 and further references in Chapter 3, n 193.

any case:[76] this would avoid the situation where a national court has to decide between safeguarding the right to judicial protection or complying with its *Foto-Frost* obligation. The result would still be, however, inconsistency and inequality across the different Member States. In conclusion, one of the main purposes of the application of supremacy to the first pillar in *Costa*, consistency in the application of EC law, would not be served in the least by the extension of primacy to the third pillar as it currently stands.

One could counter, of course, that not extending supremacy to the current third pillar does not serve consistency either, since Member States are able at the moment to adopt inconsistent national rules, as there is no principle of primacy to make them 'toe the line'. Does this mean that, in terms of consistency, we have nothing to gain by extending primacy—but also nothing to lose? Hardly: inconsistency within a third pillar without primacy does not seem to damage individuals' interests as badly as inconsistency within a third pillar with supremacy. If third pillar measures do not have direct effect (expressly excluded in the TEU) they cannot directly govern an individual's legal position; but if they have primacy, they can at least preclude the application of inconsistent national measures.[77] In the second situation, the EU measure is also changing the individual's legal position: the difference is theoretical or, at most, one of degree. Inconsistency across the Member States in the interpretation of a Union measure that cannot in any case change an individual's legal position (because it has neither direct effect nor primacy) does not seem as grave as inconsistency in the interpretation of a Union measure that is likely to affect an individual's position by deploying primacy. It is arguable that the Court has already ignored this argument when extending the duty of conform

---

[76] AG Mengozzi argued in his Opinion in *Segi* that *Foto-Frost* should not apply in the third pillar because of the need to offer proper judicial protection. Accordingly, national courts should be allowed to assess the validity of an EU measure, albeit applying EU standards rather than national ones. It is submitted that this way of dealing with the problem would still be a source of inconsistency, although admittedly far less than if national courts applied their own national standards. In practice, it is arguably also problematic to expect courts to apply EU standards only and not national ones in this sort of situation. Opinion of AG Mengozzi delivered on 26 October 2006, Case C-355/04 P *Segi and others v Council* [2004] ECR I-1657.

[77] Again, I am adopting here a narrow definition of direct effect, ie assuming that the so-called exclusionary effect is a manifestation of primacy and not of direct effect (and thus not expressly prohibited by Art 34 TEU). On these distinctions and their significance for the third pillar, A Hinarejos, 'On the Legal Effects of Framework Decisions and Decisions: Directly Applicable, Directly Effective, Self-executing, Supreme?' (2008) 14 ELJ 620.

interpretation to the third pillar, given that individuals are already being affected by these third pillar measures when national courts interpret national rules in their light. There is, however, an important difference of degree: the individual is, in this case, being affected only because—and as far as—the national rule allows a particular reading. The third pillar measure should not affect the individual's position to the extreme of yielding a result that would have been unthinkable when reading the national rule.

To sum up: if the effects that a third pillar measure can have on an individual's legal position are limited, so are the pernicious effects of inconsistency in the application of such measure across the Union. If we are going to have inconsistency within the third pillar in any case, then let us at least restrain its pernicious effects on individuals by restraining the 'force' of third pillar measures; that is, by not granting them primacy. The third pillar in its current form—without undergoing a treaty reform like the one envisaged in Lisbon—does not seem to be ready for the full-blown application of the EC principle of primacy.

2.2.2.6 A Case Study on the Legal Effects of Third Pillar Measures: Reviewing the EAW Framework Decision[78]

This section will argue that there is uncertainty among national courts as to the present status of third pillar law. This is caused by a number of factors—the decision of the ECJ in *Pupino*,[79] for one, has already been mentioned. Others include the general phenomenon of *Reflexwirkung* between the pillars,[80] in the sense that it is difficult to keep two 'integrated but separate legal orders'[81] from influencing each other, also in the way they are applied by courts. Perhaps some national courts feel a certain pressure to over-comply with EU law, lest they be criticized for their backward stance. Finally, the political efforts to unify the pillars in the Constitutional and afterwards Lisbon Treaty may have also played a role in confusing actors as to the current state of play.

---

[78] An earlier version of this section was included in A Hinarejos, 'The Lisbon Treaty versus Standing Still: A View from the Third Pillar' (2009) 5 EuConst 99.

[79] Case C-105/03 *Criminal Proceedings against Maria Pupino* [2005] ECR I-5285.

[80] C Timmermans, 'The Constitutionalisation of the European Union' (2002) 21 YEL 1, 10; M Claes, *The National Courts' Mandate in the European Constitution* (Hart: Oxford, 2006) 105.

[81] Case C-402/05 P *Kadi* [2008] ECR I-6351 [202].

In order to illustrate this uncertainty, this section will focus on the litigation generated by the Framework Decision on the EAW[82] before several national constitutional courts across the Union,[83] and recently also before the ECJ.[84] Against this background, this section will briefly showcase the different attitudes towards third pillar law taken by various national courts.

The EAW Framework Decision creates a speedy surrender procedure between judicial authorities of EU Member States that replaces traditional methods of extradition based on public international law.[85] The new procedure is based on the principle of mutual recognition of judicial decisions in criminal law and, in a large number of cases, it does away with the traditional requirement of double criminality.[86] The challenges against the EAW Framework Decision before national constitutional courts concerned the validity of the national laws implementing it, generally because they conflicted with the prohibition on the extradition of nationals contained in the national constitution.[87] In the German case, the Bundesverfassungsgericht was of the opinion that the national legislator could have found a constitutional implementation within the latitude afforded by the framework decision, but failed to do so.[88] In the Polish case, the court found that it was impossible for the legislator to find a constitutional way to

---

[82] Council Framework Decision 2002/584/JHA of 13 June 2002 on the European arrest warrant and the surrender procedures between Member States, OJ (2002) L 190/1.

[83] *Inter alia*, Bundesverfassungsgericht (German Constitutional Court), Decision of 18 July 2005 (2 BvR 2236/04) [2006] 1 CMLR 16; Trybunal Konstytucyjny (Polish Constitutional Court), Judgment of 27 April 2005, No P 1/05 [2006] 1 CMLR 36; Judgment of the Czech Constitutional Court of 3 May 2006, Pl ÚS 66/04 [2007] 3 CMLR 24; Supreme Court of Cyprus, Judgment of 7 November 2005, App No 294/2005 [2007] 3 CMLR 42; *Minister for Justice & Law Reform v Robert Aaron Anderson* [2006] IEHC 95; *Office of the King's Prosecutor v Cando Armas* [2005] UKHL 67. On the European Arrest Warrant itself, see S Peers, *EU Justice and Home Affairs Law* (OUP: Oxford, 2007) 468–73; R Blekxtoon and W van Ballegooij, *Handbook on the European Arrest Warrant* (TMC Asser: The Hague, 2005); and J Wouters and F Naert, 'Of Arrest Warrants, Terrorist Offences and Extradition Deals: An Appraisal of the Main Criminal Law Measures against Terrorism after "11 September"' (2004) 41 CML Rev 909.

[84] Case C-303/05 *Advocaten voor de Wereld* [2007] ECR I-3633.

[85] An extensive recollection of the legislative process can be found in J Spencer, 'The European Arrest Warrant' (2004) 6 Cambridge Ybk of European Legal Studies 201.

[86] For a comprehensive overview of the problems prompted by the application of the principle of mutual recognition to criminal matters, see V Mitsilegas, 'The Constitutional Implications of Mutual Recognition in Criminal Matters in the EU' (2006) 43 CML Rev 1277.

[87] Although not only—in the Czech Republic, for example, the challenge also concerned the abolition of the requirement of double criminality.

[88] For a comment of this case, A Hinarejos, (2006) 43 CML Rev 583.

implement the EU measure, but it decided to patch the conflict until the national constitution could be reformed.[89] The Czech Constitutional Court could not find a way to reconcile the national implementing measures and the national constitution through interpretation.[90] None of these courts referred the case to the ECJ. In Belgium, however, the validity of the framework decision itself was questioned and the ECJ was asked to give a preliminary ruling under Article 35 TEU in the case *Advocaten voor de Wereld*.[91] Among other things,[92] the claimant argued that, because of the suppression of the requirement of double criminality in a set number of instances, the framework decision ran counter to the principles of legality and equality.

The litigation in national courts surrounding the EAW goes right to the heart of the nature of third pillar measures and how they are perceived by national constitutional courts. The German Constitutional Court was quick to label the framework decision as international law, and deny it any effects typical of EC law (even indirect effect, thereby contradicting *Pupino*). The conflict was manageable because the framework decision allowed for a constitutional implementation; if this had not been the case, the German Court would have probably declared the framework decision inapplicable on German soil, at least under the national constitution as it

---

[89] So that Poland would not breach its EU law obligations, the Polish court delayed the entry into force of its judgment by 18 months while stating the obligation of the legislature to amend the Constitution in the meantime. For a comment of this case, D Leczykiewicz, (2006) 43 CML Rev 1181; A Lazowski, 'Constitutional Tribunal on the Surrender of Polish Citizens under the European Arrest Warrant. Decision of 27 April 2005' (2005) 1 EuConst 569. As a result of the Court's judgment, Art 55 of the Polish Constitution was amended (statutes approved by the *Sejm* on 8 September 2006, and by the Senate on 14 September 2006). It has been argued that the amended provision can still not be reconciled fully with the content of the EAW Framework Decision: A Górski, P Hofmanski, A Sakowicz, D Szumilo-Kulczyckac, 'The European Arrest Warrant (EAW) and its Implementation in the Member States of the European Union: International Research Questionnaire', part of an 'EAW Database' and available at: http://www.law.uj.edu.pl/~kpk/eaw/data/poland.html (accessed January 2009). See also A Lazowski, 'From EU with Trust: The Potential and Limits of the Mutual Recognition in the Third Pillar from the Polish Perspective' in G Vernimmen-Van Tiggelen, L Surano and A Weyembergh (eds), *The Future of Mutual Recognition in Criminal Matters in the European Union / L'Avenir de la Reconnaissance Mutuelle en Matière Pénale dans l'Union Européenne* (Éditions de l'Université de Bruxelles: Brussels, 2009).

[90] For a comment of the Czech case, J Komárek, 'European Constitutionalism and the European Arrest Warrant: In Search of the Limits of "Contrapunctual Principles"' (2007) 44 CML Rev 9.   [91] C-303/05 *Advocaten voor de Wereld* [2007] ECR I-3633.

[92] The claimant also argued that the subject-matter of the framework decision should have been implemented by way of a convention.

now stands. From the German Court's point of view, it is clear that the differences between EU and EC law remain very much in place.

The Polish Constitutional Court found a conflict between the national constitution and the third pillar measure that could not be solved through interpretation. The question was, then, whether third pillar measures have supremacy over national law. Of course, the problem before the Court concerned the compatibility of the national implementation law with the constitution, but the framework decision did not give discretion to the national legislator to implement it in a manner that did not conflict with the national constitution. The Polish Court could have annulled the implementing national law and made it clear that no possible implementation of the framework decision would be considered constitutional in the future, thereby making it inapplicable on Polish soil as long as the constitution remained unchanged. However, this would have meant that Poland would not only be in breach of its obligations under EU law, but also of Article 9 of its own constitution: '[Poland] shall respect international law binding upon it'. To be on the safe side, the Court decided to delay the annulment of the national implementation measure, while instructing the legislator to amend the national constitution in the meantime. The Polish Court's attitude as regards third pillar measures is hesitant and reflects the growing confusion on the boundaries between EU and EC law.[93] It is perhaps a shame that this national court could not put its doubts on the primacy of third pillar measures to the ECJ—something that, on the other hand, squares well with the 'silent' inter-court dialogue that often takes place in the Union.[94]

The Czech Court was also hesitant as to the position of third pillar law in the Member States' legal order. While it made it clear that there are important differences between EU and EC norms, it also remarked that '[t]he consequences of these differences for the current nature and status of such norms in relation to Member State legal orders, has not as yet been definitively and clearly settled in the case-law of the ECJ'.[95] It was possible

---

[93] Although the Court refers to the framework decision as an international agreement, it also wonders in its judgment whether third pillar law has primacy over national law as a matter of EU law: D Leczykiewicz, (2006) 43 CML Rev 1181, 1185.

[94] Even if the Polish Constitutional Court had wanted to ask the ECJ on this point (something we are not in a position to know), it would have been impossible because Poland has not accepted the jurisdiction of the ECJ in the third pillar of the EU. See n 70.

[95] Judgment of the Czech Constitutional Court of 3 May 2006, Pl ÚS 66/04 [2007] 3 CMLR 24 [58].

for the Czech Court to reconcile the national implementation law with the constitution through interpretation, which meant that it did not need to ask the ECJ to clarify the legal effects of third pillar measures any further; it concluded that the question remained open.[96]

The only national court to refer the question to the ECJ, the Belgian Arbitragehof, arguably considered that the EAW Framework Decision had primacy over national law. This can be inferred from the following: the claimant had challenged the legality of the national implementing law, yet the Arbitragehof did not simply assess the compatibility of the national law with national human rights standards. It reasoned that the national law was merely the verbatim implementation of a Union measure that did not leave any room for national discretion on the points at stake in the case, and it thus considered itself unable to assess it against national standards—presumably since that would amount to assessing the framework decision itself against national standards, something that is not allowed if the Union measure is considered supreme over national law. Instead, it referred the question to the ECJ and asked the Court to assess the validity of the framework decision against EU human rights standards.[97]

All these different approaches to the nature and legal effects of the EAW Framework Decision illustrate the uncertainty in the field; an uncertainty that was not dispelled by the ECJ. The Court subjected itself to the letter of the questions asked by the Arbitragehof, thus reflecting only on the compatibility of the framework decision with EU human rights standards in a brief and, at times, thinly argued judgment.[98] No attempt was made at clarifying the status of third pillar law fully—something that is not very surprising, given the altogether different focus that the Belgian Court gave to its questions. The ECJ did nevertheless remark that not only the institutions of the Union, but also the Member States when implementing Union law, 'are subject to review of the conformity of their acts with the Treaties and the general principles of law':[99] the precise meaning of this

---

[96] Ibid, [60].

[97] Vandamme shows that the Belgian Arbitragehof has consistently merged Belgian and EC/EU legal principles for the purpose of their interpretation. This 'merger' ensures that there is no discrepancy between EC/EU law and Belgian law. T Vandamme, 'Prochain Arret: La Belgique! Explaining Recent Preliminary References of the Belgian Constitutional Court' 4 (2008) EuConst 127.

[98] For a more general critique of the judgment, see A Hinarejos, 'Recent Human Rights Developments in the EU Courts: The Charter of Fundamental Rights, the European Arrest Warrant and Terror Lists' (2007) 7 HRL Rev 793, 795–802; D Leczykiewicz, 'Constitutional Conflicts and the Third Pillar' 33 (2008) ELR 230.   [99] *Advocaten* [45].

statement is unclear. Firstly, the Court seems to be saying that, also in the third pillar, the Treaties and the general principles of law (primary law) have a certain degree of primacy over national law, presumably at least as regards respect for fundamental rights.[100] This, in itself, is not shocking: the Member States are bound by the TEU when implementing Union law, and thus by its Article 6. It is logical for the ECJ to claim that, in theory, Article 6 TEU and the obligation enshrined in it has primacy over national law; after all, the ECJ is an international court and we cannot expect an international court to do anything other than to uphold the principle of *pacta sunt servanda*, or primacy as a theoretical claim of public international law.[101]

Secondly, however, the Court uses the words 'subject to review', meaning that it may be going further than just stating a theoretical claim. Who, we may wonder, is going to carry out this review of national action in practice? The obvious candidates are national courts, since there are no infringement proceedings in the third pillar. To the extent that a number of countries have accepted the jurisdiction of the ECJ in this area, some of the national courts may ask for guidance through the preliminary ruling procedure. It may be that, in the near future, the Court expressly imposes on national courts the duty to disapply national law within this area that is in conflict with EU fundamental rights standards as enshrined in primary law, something hinted at in *Advocaten*. The Court is also leaving the door open to deciding itself (through the preliminary ruling procedure if available) if national action complies with EU human rights standards as long as the Member State is acting within the scope of EU law.

The question is whether the process will stop here. What of third pillar primary law that does not concern the protection of fundamental rights? What of secondary law? It seems that, if any of these national courts asks the ECJ at some point whether any third pillar measure other than those at stake in *Advocaten* should prevail over national law, the answer is also likely to be 'yes': the Court, as an international court, can do nothing but uphold the principle of *pacta sunt servanda*. It has been convincingly argued in the

---

[100] D Sarmiento, 'European Union: The European Arrest Warrant and the Quest for Constitutional Coherence' 6 (2008) I-CON 171, 166–7 and 180–1. Spaventa has also argued for the primacy of fundamental rights as general principles in the third pillar: E Spaventa, 'Remembrance of Principles Lost: On Fundamental Rights, the Third Pillar and the Scope of Union Law' (2006) 25 YEL 153, 170–2.

[101] M Claes, *The National Courts' Mandate in the European Constitution* (Hart: Oxford, 2006) 167–8.

literature that the fact that the Court declared EC law supreme over national law in *Costa v ENEL* was not at all surprising, since it amounted to asking an international court about the status of international law. What made the primacy of EC law have stronger effects was that it could be ascertained by the ECJ in the middle of a case that was being heard by a national court. These stronger effects were the result of the way the judicial system is structured in the EC and, in particular, of the existence of an (*ex-ante*) preliminary ruling mechanism.[102] To the extent that this mechanism is available in the third pillar, the foundations are there for the ECJ to declare the primacy of the whole of third pillar law over the whole of national law, at least in theory. Whether this would be done in the same terms as in *Costa* and *Simmenthal* is, of course, a different matter. In *Costa*, the ECJ put forward several arguments that spoke in favour of a strong principle of primacy in the first pillar.[103] The same arguments led to imposing the *Simmenthal* duty on national courts. To the extent that these other arguments are not present in the third pillar and that other policy considerations would have to be weighed, the ECJ may feel obliged to adopt a more ambiguous or even weaker position on the primacy of third pillar law: by even avoiding to answer if at all feasible, for example, or by stating such primacy in a theoretical manner but not spelling out its effects in practice, leaving them for national courts to decide. In any case, the discussion as to the status of third pillar law continues; the only remark that the ECJ made in *Advocaten* in this regard did not fully clarify the matter, although it did make it clear that the 'slippery slope' towards full-fledged primacy in the third pillar may be closer than we think.

To sum up: national courts view and deal with third pillar law in very different manners. The spectrum goes from considering it public international law to considering it akin to EC law, with intermediate stages. This section has pointed to some likely causes for what seems to be uncertainty as to the current state of play in the third pillar, something that is manifest in both the academic discussion as to what the nature of third pillar law is and should be, and in an array of different judicial attitudes towards it.

---

[102] See on this point D Wyatt, 'New Legal Order, or Old' 7 (1982) ELRev 147; M Claes, *The National Courts' Mandate in the European Constitution* (Hart: Oxford, 2006) 167–8; B de Witte, 'The European Union as an International Legal Experiment' forthcoming EUI Working Paper, on file with the author.

[103] An autonomous legal system that demands consistency, a Community of unlimited duration with its own institutions and legal personality, resulting from a limitation of sovereignty/transfer of powers from the Member States: Case 6/64 *Costa v ENEL* [1964] ECR 585.

We have also seen how the ECJ itself has not clarified the status of third pillar law. It has been argued, however, that it may be only a matter of time until the ECJ is asked to make a pronouncement in this respect, with unforeseeable results.

In the absence of a Treaty reform that addresses the nature of third pillar measures, judicial uncertainty may result in a gradual change in the way these measures are applied by courts, either national or EU ones. It has been argued that these measures may progressively be allowed to deploy effects similar to those of measures adopted within the first pillar. In turn, this process would lead to gaps in judicial protection and inequality throughout the Union if it does not come paired with a necessary extension of the first pillar system of judicial protection.

Moreover, if the strengthening of these measures comes as a result of ECJ case-law, it is most likely to cause new conflicts between the latter court and national constitutional courts. In its famous *Maastricht* decision,[104] the German Constitutional Court had to decide whether the transfer of powers to the Community had gone beyond what the *Grundgesetz* permitted. The Court replied in the negative, after a careful examination of several arguments put forward by the complainant. One of them may be of interest for our discussion: the argument was that, since the jurisdiction of the European Court of Justice was excluded in the second and third pillars, there was a gap in the protection of individuals.

The Bundesverfassungsgericht considered that the ECJ's jurisdiction was only excluded 'in respect of provisions of the Union Treaty which do not confer powers on the Union to take measures which have direct effects on holders of constitutional rights within the territory of member-States'.[105] Considering decisions adopted within the third pillar specifically, the Court stated that 'regardless of the binding effect on the member-states in international law of such council decisions [...] no law may be passed by them which is directly applicable in member-states and *can claim precedence*.'[106] What convinced the Court, then, that there was no legal gap was the nature of the measures adopted within the second and third pillars: measures of public international law, which could not directly affect German citizens. Furthermore, if those measures obliged Member States to 'make encroachments which are of constitutional relevance, all such

---

[104] BVerfGE 89, 155; *Manfred Brunner and Others v The EU Treaty* (Cases 2 BVR 2134/92 & 2159/92) [1994] 1 CMLR 57.   [105] Ibid, [14].
[106] Ibid, [17] emphasis added.

encroachments, if they occur[red] in Germany, [would] be subject to review in full by the German courts.'[107]

The reason why this argument could not be used to prove the uncon-stitutionality of the transfer of powers to the European Union was that 'the protection of basic rights provided by the Constitution is not displaced by supra-national law that could claim precedence'.[108] There is an important distinction between the Community and the intergovernmental pillars as regards the effects of the measures adopted within them. Foreign and security policy and justice and home affairs are objects of European cooperation, but the Member States 'have deliberately not incorporated them into the supra-national jurisdiction system of the European Com-munities'.[109] The Court emphasized that this separation is clear and per-manent, to the extent that a transfer from the realm of intergovernmental cooperation into the first pillar would have to be preceded by a Treaty amendment, ratified by all Member States.

The way in which the different nature of the pillars, in general, and the lack of primacy, specifically, were used by the German Constitutional Court to justify the constitutionality of a restricted judicial control at European level is meant to show that an extension of primacy to the third pillar and the blurring of the distinction between first and third pillar could under-standably reawaken old but persisting concerns about the legitimacy and constitutionality of this intergovernmental area among national courts. These concerns would be fuelled by the fact that measures adopted within the third pillar, which do not undergo the same controls of validity as EC law measures, can nevertheless affect an individual's legal position in a comparable, albeit not identical, way. From this point of view, primacy is liable to erode the protection of constitutional (national) fundamental rights, and this can be used as a sound argument for the unconstitutionality or illegitimacy of the transfer of sovereign powers to the Union that has taken place in the third pillar. The time may come when a national constitutional court deems it necessary to exercise its reserved 'subsidiary emergency jurisdiction'[110] because the ECJ cannot properly protect the rights of indi-viduals against third pillar measures that have primacy over national law.

---

[107] Ibid, [22].

[108] Ibid, [22].

[109] Ibid, [18].

[110] A Peters, 'The Bananas Decision 2000 of the German Federal Constitutional Court: Towards Reconciliation with the ECJ as regards Fundamental Rights Protection in Europe' (2000) 43 German Yearbook of International Law 276, 281.

It seems, finally, that allowing third pillar measures to be granted supremacy as a matter of EU law is not only dangerous from the EU point of view of judicial protection, consistency, and equality; it could also be a cause of conflict between the ECJ and national constitutional courts.

2.2.3 Legal Effects of AFSJ Measures after the Lisbon Treaty

Although the AFSJ is an area in evolution, I have argued until now that this slow process of approximation to the EC legal system does not yet warrant the conclusion that third pillar law should be treated in the same way as EC law. A prior wide-ranging reform would be necessary. It is the case, nevertheless, that the necessary political will—at least among political elites—seems to be there for the third pillar to undergo such a reform. The Member States thus accepted and signed the Constitutional Treaty, which envisaged the integration of the three pillars into a single structure. In the wake of its failure, various possible legislative reforms with a similar effect as regards the third pillar were put forward. Finally, the Lisbon Treaty also envisages the extension of what is currently termed the Community method to the third pillar.

This section will deal with the nature and effects of the range of AFSJ measures foreseen in the Lisbon Treaty. As a general observation, it should be remembered that the unification of EC and EU law means that under the Lisbon Treaty there would only be EU law, which would have the current features of EC law. Accordingly, what are now third pillar measures would, under the Lisbon Treaty, have primacy over national law and possible direct effect. The current discussion on the nature of third pillar measures and their possible primacy would thus be superseded. Equally, it was said earlier that, as the third pillar now stands, national courts could theoretically assess the validity of EU law measures against national standards and ultimately disapply them. This would, of course, depend on their competence as a matter of national law, but it would not be precluded as a matter of EU law. This would also change with the Lisbon Treaty: as a consequence of the principle of primacy, it would not be possible to review the same measures against national standards and,[111] furthermore, the *Foto-Frost* principle would allow only the ECJ to review their validity effectively.[112]

---

[111] eg Case 11/70 *Internationale Handelsgesellschaft mbH v Einfuhr- und Vorratstelle für Getreide und Futtermittel* [1970] ECR 1125.

[112] Case 314/85 *Foto-Frost v Hauptzollamt Lübeck-Ost* [1987] ECR 04199.

2.2.3.1 Types of Measures

The unification of first and third pillars in the Lisbon Treaty results in a common range of measures to be adopted across the board. The current binding instruments of EC law at present (directives, regulations, and decisions) become the instruments of all Union law and may therefore be adopted across the AFSJ. These instruments are described in Article 288 TFEU in the same terms as they are described at the moment in Article 249 EC: I will therefore not dwell on their features, since they are well known. Of note is that all of these instruments may be of a legislative or non-legislative nature, depending on whether they are adopted following the legislative procedure set out in Article 289 TFEU.[113] The next section will map out the legal effects of each of these measures within the framework of the Lisbon Treaty.

2.2.3.2 Legal Effects

2.2.3.2.1 Direct Applicability.   It has been pointed out earlier that direct applicability is absent in the current third pillar: Article 34(2) TEU makes no mention of direct applicability, which should lead us to believe that the Union has no claim as to how these measures penetrate the national legal order. In theory, then, there is no corresponding obligation on the part of the Member States to consider any of these measures as law of the land directly after their adoption and in their original form. The way and the shape in which they penetrate the national legal system may differ among the Member States, depending on their national rules on the matter.[114]

The Lisbon Treaty, however, would change this scenario. Article 288 TFEU does claim the direct applicability of regulations; in their original form, regulations shall automatically become the law of the land in the

---

[113] Art 289 TFEU refers both to an ordinary legislative procedure (co-decision, further regulated in Art 294 TFEU in the same terms as the current Art 251 EC) and to special legislative procedures where the Treaty so provides. These special legislative procedures would require the Council to act with the participation of the European Parliament, or the European Parliament to act with the participation of the Council. In the first case, the Council may be required to obtain the Parliament's consent or only to consult with it. On the legislative/non-legislative/regulatory distinction, see also section 2.5.1.

[114] K Lenaerts and P Van Nuffel, *Constitutional Law of the European Union* (2nd edn Sweet & Maxwell: London, 2005) 804–7.

Member States and do not need any sort of incorporation to do so. This feature is understandably absent from the description of directives given in the same Article, but can be presumed in the case of decisions, which are described as binding in their entirety.

2.2.3.2.2 Direct Effect. The current framework decisions and decisions, the most significant types of current third pillar measures, can have no direct effect because of the explicit prohibition of Article 34 TEU. Direct effect can also be safely excluded in the case of common positions—more political declarations than orthodox legal measures—and, as regards conventions, suffice it to say that the TEU has no claim as to their legal effects; they depend on the way national law deals with public international law measures. In sum, none of the current third pillar measures can deploy the direct effect to which some measures of Community law have a claim.

Two observations can made as regards the Lisbon Treaty in this respect: one, that there is no specific ban on the direct effect of the Union measures adopted within the AFSJ, a limitation that would have been comparable to some extent to the one found in Article 34 TEU at present. And two, that although the range of 'normal' Union law measures (with the current effects of Community measures) is made available across the board, not all AFSJ measures would necessarily have direct effect—just as not all Community measures adopted under the current first pillar have it. Rather, this would continue to depend on the type of measure used and on the general rules on direct effect. Since the Lisbon Treaty only extends the 'classic' effects of EC measures to the AFSJ, it is foreseeable how direct effect would be deployed in this area: it is fair to expect that regulations, directives, and decisions would have direct effect under the same conditions that apply in the current first pillar.

2.2.3.2.3 Indirect Effect. It has already been explained that the duty of conform interpretation, or the indirect effect of certain measures, is a judicial invention. It is not included in the current Treaties, and neither is it included explicitly in the Lisbon Treaty. The latter document does not contain a general clause on the continuity of previous ECJ case-law either (contrary to its predecessor, the Constitutional Treaty),[115] but it is

---

[115] Art IV-438(4) of the Treaty establishing a Constitution for Europe: 'The case-law of the Court of Justice of the European Communities and of the Court of First Instance on the interpretation and application of the treaties and acts repealed by Article IV-437, as well as of the acts and conventions adopted for their application, shall remain, mutatis mutandis, the source of interpretation of Union law and in particular of the comparable provisions of the Constitution.' [2004] OJ C310/01.

arguable that such continuity should be the default approach, and no reminder is strictly necessary. Further, the fact that the current range of first pillar measures is extended to the AFSJ speaks in favour of the existence of indirect effect in the same terms as it now does in EC law.

2.2.3.2.4 Self-Executing Measures in the Lisbon Treaty.

As explained above, I will use this label to refer only to the level of detail in the substance of a measure; that is, the question is whether a measure is detailed enough to be able to achieve its aim without implementation or to be applied by a court, in theory. I do not refer here to whether these measures would actually be applied by a court in practice—this depends on other factors such as direct effect or primacy.

On the one hand, self-executing can mean that a measure is detailed enough to achieve its aim without further implementation: in that sense, and according to the depiction of these measures in the Lisbon Treaty, only regulations and decisions (as opposed to directives) are likely to have the necessary level of detail to be self-executing in this sense. On the other hand, self-executing can also mean that a measure is detailed enough to be applied by a court, be it as the rule governing the substance of the matter or as a standard of legality: of course, the level of detail needed varies with the purpose for judicially applying the measure. Bearing this in mind, the more specific instruments foreseen in the Lisbon Treaty (regulations and decisions) could have the level of detail needed to perform both functions. This, however, seems unlikely in the case of more general instruments (such as directives), which probably have the level of detail necessary to function as a standard of legality in some cases,[116] but which are much less likely to have the level of detail necessary to function as the rule governing the substance of the matter.

2.2.3.2.5 Primacy in the Lisbon Treaty.

The failed Constitutional Treaty established that 'the Constitution and law adopted by the

---

[116] In the context of judicial application, if we wish to use a Union measure as a standard of legality against a national rule, it may only be necessary to be able to construe the Union measure as imposing an obligation on the state. The measure may not need to be very detailed in the way this obligation is to be discharged, for instance, but it may suffice to be able to extract a clear obligation from it. See Case C-431/92 *Commission v Germany (Grosskrotzenburg)* [1995] ECR I-2189.

institutions of the Union in exercising competences conferred on it shall have primacy over the law of the Member States',[117] a provision which would have explicitly extended the principle of primacy to the third pillar. The Lisbon Treaty does not contain a similar provision; the fact that the differences between EC and EU law disappear and that the current effects of EC law are extended across the board, however, speaks in favour of an extension of primacy all the same. Furthermore, the Intergovernmental Conference did recall in one of its declarations annexed to the Lisbon Treaty 'that, in accordance with well settled case law of the Court of Justice of the European Union, the Treaties and the law adopted on the basis of the Treaties have primacy over the law of the Member States, under the conditions laid down by the said case law'.[118]

The extension of primacy within the current legislative framework to the intergovernmental pillars—and especially to the third one—poses many questions. The first one arises from the fact that there is currently no agreement in the literature on whether the most important manifestation of primacy, or the duty to disapply conflicting national rules (the *Simmenthal* duty), applies only where the Community measure is directly effective—regardless of whether it subsequently governs the substance of the matter (substitutionary effect) or it does not (exclusionary effect). The discussion goes back to the well-known debate on whether the exclusionary effect is direct effect. This may almost be a moot point within the first pillar, where it is clear that exclusionary effect is a fact, and there is no formal problem in calling it direct effect: in these circumstances, whether we believe that a directive has been allowed to exclude the application of a national rule because it is supreme and directly effective, or only supreme, is of limited significance. That is, however, not the case within the current third pillar, where the direct effect of framework decisions and decisions is prohibited (Article 34 TEU). It has already been argued that, if we assume that the exclusionary effect is direct effect, we are assuming that primacy and direct effect always appear together in the first pillar. In that case, the prohibition of direct effect in the third pillar means that there can also be

---

[117] Art I-6 of the Treaty establishing a Constitution for Europe, [2004] OJ C310/01.

[118] Declaration 17, Declarations annexed to the Final Act of the Intergovernmental Conference which adopted the Treaty of Lisbon, signed on 13 December 2007 [2008] OJ C115/335, 344.

no supremacy—at least in its typical manifestation, the *Simmenthal* duty—since there is no primacy without direct effect. Conversely, if we believe that the exclusionary effect is not direct effect, we may infer that supremacy is possible without direct effect in the first pillar. It would follow that it would also be possible within the third one, despite the prohibition of Article 34 TEU.

Consider now the situation envisaged in the Lisbon Treaty, where there is no ban on direct effect and so directives, regulations, and decisions may be able to deploy direct effect if they comply with the necessary conditions. The extension of primacy orchestrated within this framework would be far less problematic than an extension of primacy within the framework of the current third pillar. In the latter case, a series of clear choices would have to be made beforehand: for supremacy to deploy any effects, we would have to accept that supremacy and direct effect do not necessarily come hand in hand. That, in turn, entails accepting that the exclusionary effect is not direct effect, but only a manifestation of supremacy, and is therefore not prohibited within the third pillar. Within the proposed framework of the Lisbon Treaty, on the other hand, the extension of primacy to what is at present the third pillar requires no such preliminary choices. The interaction between supremacy and direct effect is exactly the same as within the current first pillar, and it is therefore still possible to support opposing views on their relationship. The question is no more whether the exclusionary effect falls within the prohibition on direct effect, since there is no such prohibition. Hence the exclusionary effect can appear and can be explained away both on the basis of supremacy and direct effect acting together, and on the basis of supremacy alone.

To sum up: the discussion prompted by the proposed extension of supremacy in the Lisbon Treaty would be the same one that we have now within the first pillar—whether supremacy applies only when there is direct effect, or whether it can also apply in its absence. Authors such as Arnull and Besselink subscribe to the first view,[119] whereas Craig supports the second one, albeit clarifying that where a measure has direct effect, supremacy is 'more keenly felt'.[120] In its submissions on the matter, the

---

[119] EU Committee of the House of Lords, 'The Future Role of the European Court of Justice: Report with Evidence' (6th Report of Session 2003–4, HL Paper 47) 15.

[120] Presumably because the measure can, in such cases, deploy not only exclusionary but also substitutionary effect. Ibid.

UK Government remains ambiguous on its understanding of primacy.[121] In any case, the scope of primacy itself is not being contested, but rather whether, when supremacy appears, we are necessarily in the presence of direct effect as well. This is not a debate on supremacy, but rather on what it tells us about direct effect. The *quid* of the question, as it surprisingly often seems to happen, is the scope of direct effect.

2.3 The Jurisdiction of the ECJ at Present

Now that the current and intended future features of third pillar measures have been explained, this chapter will now map out the powers that the ECJ has at present to control those measures, as well as, later on, the reform proposed by the Lisbon Treaty.

Judicial control in matters pertaining to the Area of Freedom, Security and Justice has come a long way since the creation of the third pillar at Maastricht, where the Court was given little jurisdiction.[122] The Treaty of Amsterdam subsequently extended the jurisdiction of the Court to the third pillar (Title VI TEU) and to the new provisions on visa, asylum and immigration policies, which previously fell within the third pillar and were

---

[121] EU Committee of the House of Lords, 'The Constitutional Treaty: Role of the ECJ. Primacy of Union Law—Government Response and Correspondence' (3rd Report of Session 2005–6, HL Paper 15). The view is repeatedly stated that supremacy can only apply 'where the EU can generate directly effective or directly applicable law' (p 18); this seems to support the view that supremacy can appear independently of direct effect, with the Union measure being merely directly applicable. Later on, however, the opposite view seems to be supported. When discussing the primacy of CFSP measures, it is said that 'because of their content and subject matter, they will be highly unlikely in practice to contain provisions that are directly effective or directly applicable' (pp 18–19). This seems to indicate that the expressions 'directly effective' and 'directly applicable' are being used as synonyms and both denote a feature that depends on the substance of the measure. The other, more extended use of the label 'directly applicable' is not a synonym of 'directly effective' and relates only to how the measure penetrates the national legal system, independently of its contents. If both labels were being used as synonyms throughout, the Government's position is that supremacy and direct effect must go hand in hand. It nevertheless seems that a certain degree of ambiguity has been purposely maintained throughout the submissions.

[122] The Court has played a role in JHA matters since 1971, given that it was given jurisdiction by the Member States over specific Protocols and Conventions. At Maastricht, Art K.3(2), (c), the Treaty itself recognized this practice; the Court was also able after Maastricht to police the boundaries between the first and third pillars. For an overview, see S Peers, 'Who's Judging the Watchmen: The Judicial System of the "Area of Freedom, Security and Justice" ' (1998) 17 YEL 337, 340–50.

then transferred to the first one (Title IV EC).[123] The Court's jurisdiction is limited under both Titles, albeit in different manners, and they will be studied in turn. The Urgent Preliminary Ruling Procedure applies throughout the AFSJ, but will be discussed under Title VI TEU.

2.3.1 The Area within the First Pillar (Title IV EC)

2.3.1.1 Powers of Review

2.3.1.1.1 Procedural limitations.   The powers of the Court to review measures adopted under Title IV EC directly are, in principle, the same as in other areas pertaining to the first pillar. In all cases, the Court exercises this competence pursuant to Article 230 EC.[124]

On the contrary, the power of the Court to give preliminary rulings pursuant to Article 234 EC can only be exercised under special conditions, laid down in Article 68 EC. The first paragraph of this provision establishes that only national courts of last resort shall request a preliminary ruling from the ECJ.[125] The choice of words seems to

---

[123] For a more detailed account of these changes, A Albors-Llorens, 'Changes in the Jurisdiction of the European Court of Justice under the Treaty of Amsterdam' (1998) 35 CML Rev 1273; P Eeckhout, 'The European Court of Justice and the "Area of Freedom, Security and Justice": Challenges and Problems' in D O'Keeffe (ed), *Judicial Review in European Union Law: Liber Amicorum in Honour of Lord Slynn of Hadley* (Kluwer: London, 2000); AM Arnull, *The European Union and its Court of Justice* (Oxford EC Law Library, OUP: Oxford, 1999) 69–74; S Douglas-Scott, 'The Rule of Law in the European Union: Putting the Security into the EU's Area of Freedom Security and Justice' (2004) 29 ELR 219; D Boer, 'Justice and Home Affairs Co-operation in the Treaty on European Union: More Complexity Despite Communautarization' (1997) 4 Maastricht J 310; K Hailbronner, 'European Immigration and Asylum Law under the Amsterdam Treaty' (1998) 35 CML Rev 1047, 1055–7; J Monar, 'Justice and Home Affairs in the Treaty of Amsterdam: Reform at the Price of Fragmentation' (1998) 23 ELR 320; for a general study on institutional evolution that includes the European Constitution, P Kuijper, 'The Evolution of the Third Pillar from Maastricht to the European Constitution: Institutional Aspects' (2004) 41 CML Rev 609.

[124] For two recent examples: Cases C-133/06 *Parliament v Council* [2008] ECR I-3189; C-77/05 *United Kingdom v Council* [2007] I-11459.

[125] As to what constitutes a court of last resort for the purposes of Art 68 EC, see the Opinion of AG Ruiz-Jarabo Colomer in Case C-14/08 *Roda Golf & Beach Resort SL* (pending), delivered 5 March 2009; S Peers, *EU Justice and Home Affairs Law* (OUP: Oxford, 2006) 38. For a critique of the restrictions included in Article 68 EC, see N Fennelly, 'The "Area of Freedom, Security and Justice" and the European Court of Justice: A Personal View' (2000) 49 ICLQ 1; D Thym, 'The Schengen Law: A Challenge for Legal Accountability in the European Union' (2002) 8 ELJ 218; S Peers, 'The Jurisdiction of the Court of Justice over EC Immigration and Asylum Law: Time for a Change?' in H Toner, E Guild, and A Baldaccini (eds), *Whose Freedom, Security and Justice? EU Immigration and Asylum Law and Policy* (Hart: Oxford, 2007).

indicate an obligation on the part of such courts, just as in the first pillar.[126]

This procedural restriction presents significant disadvantages. Individuals following the indirect path of review are forced to go through a national judicial system and take their case to the highest court before they can have access to the ECJ. Many may not have the time nor the resources to do this;[127] as regards time, the situation has been improved by the fact that, if and when the question gets to the ECJ, the latter may at least be faster in giving a ruling because of the Urgent Preliminary Ruling Procedure, studied in Section 2.3.2.2. References under Article 68 EC that concern civil procedure are relatively common;[128] in the field of immigration and asylum law, however, the ECJ has only received until now three references from national courts: two of them were inadmissible because the court could not be considered a court of last resort within the meaning of Article 68 EC.[129] Interim measures present us also with an interesting dilemma: in normal circumstances (that is, in the first pillar) any national court can protect the applicant's interests by suspending the application of EC law or its implementation, as long as it makes a reference on its validity to the ECJ. The fact that lower national courts are not able to make such a reference within Title IV EC leads to the unsettling result that they are equally unable to grant interim measures. Different possible ways to deal with this problem have been put forward: Peers has submitted that any

---

[126] Art 68(1) EC: 'Article 234 shall apply to this title under the following circumstances and conditions: where a question on the interpretation of this title or on the validity or interpretation of acts of the institutions of the Community based on this title is raised in a case pending before a court or a tribunal of a Member State against whose decisions there is no judicial remedy under national law, that court or tribunal shall, if it considers that a decision on the question is necessary to enable it to give judgment, request the Court of Justice to give a ruling thereon.' Art 234(3) EC: 'Where any such question is raised in a case pending before a court or tribunal of a Member State against whose decisions there is no judicial remedy under national law, that court or tribunal shall bring the matter before the Court of Justice.'

[127] eg asylum-seekers, applicants for family reunification, third-country nationals challenging expulsion orders.

[128] For some recent examples see Cases C-68/07 *Sundelind Lopez* [2007] ECR I-10403; C-386/05 *Color Drack* [2007] ECR I-3699; C-283/05 *ASML* [2006] ECR I-12041.

[129] Cases C 51/03 *Georgescu* [2004] ECR I-3203 and C-45/03 *Dem'Yanenko* Judgment of 18 March 2004 (unpublished). The admissible case concerned the freedom to travel rules that apply to non-EU citizens and came from the French Conseil d'État: Case C-241/05 *Bot* [2006] ECR I-9627. See further S Peers, 'The Jurisdiction of the Court of Justice over EC Immigration and Asylum Law: Time for a Change?' in H Toner, E Guild, and A Baldaccini (eds), *Whose Freedom, Security and Justice? EU Immigration and Asylum Law and Policy* (Hart: Oxford, 2007) 90–2. For a critique of the fact that lower courts cannot refer: ibid, 101–7; E Guild and S Peers, 'Deference or Defiance? The Court of Justice's Jurisdiction over Immigration and Asylum' in E Guild and C Harlow (eds), *Implementing Amsterdam* (Hart: Oxford, 2001) 284–7.

national court must be able to grant interim measures provisionally, on the condition that an appeal must be undertaken within the national legal system —along with satisfaction of the other conditions applying to the grant of such measures (*Zuckerfabrik* and *Atlanta*).[130] Eeckhout considers this solution unsatisfactory, and has stated that it may be better simply to allow lower courts to declare a Community act invalid.[131]

2.3.1.1.2 Substantive limitations.   The limitations *ratione materiae* on the Court's powers of review across the whole of the AFSJ concern the maintenance of law and order and the safeguarding of internal security; Title IV EC is no exception in this respect.

The maintenance of law and order and the safeguarding of internal security are competences at the very core of national sovereignty. It is therefore understandable that, within the framework of an ever more dynamic AFSJ, the Member States have sought to emphasize that neither the EC nor the EU may lay claim to these competences, or regulate the way in which the Member States discharge them. When studying together the law and order and internal security provisions that can be found in Title IV EC, Title VI TEU, and the Lisbon Treaty, it becomes clear that the Member States have tried to assuage their concerns by introducing two different kinds of provisions: general clauses clarifying the separation of competences between the EC (or EU) and themselves, and more specific provisions that explicitly limit the jurisdiction of the Court of Justice. Each of the relevant Treaties mentioned contains a pair that consists of one provision of each type. My first claim in this respect will be that the general clause contained in each of the Treaties studied is better understood as a clause that indicates where the limits of EC/EU legislative competence lie, rather than as a derogation similar to those available to the Member States within the single market. Ultimately, however, the Court's case-law shows that this does not exclude eventual review of national action at EC/EU level. Possibly as a reaction, a safeguard has been added—again, in all three Treaties—in the form of another provision that explicitly curtails the ECJ's jurisdiction, minimally in the case of Title IV EC, but more extensively in the TEU and in the Lisbon Treaty, as we shall see later. The introduction

---

[130] S Peers, 'Who's Judging the Watchmen: The Judicial System of the "Area of Freedom, Security and Justice"' (1998) 17 YEL 337, 354–5. Joined Cases C-143/88 and 92/89 *Zuckerfabrik* [1991] ECR I-415; Case C-465/93 *Atlanta* [1995] ECR I-3761.

[131] P Eeckhout, 'The European Court of Justice and the "Area of Freedom, Security and Justice": Challenges and Problems' in D O'Keeffe (ed), *Judicial Review in European Union Law: Liber Amicorum in Honour of Lord Slynn of Hadley* (Kluwer: London, 2000) 157–9.

of these restrictions may prove problematic: not only because they may affect national action that does fall within the scope of EU law, but also because they may hamper the Court's capacity to give useful preliminary rulings on the interpretation of EU law in certain situations.

Within Title IV EC, Article 64(1) EC states that '[t]his title shall not affect the exercise of the responsibilities incumbent upon Member States with regard to the maintenance of law and order and the safeguarding of internal security'. This provision belongs to the first group mentioned earlier, that of general clauses. The first question to come to mind when reading Article 64 (1) EC is whether it should be considered a derogation from EC law comparable to the derogations from the Single Market contained, for example, in Article 30 EC. This is significant for the purposes of judicial control: the Court has stated that, in those situations where a Member State seeks to derogate from EC law (*ERT, Familiapress*),[132] it will still be controlled for compliance with the general principles of EC law. This question is of particular interest in the case of Article 64(1) EC, since there is no subsequent provision explicitly excluding the jurisdiction of the Court as regards all national action caught by it (this, as we will see later, is what happens in the TEU with Articles 33 and 35(5) TEU). If we were to conclude that Article 64(1) EC is a derogation equivalent to that of Article 30 EC, we could safely assume that the *ERT* case-law would apply to national action caught by this provision, making the ECJ competent to assess its compliance with general principles of EC law.[133] Several authors support this view, if acknowledging the fact that the sensitive nature of 'law and order' and 'internal security' would make the Court exercise a light review of proportionality.[134]

---

[132] Cases C-260/89 *ERT/DEP* [1991] ECR I-2925; C-368/95 *Vereinigte Familiapress Zeitungsverlags- und vertriebs GmbH/Bauer Verlag* [1997] ECR I-3689.

[133] Although it is, of course, unclear how extensive this control should be. AG Jacobs claimed that this second test or substantive control should only involve checking the compliance with the principles of proportionality and non-discrimination on grounds of nationality: F Jacobs 'Human Rights in the European Union: The Role of the Court of Justice' (2001) 26 ELR 331, 337–9. On the other hand, the scope of *ERT, Familiapress* and later case-law is wider.

[134] S Peers, 'National Security and European Law' (1996) 16 YEL 363; D Thym, 'The Schengen Law: A Challenge for Legal Accountability in the European Union' (2002) 8 ELJ 218; G Simpson, 'Asylum and Immigration in the European Union after the Treaty of Amsterdam' (1999) 5 Eur PL 91. These authors (especially Peers and Thym) consider this provision analogous to all the 'public policy' derogations in the EC Treaty, and accordingly believe that the ECJ should be competent to conduct, at least, a review of proportionality. On how the Court has dealt with the public policy derogations, see S Peers, 'National Security and European Law' (above) 364–92. On the 'light' review of proportionality in these cases, see T Tridimas, *The General Principles of EU Law* (2nd edn, OUP: Oxford, 2006) 225–9.

On the other hand, it is possible to argue that Article 64(1) EC is not a derogation from EC law obligations that therefore falls within the scope of EC law, but rather an indication as to where the limits of EC competence lie.[135] This would mean that all national action covered by Article 64(1) EC is outside the legislative competence of the EC, but it does not necessarily put this national activity outside the jurisdiction of the ECJ: the Court has already stated that, even though a certain measure does not fall within the scope of EC law (in the sense of EC legislative competence) and remains in the exclusive competence of the Member States, the latter must nevertheless, when exercising said competence, respect the Treaty rules. In *Commission v France ('Spanish Strawberries')*, the Court stated that maintenance of public order and the safeguarding of internal security are matters of national competence that are nevertheless reviewable insofar as their pursuit impedes cross-border trade.[136] In *Centro-Com*, the Court recognized the Member States' competence to protect their security, but asserted that, in doing so, EC law had to be complied with.[137] In its case-law dealing with sex discrimination and the armed forces, the Court has made it clear that there is no 'general exception excluding from the scope of Community law all measures taken for reasons of public security':[138] meaning that, while it is clear that the organization of the armed forces still falls within the competences of the Member States and not of the EC, the national regulation of such matter has, nevertheless, to comply with EC law. The distinction at play is that between legislative competence and the much wider reach of EC rules (on non-discrimination, in this case). Of course, the Court is dealing here in shades of grey: as it turned out, the British rule preventing women from joining the Royal Marines in *Sirdar* and the German rule confining women's access to the army to medical and military-music services in *Kreil* could only remain in force if they were consistent with the EC rules on sex discrimination (which they were not),[139] whereas the

[135] A distinction used by J Weiler, 'Fundamental Rights and Fundamental Boundaries: On Standards and Values in the Protection of Human Rights' in N Neuwahl and A Rosas (eds), *The European Union and Human Rights* (Martinus Nijhoff Publishers: The Hague, 1995) 69; T Tridimas, *The General Principles of EU Law* (2nd edn, OUP: Oxford, 2006) 325.

[136] C-265/95 *Commission v France ('Spanish Strawberries')* [1997] ECR I-6959 [33]–[35], [56]–[57]. See written evidence given by Dutheil de la Rochere in EU Committee of the House of Lords, 'The Future Role of the European Court of Justice. Report with Evidence' (6th Report of Session 2003–4. HL Paper 47) 73.

[137] C-124/95 *The Queen, ex parte Centro-Com Srl v HM Treasury and Bank of England* ECR [1997] I-81 [25].

[138] Case C-285/98 *Tanja Kreil v Bundesrepublik Deutschland* [2000] ECR I-69 [16].

[139] Cases C-273/97 *Angela Maria Sirdar v The Army Board and Secretary of State for Defence* [1999] ECR I-7403; *Kreil*, ibid.

rule that makes military service compulsory only for men in Germany—at stake in *Dory*—could not be affected by the same EC rules. The reason, according to the Court, was the first two situations concerned mere 'decisions of the Member States concerning the organisation of their armed forces', whereas the latter was one of the Member States' 'choices of military organization for the defence of their territory or of their essential interests'.[140] The Court seems to have distinguished between situations which involve a fundamental policy choice, where allowing the EC rules to have an effect would be close to allowing the EC to regulate the matter, and situations which do not involve such a fundamental policy choice and where the Member State's decision is therefore subject to a proportionality test if it breaches a rule of EC law.[141] Needless to say, the line may be difficult to draw.

National security is not the only field where case-law of this sort is at hand.[142] The Court has taken a similar approach (recognizing national competence, yet claiming that EC law needs to be complied with) as regards, for example, Article 295 EC, which states that '[the] Treaty shall in no way prejudice the rules in Member States governing the system of property ownership'. Yet EC law (and hence the ECJ, if there is no express restriction to its jurisdiction) can affect it in many ways through other provisions of the EC Treaty. In *Salzmann*, the Court stated that 'although the legal regime applicable to property ownership is a field of competence reserved for the Member States under Article 222 of the EC Treaty (now Article 295 EC), it is not exempted from the fundamental rules of the Treaty'.[143] As a result, the national rules at stake—on the establishment of secondary residences in certain areas—had to comply with the EC Treaty provisions on free movement of capital. It is possible to find further examples of the Court's attitude in the fields of social security, taxation, sport, etc.[144]

To sum up: Article 64(1) EC may be considered a derogation within the scope of EC law or an indication as to where the limits of EC law lie,

[140] Case C-186/01 *Alexander Dory v Bundesrepublik Deutschland* [2003] ECR I-2479 [35].

[141] See N Grief, 'EU Law and Security' (2007) 32 ELR 752 763–4; Koutrakos distinguishes between Member States' primary and secondary choices: P Koutrakos, 'How Far is Far Enough? EC Law and the Organisation of the Armed Forces after Dory' (2003) 66 MLR 759, 765.

[142] 'National security' encompasses both internal and external security: *Kreil* [17]. For the use of these and related concepts, see N Grief, 'EU Law and Security' (2007) 32 ELR 752, 755.

[143] Case C-300/01 *Salzmann* [2003] ECR I-4899 [39].

[144] Cases C-372/04 *Watts* [2006] ECR I-4325 and C-512/03 *Blanckaert* [2005] ECR I-7685 on social security; C-446/03 *Marks & Spencer* [2005] ECR I-10837 on taxation; C-415/93 *Bosman* [1995] ECR I-4921 on sport. For two recent and notorious examples of this reasoning, see also Cases C-438/05 *The International Transport Workers' Federation and The Finnish Seamen's Union* [2007] ECR I-10779; C-341/05 *Laval un Partneri* [2007] ECR I-11767.

a provision on separation of competences.[145] From the point of view of judicial control at EC level, the distinction may not be of great significance in practice, as long as there is a conflict between the national activity and a rule of EC law: in the first case, that is, if the provision is used as a derogation in order not to comply with a specific EC law obligation, the Court could check the compatibility of the national action with the general principles of EC law straight away (since the derogation is within the scope of EC law already). In the second case, the Court could act because the national action, albeit outside the legislative competence of the EC, can fall within the scope of the Treaty if it breaches a rule of EC law: according to the case-law, this has so far happened where national action of this kind has come into conflict with EC rules on free movement, competition, and non-discrimination. As regards national security, specifically, the Court has further distinguished between Member States' decisions that involve fundamental policy choices and those that do not, making EC rules apply only to the latter: anything else would come too close to allowing the Community to regulate the matter, breaching the division of competences at play.

Thus the result of both approaches—considering this sort of general provision as equivalent to a single market derogation or not—may not differ much in practice. Ultimately, the Court's theoretical take would depend on the particular circumstances of the case; it is likely, however, that a 'light' control of proportionality would ensue at any rate, given the sensitivity of the field at stake. Until now, the Court has never had to directly clarify the interpretation and use to be given to Article 64(1) EC. It has included it on two occasions in the list of EC Treaty 'derogations applicable in situation which may involve public safety', together with Articles 30, 39, 46, 58, 296, and 297 EC,[146] but this is not sufficient evidence to assume that the Court

---

[145] Indeed, Art 64(1) EC could have either of these functions (derogation within EC law, limiting the scope of EC law), depending on the circumstances of the case. Art 296 EC is another example of a similar provision, if more specific in its scope. In Case C-414/97 *Commission v Spain* [1999] ECR I-5585, Spain used Art 296 EC as a derogation within the scope of EC law and the Court treated the provision accordingly. It is nevertheless possible to imagine a Member State using Art 296 EC as a 'sword' to attack the validity of an EC law measure that regulates or affects issues of national security connected with the production of or trade in arms, munitions, and war material.

[146] Cases C-337/05 *Commission v Italy* [2008] ECR I-2173 [43]; C-186/01 *Alexander Dory v Bundesrepublik Deutschland* [2003] ECR I-2479 [31]. This very same list had previously been used by the Court without including Art 64(1) EC on two occasions since this provision had entered into force: Cases C-273/97 *Angela Maria Sirdar v The Army Board and Secretary of State for Defence* [1999] ECR I-7403 [16]; C-285/98 *Tanja Kreil v Bundesrepublik Deutschland* [2000] ECR I-69 [16].

would treat Article 64(1) EC in the same way as a single market derogation, were it to face a case that came directly within its scope. On the contrary, it is submitted that, from a theoretical point of view, the best reading of Article 64(1) EC and its counterparts in the TEU and the Lisbon Treaty is that of a general clause on division of competences, rather than as the equivalent of Articles 30, 39, or 46 EC.

Still within Title IV EC, Article 68(2) EC contains a further reference to law and order and internal security, in stating that 'the Court of Justice shall not have jurisdiction to rule on any measure or decision taken pursuant to Article 62(1) relating to the maintenance of law and order and the safeguarding of internal security'. This provision belongs to the second kind of provisions mentioned above, in that it explicitly curtails the jurisdiction of the ECJ with regard to the national measures at stake. Nevertheless, this restriction arguably affects only the jurisdiction of the Court to give preliminary rulings (the subject-matter of Article 68 EC), leaving its jurisdiction to review such measures directly in infringement proceedings unaffected.[147]

Article 62(1) EC provides for Council measures to ensure 'the absence of any controls on persons, be they citizens of the Union or nationals of third countries, when crossing internal borders'. This provision is the legal base of Article 2(2) of the Schengen Implementing Convention (now Article 23 of the Schengen Borders Code)[148] which allows Member States

---

[147] Arnull rightly points out that 'the Court's jurisdiction should be regarded as capable of being limited only by the clearest of language': A Arnull, *The European Union and its Court of Justice* (2nd edn, OUP: Oxford, 2006) 133; similarly, Peers, believes that 'there is a presumption of full applicability that can only be ousted by express language': S Peers, 'Who's Judging the Watchmen: The Judicial System of the "Area of Freedom, Security and Justice" ' (1998) 17 YEL 337, 352. A more pessimistic approach has been adopted by the Commission, which seems to believe that Art 68(2) EC excludes any kind of jurisdiction—not only the competence to give preliminary rulings. This can be inferred from the Communication from the Commission to the European Parliament, the Council, the European Economic and Social Committee, the Committee of the regions, and the Court of Justice of the European Communities: Adaptation of the Provisions of Title IV of the Treaty establishing the European Community relating to the jurisdiction of the Court of Justice with a view to ensuring more effective judicial protection. Brussels, 28 June 2006 COM(2006) 346 final, 6: 'The wording of this paragraph appears to exclude any review by the Court of Justice of Community measures adopted by the legislature on the basis of Article 62(1) of the EC Treaty [...] Since, by definition, the national courts cannot rule either on the validity of such Community rules, the result is to exclude any possibility of judicial review'.

[148] Convention implementing the Schengen Agreement of 14 June 1985 [2000] OJ L 239/0019; Schengen Borders Code, EC Regulation 562/2006 [2006] OJ L 105/01.

to reintroduce internal border checks where public policy or national security so require; this has often been used to restrain cross-border political activity.[149] In fact, it has been suggested that Article 68(2) EC was drafted with the application of Article 2(2) of the Schengen Implementing Convention specifically in mind.[150] At any rate, Article 68(2) EC encompasses, in practice, measures which may encroach upon fundamental rights (for example, freedom of association and expression) along with the free movement rights of EU citizens—yet these measures are specifically left outside the ECJ's competence to give preliminary rulings. The restriction may be considered problematic as regards the protection of individuals, who are very rarely able to bring a direct action and must normally rely on an indirect challenge through the preliminary reference procedure.[151]

Article 62(1) EC is the legal base of measures which deal with internal borders and which allow Member States to derogate from the obligations they create—by reintroducing border checks—in a situation where national security is at stake. The result is that, although measures of EC law are the potential object of Article 68(2) EC, its practical object is most likely to be national action. Such action is not the necessary result of the EC law measure, but rather a derogation from it. A sufficient standard

[149] After the integration of the Schengen acquis into EC law, the Council attributed the legal base of Art 62(1) EC to the provisions of Art 2(1) to (3) of the Schengen Convention and the three relevant Executive Committee Decisions: Council Decision 1999/436/EC [1999] OJ L176/17. The power to reintroduce border checks has been used often to prevent EU citizens from taking part in political demonstrations: K Groenendijk, 'Reinstatement of Controls at Internal Borders: Why and Against Whom?' (2004) 10 ELJ 150; S Peers, *EU Justice and Home Affairs Law* (OUP: Oxford, 2006) 132–5; S Peers, 'National Security and European Law' (1996) 16 YEL 363, 388–93.

[150] P Eeckhout, 'The European Court of Justice and the "Area of Freedom, Security and Justice": Challenges and Problems' in D O'Keeffe (ed), *Judicial Review in European Union Law: Liber Amicorum in Honour of Lord Slynn of Hadley* (Kluwer: London, 2000) 164; D Thym, 'The Schengen Law: A Challenge for Legal Accountability in the European Union' (2002) 8 ELJ 218, 233.

[151] For a critique of the restrictions included in Article 68 EC, see generally N Fennelly, 'The "Area of Freedom, Security and Justice" and the European Court of Justice: A Personal View' (2000) 49 ICLQ 1; S Peers, 'Who's Judging the Watchmen: The Judicial System of the "Area of Freedom, Security and Justice" ' (1998) 17 YEL 337, 351–7; D Thym, 'The Schengen Law: A Challenge for Legal Accountability in the European Union' (2002) 8 ELJ 218; S Peers, 'The Jurisdiction of the Court of Justice over EC Immigration and Asylum Law: Time for a Change?' in H Toner, E Guild, and A Baldaccini (eds), *Whose Freedom, Security and Justice? EU Immigration and Asylum Law and Policy* (Hart: Oxford, 2007). On the potential conflict between this restriction and Art 47 of the EU Charter of Fundamental Rights, A Ward, 'Access to Justice' in S Peers and A Ward (eds), *The EU Charter of Fundamental Rights* (Hart: Oxford, 2004).

of protection for individuals may be achieved in practice if the national court, albeit not able to review the EC measure dealing with internal borders,[152] is able to review the national authorities' decision to reintroduce border checks. Yet this argument forgets that such an arrangement can only be satisfying to the extent that national courts review the national measure for compliance with national human rights standards and national law in general. When the question, however, comes to checking the national measure for compatibility with the EC measure that allows the derogation or for compatibility with rights flowing from EC law, we are still left with the problem of fragmentation of EC law because the ECJ would have no jurisdiction and would thus be unable to offer guidance to the national courts; without it, in fact, it is even doubtful that national courts would be willing to undertake such control. As a result, the EC rights of individuals may be left unprotected.[153]

Title IV EC, to conclude, contains both a general clause on competence (Article 64(1) EC) and a specific restriction to the Court's jurisdiction (Article 68(2) EC) that concern the Member States' responsibilities as regards law and order and internal security. The Court has never had to directly clarify the way in which Article 64(1) EC is to be applied: all we can do, therefore, is guess what the Court would do if it had such an opportunity. Article 64(1) EC is a vague provision that leaves open the possibility for the Court to check, at least, the proportionality of national action in some cases—something the Court has shown itself willing to do in comparable circumstances. Against this backdrop, Article 68(2) EC (which puts the Schengen reintroduction of internal borders by Member States because of law and order and internal security concerns outside of the jurisdiction of the Court) may have been a safeguard

---

[152] National courts would not be able to consider the validity of a Community measure falling within the scope of Art 68(2) EC other than to uphold it, if we accept that the *Foto-Frost* principle applies in this area: Case 314/85 *Foto-Frost v Hauptzollamt Lübeck-Ost* [1987] ECR 04199. Arnull, however, believes that *Foto-Frost* should not be deemed to apply in the absence of a preliminary ruling mechanism: A Arnull, *The European Union and its Court of Justice* (2nd edn, OUP: Oxford, 2006) 134–5. AG Mengozzi resorted to the same rationale in *Segi* when arguing that *Foto-Frost* should not apply in the third pillar because of the need to offer proper judicial protection: Opinion of AG Mengozzi delivered on 26 October 2006, Case C-355/04 P *Segi and others v Council* [2007] ECR I-1657.

[153] The paradigmatic case would be where border checks are discriminatory or where they are conducted under such conditions that they represent an obstacle to the free movement of citizens (eg where checks are so slow that they act as a deterrent).

introduced by the drafters of the Treaty to make sure that there is a hard and fast rule keeping at least this particular instance of national action from being reviewed.[154]

2.3.1.2 Infringement Proceedings, Failure to Act, Damages

Apart from the restrictions on the powers of the Court to give preliminary rulings under Article 68 EC, all its other powers remain untouched. The provisions of Title IV EC on 'visas, asylum, immigration and other policies related to free movement of persons' are part of the first pillar and, as such, are under the traditional supervisory powers of the Commission. Thus, Article 226 EC is applicable in case of infringement on the part of the Member States.[155]

According to Article 226 EC,

> If the Commission considers that a Member State has failed to fulfil an obligation under this Treaty, it shall deliver a reasoned opinion on the matter after giving the State concerned the opportunity to submit its observations.
>
> If the State concerned does not comply with the opinion within the period laid down by the Commission, the latter may bring the matter before the Court of Justice.[156]

If the Court finds that the Member State has infringed Community law, the latter is obliged to take all measures necessary to comply with the judgment. If the Member State fails to do so, the Commission may use Article 228 EC to ask the Court to order payment of a lump sum or penalty payment; in determining the specific sum, the Commission shall take into account not only the seriousness and duration of the breach, but also the desired deterrent effect. The Commission's suggestion is, however, not binding on the Court.[157] Infringement proceedings can also be brought against a

---

[154] Two of the cases mentioned earlier (*Spanish Strawberries* and *Centro-Com*) had already been decided by the time Art 68(2) and 62(1) EC were introduced at Amsterdam.

[155] For some examples of infringement proceedings brought by the Commission in this area, see C-449/04 *Commission v Luxembourg* Judgment of 21 July 2005 (unpublished); C-462/04 *Commission v Italy* Judgment of 8 December 2005 (unpublished); C-448/04 *Commission v Luxembourg* Judgment of 8 September 2005 (unpublished).

[156] In exceptional cases, the Commission may skip the first step and summon the Member State directly before the Court of Justice: see Arts 95(9) and 298 EC, plus the special procedure related to Art 226 found in Art 88(2) EC. K Lenaerts and P Van Nuffel, *Constitutional Law of the European Union* (2nd edn, Sweet & Maxwell: London, 2005) 428–9.

[157] Although it is considered a 'useful point of reference': Case C-387/97 *Commission v Greece* [2000] ECR I-5047 [89].

Member State by another Member State, according to Article 227 EC. This mechanism of control has, however, hardly been used.[158]

Finally, the action for failure to act is available to the Member States, the institutions, and natural or legal persons, under the conditions set out in Article 232 EC; the non-contractual liability of the Community may be established, and damages may be awarded, pursuant to Articles 235 and 288 EC.

2.3.2 The Third Pillar (Title VI TEU)

2.3.2.1 Powers of Review

2.3.2.1.1 Procedural Limitations. The Treaty of Amsterdam extended the jurisdiction of the Court of Justice to the provisions on police and judicial cooperation in criminal matters (Title VI TEU)—albeit under the conditions set out in Article 35 TEU. As regards direct review of legislation, Article 35(6) TEU provides for the direct review of validity of framework decisions and decisions of the Council. Direct actions can only be brought by the Commission and the Member States; individuals are not contemplated as potential applicants.

Article 35 TEU also limits the competence of the Court to give preliminary rulings. Firstly, it can only do so 'on the validity and interpretation of framework decisions and decisions, on the interpretation of conventions established under this title and on the validity and interpretation of the measures implementing them.' Secondly, a special 'limited system of judicial protection'[159] has been designed for this area. The preliminary reference procedure is available to national courts only if the particular Member State has expressly accepted the jurisdiction of the Court of Justice; this acceptance can include all national courts or only

---

[158] For two examples, see Cases C-145/04 *Spain v United Kingdom* [2006] ECR I-7917 and C-388/95 *Belgium v Spain* [2000] ECR I-3123.

[159] A Albors-Llorens, 'Changes in the Jurisdiction of the European Court of Justice under the Treaty of Amsterdam' (1998) 35 CML Rev 1273, 1278. For more recent critiques of the arrangements for judicial control in the third pillar, see S Peers, 'Salvation Outside the Church: Judicial Protection in the Third Pillar after the Pupino and Segi Judgments' (2007) 44 CML Rev 885; S Douglas-Scott, 'The Rule of Law in the European Union: Putting the Security into the EU's Area of Freedom Security and Justice' (2004) 29 ELR 219. On the connected issue of effectiveness in the third pillar, M Ross, 'Effectiveness in the European Legal Order(s): Beyond Supremacy to Constitutional Proportionality' (2006) 31 ELR 476.

those of last resort, and it is for national law to determine the scope of the obligation to refer.[160]

In general, the jurisdiction 'à la carte' offered to Member States within Title VI TEU is, at first sight, problematic.[161] It is not surprising that individuals have no direct access to the Court; but the arrangements for indirect access are not satisfactory either. The indirect protection offered to individuals from different Member States of the Union can vary enormously; it can range from none (where no court is allowed to make a reference) to cases in which only the court of last resort may (or must) refer and cases where all national courts can make use of the preliminary reference procedure. Equality does not seem to be one of the purposes served by these special arrangements, which hardly conform to the vision of 'citizenship of the Union'. Again, if national courts are not able to ask the ECJ for an authoritative interpretation of a Union measure, application may vary across the Member States.[162]

As regards the third pillar measures that can be reviewed, Article 35 refers only to framework decisions and decisions.[163] The review of common positions, be it direct or indirect, is not explicitly foreseen in the TEU because, in theory, this type of measure is not supposed to have effects on third parties. This is nevertheless an assumption that does not sit well with

---

[160] Member States may impose an obligation on courts of last resort to refer as a matter of national law: Declaration on Art 35 TEU adopted by the Intergovernmental Conference (Declaration 10). All the Member States of the Union of 15 have accepted the jurisdiction of the Court with the exception of Denmark, Ireland, and the UK ([1999] OJ C120/24). Of the Member States that have acceded since 2004, the Czech Republic and Hungary accepted in 2005 ([2005] OJ L327/19) and Latvia, Lithuania, and Slovenia in 2008 (in that year, Hungary also extended its acceptance from only courts of last resort to all national courts): [2008] OJ C69/1. Of the 17 Member States that have accepted, only Spain currently restricts its acceptance to courts of last resort, and 10 Member States have reserved the right to make provision in their national law to oblige their courts of last resort to refer (the exceptions are Finland, Greece, Portugal, Sweden, Hungary, Latvia, and Lithuania). The Court published a scorecard in March 2008 that indicates which of these 10 Member States have made use of that right and have imposed the duty to refer through national legislation: http://curia.europa.eu/en/instit/txtdocfr/txtsenvigueur/art35.pdf (accessed April 2009).

[161] On the potential conflict between this restriction and Art 47 of the Charter of Fundamental Rights, A Ward, 'Access to Justice' in S Peers and A Ward (eds), *The EU Charter of Fundamental Rights* (Hart: Oxford, 2004), 136–7.

[162] Apart from the restrictions explicitly imposed by Art 35 TEU, it can be assumed that the (judicially developed) rules on the application of Art 234 EC—on eg the admissibility of references or what is a 'court or tribunal of a Member State'—apply here as well.

[163] The ECJ can also give preliminary rulings on the interpretation of conventions—a measure that has fallen into disuse since the Treaty of Amsterdam entered into force: S Peers, *EU Justice and Home Affairs Law* (OUP: Oxford, 2006) 33–5.

the—relatively recent—practice of putting together lists containing the names of individuals and organizations that are labelled as terrorists, and attaching said lists as annexes to common positions that may be adopted under both the second and the third pillars or only under the second one, depending on whether or not there is a 'domestic' component. It is standard for a CFSP common position of this kind to be implemented by EC measures that impose the freezing of assets of listed individuals and that are fully amenable to review. The EC, however, cannot adopt such implementing measures in relation to 'domestic' terrorists.[164] In *Segi*,[165] the common position at stake had been adopted jointly under both intergovernmental pillars;[166] there were Community implementing measures affecting the 'foreign' listed individuals, but not the 'domestic' ones. The applicants belonged to the second group and they sought redress for the damage caused by the adoption of the common position, since it labelled them as terrorists. Whereas the CFI adopted a literal reading of the TEU that did not allow for the award of damages or the review of common positions, the ECJ took a more creative approach and substantially extended judicial control in the third pillar.[167]

The claimants had sought damages for the disadvantages they had faced as a consequence of being listed—if their action was rejected, they argued, they would have no access to judicial protection.[168] When the CFI rejected their claim, they appealed to the ECJ. They were not successful in their first endeavour: the ECJ agreed with the CFI that there was no jurisdiction to entertain an action for damages in the intergovernmental

---

[164] According to Eckes: this is because 'with regard to EU-internal terrorist suspects there is no political consensus whether the EU is in fact competent to adopt sanctions against them', with the result that 'autonomous sanctions against EU-internal terrorists are considered to be outside the realm of Article 301 EC': C Eckes, 'Sanctions against Individuals: Fighting Terrorism within the European Legal Order' (2008) 4 EuConst 205, 221.

[165] Case T-338/02 *Segi* [2004] ECR II-01647 ('CFI *Segi*').

[166] Council Common Position 2001/931/CFSP of 27 December 2001 on the application of specific measures to combat terrorism [2001] OJ L344/93; Council Common Position 2002/340/CFSP of 2 May 2002 updating Common Position 2001/931 [2002] OJ L116/75; Council Common Position 2002/462/CFSP of 17 June 2002 updating Common Position 2001/931 and repealing Common Position 2002/340 [2002] OJ L160/32.

[167] Case C-355/04 P *Segi* [2007] ECR I-1657 ('ECJ *Segi*'). See also the analysis of *Segi* and what it means for judicial control in the third pillar in S Peers, 'Salvation outside the Church: Judicial Protection in the Third Pillar after the Pupino and Segi Judgments' (2007) 44 CML Rev 885, 885–902.

[168] This was a common position adopted both under the second and third pillars of the EU, on the basis of Arts 15 and 34 TEU.

pillars of the Union.[169] The surprise came when the ECJ had to deal with the applicants' right to judicial protection in the face of a common position: whereas the CFI had stated that the fact that the plaintiffs have no access to judicial protection cannot lead to the court pushing the limits of its competence,[170] the ECJ found a way to do exactly that.

First of all, it must be borne in mind that the Court considered the common position a third pillar measure insofar as it affected the applicant. The ECJ argued that the review, be it direct or indirect, of common positions is not foreseen in the TEU because these measures are not supposed to produce legal effects in relation to third parties. The intention of the Treaty (Article 35 TEU) is to allow for review of all measures that do produce such effects. Consequently, if a common position intends to produce such effects, it may be reviewed under Article 35 TEU.[171] This means that, on the one hand, common positions may be reviewed indirectly: individuals may challenge their validity through national courts, and the latter may ask for a preliminary ruling from the ECJ. On the other hand, a direct action for annulment may be brought before the ECJ by a Member State or the Commission. It follows that individuals cannot challenge a common position directly—the TEU does not foresee this for any measure adopted under the intergovernmental pillars—but they can at least hope for indirect review.

The fact that individuals can only hope for indirect review of common positions through Article 35 TEU is not ideal; the problems of this approach are well known and include the need for national implementation in order to have access to a national court and the fact that the individual has no right to a reference to the ECJ and no influence on how the question is framed.[172] More importantly, availability of the reference procedure in

---

[169] In the intergovernmental pillars, the Courts only have the jurisdiction conferred upon them by Art 35 TEU—which does not include actions for damages. ECJ *Segi* [45]–[48].

[170] CFI *Segi* [38]. During the appellate proceedings, AG Mengozzi offered a different view: protection had to reside at the level of the Member States—they should therefore be able to review EU law, free of the *Foto-Frost* mandate. Opinion of AG Mengozzi in *Segi*, delivered on 26 October 2006 [121]–[132].   [171] ECJ *Segi* [52]–[56].

[172] According to Eckes, a further problem is that individuals do not know which Member State instigated the listing, a fact the individual may need to know in order to decide which national court to address. This may have been solved to some extent by the CFI's decision in *Sison* (concerning the right to a personalized statement of reasons, including the identification of the designating Member State): T-47/03 *Jose Maria Sison* [2007] ECR II-73. See C Eckes, 'Sanctions against Individuals: Fighting Terrorism within the European Legal Order' (2008) 4 EuConst 205, 212–23.

the third pillar varies across Member States.[173] Accordingly, the Court sought to remind Member States of their 'UPA obligation' to make it as easy as possible for individuals to have access to an indirect action.[174] In *Segi*, we see a constitutional court that is at pains to extend its jurisdiction so as to allow for more, much needed, judicial control in the intergovernmental pillars.[175] The evolution in the type of action that the Union is undertaking in the intergovernmental areas must be coupled with an evolution in the pattern of judicial control: consequently, the Court is willing to push the boundaries of its own jurisdiction until the Treaty undergoes the needed reforms. The Court seems to have done this, however, conscious of its limitations: since individuals are not allowed to challenge any type of third pillar measure directly, allowing it in the case of common positions would have clearly gone beyond the boundaries of purposive interpretation. The Court could, however, give preliminary rulings on all third pillar measures other than common positions. Pushing the boundaries of its competence to include common positions among this group as well does not seem so out of touch, by comparison, with the letter of the Treaty.

Finally, it may be argued that the shortcomings in the system of judicial control of third pillar measures (be it the one addressed by the Court in *Segi*, or the limited system of judicial review available to national courts) need not result, at least in theory, in the defencelessness of the individual. This is because this area currently remains intergovernmental in nature and we are considering measures of Union, not EC, law. In a situation where a national court is not able to call upon the ECJ to review an EU measure because of the limited preliminary ruling procedure available, or because the measure at stake is not reviewable in such a way, national courts may be able to offer protection. Whether or not national courts would be able to do so would depend on national law, that is, whether national courts can

---

[173] As a result of the system of voluntary acceptance introduced in Art 35(2) and (3) TEU.

[174] ECJ *Segi* [56]. Under Art 230(4) EC, the ECJ continues to apply a very restrictive test to grant standing to individuals, and this can in turn lead to a gap in judicial protection. The ECJ dealt with this in *UPA* by imposing an obligation on Member States to make it easier for individuals to challenge EC legislation indirectly before national courts: C-50/00 *Unión de Pequeños Agricultores v Council* [2002] ECR I-6677.

[175] But it is not clear whether the Court would extend Art 35 TEU to cover a purely CFSP common position if necessary. Although common positions may be adopted in either of the intergovernmental pillars and the one at stake in *Segi* was adopted under both, the Court considered that the latter was a third pillar measure to the extent that it affected the applicants. Furthermore, Art 35 TEU confers powers on the Court within Title VI TEU only.

review the compatibility of a measure of public international law with national standards, and if necessary deny it any effects within national territory. As this is not a matter of EC law, the *Foto-Frost* principle would not apply. This is, of course, the theory: in practice, I have already argued that different national courts perceive measures of EU law in different manners, treating them as public international law in some cases,[176] and as something very close to EC law in others.[177] In between, several national courts are just uncertain as to how they should treat these measures, which is, needless to say, not conducive to legal certainty. At any rate, even though the characterization of third pillar measures as public international law may offer a theoretical shield from the shortcomings of the EU system of judicial protection, it is unclear to what extent national courts would follow this path in practice. Even if they did, the situation could not be regarded as satisfactory, since national courts that decided to disapply EU measures would still cause their Member State to breach its EU law commitments, and EU measures would be applied inconsistently throughout the Union.

AG Mengozzi similarly considered the role of national courts in his Opinion in *Segi*; he argued that *Foto-Frost* should not apply in the third pillar because of the need to offer proper judicial protection, but nevertheless tried to find a 'third way' to fill the gap by instructing national courts to review third pillar measures against EU, rather than national, standards. It is submitted that this way of dealing with the problem would still be a source of inconsistency, although admittedly far less than if national courts applied their own national standards. In practice, it is arguably also problematic to expect courts to apply EU standards instead of national ones in this sort of situation. Finally, any sort of 'emergency role' that national courts may exercise cannot change the fact that, as a general normative claim, the legal system of the European Union should be in a position to offer satisfactory protection from the measures it produces. Further, the damage caused by a common position like the one at stake in *Segi* may be purely reputational; in that case, merely leaving the act without effects within the territory of one Member State does not solve the problem satisfactorily.

---

[176] Bundesverfassungsgericht (German Constitutional Court), Decision of 18 July 2005 (2 BvR 2236/04) [2006] 1 CMLR 16.

[177] Reference for a preliminary ruling of 13 July 2005 from the Arbitragehof (Belgium) in the proceedings between Advocaten voor de wereld, a non-profit-making association, and the Council of Ministers [2005] OJ C271/26.

2.3.2.1.2 Substantive limitations. The limitations *ratione materiae* within the third pillar proper are comparable to those in the first pillar that were already examined in the previous section. They too concern the maintenance of law and order and the safeguarding of internal security.

Title VI TEU, just as Title IV EC, contains both a general clause or 'reminder' in the form of Article 33 TEU ('[t]his title shall not affect the exercise of the responsibilities incumbent upon Member States with regard to the maintenance of law and order and the safeguarding of internal security') and a specific limitation of the Court's competence. The latter is Article 35(5) TEU, which puts 'operations carried out by the police or other law-enforcement services of a Member State or the exercise of the responsibilities incumbent upon Member States with regard to the maintenance of law and order and the safeguarding of internal security' outside the jurisdiction of the Court to give preliminary rulings. It should also be borne in mind that the indirect path of the preliminary ruling procedure is the only one available in the third pillar to control national action, in the absence of fully fledged infringement proceedings.[178]

Is it not the case, however, that the Court never—in theory—controls national measures under the preliminary ruling procedure? The restriction of Article 35(5) TEU could be quite limited by the fact that the Court is only ever supposed to interpret EC/Union law, spell out its requirements and leave it up to the national court to apply these requirements to national measures.[179] And yet, albeit not supposed to control national rules within the preliminary reference procedure, the Court definitely does so in practice. At the same time, the Court is aware of this anomaly and is commonly careful to formulate its rulings in a manner that is at once effective as regards national control and faithful to the constitutional 'fiction'

---

[178] The only mechanism of this sort available in the TEU can be found in Art 35(7), on disputes between the Commission and a Member State regarding the interpretation or application of a convention. In practice, conventions have been phased out since the Treaty of Amsterdam entered into force: S Peers, *EU Justice and Home Affairs Law* (OUP: Oxford, 2006) 33–5.

[179] The Court has emphasized in its case-law that it has no jurisdiction under Art 234 EC 'either to apply the Treaty to a specific case or to decide upon the validity of provision of domestic law in relation to the Treaty, as it would be possible for it to do under Article 169 [now 226, infringement proceedings]'. Case 6/64 *Costa v ENEL* [1964] ECR 585, 592–3. The distribution of competences between the ECJ and the national courts in this field is reiterated in Declaration 7 on Art 30 TEU annexed to the Final Act of the Intergovernmental Conference of Amsterdam: 'Action in the field of police cooperation under Article TEU, including activities of Europol, shall be subject to appropriate judicial review by the competent national authorities in accordance with rules applicable in each Member State'.

concerning the separation of competences between itself and the national courts. It is arguable that the additional restriction of Article 35(5) TEU is not without effects; rather, this provision is bound to influence the way the Court exercises its competence to give preliminary rulings in practice, since it may feel the need to be more cautious than normal when controlling national action.

(a) The first restriction within Article 35(5) TEU: actions of the police and law-enforcement services   From this understanding of the significance of Article 35(5) TEU, we will now examine the first part of this restriction, on the action of national law-enforcement services. It should be noted that the wording of this provision seems to catch the action of the police and law-enforcement services that has its origins in national law, but also action that comes as a result of EU law. The following paragraphs will deal with the latter situation, in which the national law-enforcement services could be considered to be acting as 'agents' of the Union, and where the lack of control on the part of the ECJ may seem more striking. The action of police or law-enforcement services that is purely a matter of national law will, for the purposes of this study, be subsumed into the heading of 'exercise of responsibilities incumbent upon Member States with regard to the maintenance of law and order and the safeguarding of internal security', the second restriction contained in Article 35(5) TEU, and discussed later in this section.

   The first part of Article 35(5) TEU excludes from the jurisdiction of the Court 'the validity or proportionality of operations carried out by the police or other law-enforcement services of a Member State'. It could be considered unsatisfactory that the actions of a law-enforcement service that have their origins in EU law cannot be controlled by the ECJ in any way; on the other hand, such actions may be controlled by national courts. In practice, this is a further manifestation of the division of competences between the ECJ and the national courts, and one should therefore be prepared to admit that the complexities of the EU system mean that it is not possible (or even desirable) for the Union itself—the ECJ—to have full power of review over the actions of its agents, as long as national courts do. The only problem is, arguably, that this national action will be checked for compliance with national standards of fundamental rights and other national rules, leaving the ECJ unable to set the standard of respect for fundamental rights that its agents must respect. Further, it is unlikely that national courts will control the national action for compliance with EU law in general and, if they do so, it may have to be without the ECJ's guidance. This, however, fits with the logic of an intergovernmental forum like the current third pillar, where the supremacy of EU law has not been established.[180]

On a slightly different note, it may be that the first restriction of Article 35(5) TEU somehow impairs the Court's role as authoritative interpreter of EU law, in the sense that this restriction may make it difficult for the Court to give a useful interpretation of the requirements of EU law to a national court, when the question submitted by the latter involves, to some extent, the action of the law-enforcement services. Under these circumstances, the Court may have difficulties separating both issues and providing useful guidance on how the measure of EU law is to be interpreted while at the same time not appearing to intrude into forbidden territory.

This difficulty is likely to be greater in a situation where national law-enforcement services act in order to enforce a Union measure directly. This is because the Court would probably feel more conscious of the limits of its jurisdiction due to the fact that there is no intermediate element (national implementing law) between the interpretation of the Union rule and the—off-limits—action of the national police. Normally, when spelling out the requirements of a rule of EU law, the Court is indirectly assessing whether the national action involved complies or not with them. In the standard situation, the Court could provide a useful interpretation of EU law by reference to the national implementing legislation, without having to refer to the action of the national police or law-enforcement services. If there is no national implementing legislation, the Court may need to frame its answer by reference to the action of the national police or law-enforcement services, something that comes too close to assessing its validity. That is why, depending on how the preliminary question is framed, the Court may not be able to give a very useful preliminary ruling, or it may have to deem itself incompetent. This is, of course, assuming that the Court strives to comply with the letter of Article 35(5) TEU. In practice, the Court may be willing to risk criticism by encroaching upon the national courts' role to the extent that it is necessary to clarify an EU law measure. Even in this scenario, the Court should leave the application of the ensuing proportionality test to its national counterparts.[181]

---

[180] Lenaerts and Corthaut have nevertheless argued that the principle of primacy applies already both in the second and in the third pillar: K Lenaerts and T Corthaut, 'Of Birds and Hedges: The Role of Primacy in Invoking Norms of EU Law' (2006) 31 ELR 287. For a defence of the 'orthodox' view, see A Hinarejos, 'The Lisbon Treaty versus Standing Still: A View from the Third Pillar' (2009) 5 EuConst 99.

[181] For examples of this approach within the EC pillar, see n 295.

It is furthermore unlikely that we would encounter, in practice, a situation where a law-enforcement service of a Member State is carrying out a third pillar measure directly within the current third pillar framework. Council Decisions (implementing or otherwise) may seem the likeliest candidate, since the Treaty describes them as 'binding in their entirety', in rather similar terms to EC regulations. In reality, however, these measures are not self-executing: they are not detailed enough and normally refer to the need for national implementation.[182]

(b) The second restriction within Article 35(5) TEU: law and order, internal security responsibilities   Let us now deal with the second restriction contained in Article 35(5) TEU, on 'the exercise of responsibilities incumbent upon Member States with regard to the maintenance of law and order and the safeguarding of internal security'. This provision mirrors the wording of the general clause contained in Article 33 TEU: '[t]his title shall not affect the exercise of the responsibilities incumbent upon Member States with regard to the maintenance of law and order and the safeguarding of internal security'.

The very same discussion on the meaning of Article 64(1) EC—and whether it is to be construed as a derogation within the scope of EC law or as an indication as to where the limits of EC legislative competence lie— can be applied to Article 33 TEU. There are only two differences between these provisions: the first one is that, whereas Article 64(1) EC could come into play within the framework of either the preliminary ruling procedure or infringement proceedings, Article 33 TEU would be most likely used in situations where the Court is asked to clarify in a preliminary ruling

---

[182] For example, Art 36 of the Prüm Decision establishes that 'Member States shall take the necessary measures to comply with the provisions of this Decision within one year of this Decision taking effect [...]. Member States shall inform the General Secretariat of the Council and the Commission that they have implemented the obligation imposed on them under this Decision [...]'. Council Decision 2008/615/JHA of 23 June 2008 on the stepping up of cross-border cooperation, particularly in combating terrorism and cross-border crime (Prüm Decision) [2008] OJ L210/1. This seems to be a common clause; for a further example see also Art 6, Council Decision 2005/671/JHA of 20 September 2005 [2005] OJ L253/22. It is, however, difficult to evaluate to what extent and in what way Member States implement third pillar decisions, since there is normally no need to notify the Commission and no provision for monitoring reports: Communication from the Commission to the Council and the European Parliament, Report on Implementation of the Hague Programme for 2007, COM(2008) 373 final, 13. See also the scoreboard on national implementation attached to this report, including three third pillar decisions: Commission staff working document, Report on the implementation of The Hague programme for 2007: Follow-up of the implementation of legal instruments in the fields of justice, freedom, and security at national level. 2007 Implementation Scoreboard— Table 2, 18–19, 33.

whether a particular EU law provision precludes a particular instance of national action—an action defended by the Member State as being covered by Article 33 TEU.[183] The second difference is a crucial one: Article 35(5) TEU has the effect of placing all national action that is covered by Article 33 TEU outside the jurisdiction of the Court, contrary to what happens with Article 64(1) EC—where only a small group of measures is placed outside the Court's jurisdiction via Article 68(2) EC. Regardless of whether one considers Article 33 TEU as a derogation that the Court would normally be competent to control, or as a provision delimiting the scope of EU law (but which the ECJ would presumably claim to be able to control if it affects certain rules in the treaties), Article 35(5) TEU makes it impossible for the Court to exercise any review of the sort of national action at stake, apart from determining that it indeed falls within the scope of Article 35(5) TEU. It seems plausible that the drafters of the Treaty foresaw the possibility of the Court exercising control over Article 33 TEU in one of the described ways or another—as it has done, in fact, with other comparable clauses—and subsequently decided to avoid that danger by introducing Article 35(5) TEU. It should also be borne in mind that by placing this sort of action outside the indirect control of the Court within the preliminary reference procedure, it is effectively beyond any EU-level judicial control within the third pillar, since there is no equivalent of Article 227 EC (fully fledged infringement proceedings) in the TEU. A Member State's action may nevertheless be controlled by its national courts, if national law so provides. The limitations of this arrangement have already been pointed out.

Finally, again, the Court's role as interpreter of EU law may be somehow restricted if, when asked by a national court whether a rule of EU law forbids certain Member State action (defended by the Member State as necessary to maintain law and order and internal security), the Court feels limited by the fact that it should not be seen to be assessing this sort of national action.

---

[183] This is because of the very limited nature of the 'special' infringement proceedings within the TEU. A very unlikely alternative scenario would present itself if the Court had to intervene in a dispute between the Commission and a Member State on the interpretation or application of a Convention (Art 35(7) TEU), and the source of the conflict were the Member State's action, regarded as within Art 33 TEU by the Member State but not by the Commission. Alternatively, Art 33 TEU could be used within the framework of a direct challenge to a framework decision or decision on grounds of lack of competence.

2.3.2.2 *The Urgent Preliminary Ruling Procedure*

Since 1 March 2008 a new urgent procedure makes it possible for the Court to deliver preliminary rulings much more quickly within the Area of Freedom, Security and Justice, or Titles IV EC and VI TEU.[184]

This proposal for reform was put on the table in September 2006, when the President of the ECJ sent a discussion paper on the 'Treatment of questions referred for a preliminary ruling concerning the area of freedom, security and justice' to the President of the Council.[185] The paper arose from the need to provide for a speedier preliminary ruling mechanism in the AFSJ, a need pointed out by the Brussels European Council of 4 and 5 November 2004.[186] This 'emergency preliminary ruling procedure' would apply in AFSJ cases 'where the urgent need to give a ruling does not, practically speaking, allow the time-limits under the normal procedure or the accelerated procedure to be observed'.[187]

As regards the substance of the proposal, the Court presented the Council with two different options:[188] in the first one, there would be a first stage where the only parties to participate in the procedure would be the parties to the dispute before the national court, the Member State of the national court, the Commission, and the institutions responsible for the measure at stake. At the end of this first stage, the Court would deliver an order. A second stage would then be possible if the order was challenged. In that case, all other Member States and Institutions would be able to participate, and a judgment, which would substitute the order, would be delivered. In the second option, all parties included in Article 23 of the Statute of the Court would have a right to participate,[189] but there would

---

[184] Council Decision of 20 December 2007 amending the Protocol on the Statute of the Court of Justice, OJ [2008] L 24/42 and amendments to the Rules of Procedure of the Court of Justice adopted by the Court on 15 January 2008, OJ [2008] L 24/39.

[185] Document 13272/06 'Treatment of questions referred for a preliminary ruling concerning the area of freedom, security and justice' Brussels, 28 September 2006.

[186] Brussels European Council, 4/5 November 2004. Presidency Conclusions, Brussels, 8 December 2004. 14292/1/04 REV 1.

[187] Document 13272/06, 5. The mentioned accelerated procedure was introduced in 2000 (Art 104a of the Rules of Procedure). For a recent example of application see Case C-127/08 *Metock* [2008] ECR I-6241. The process took four months.   [188] Document 13272/06, 6.

[189] The parties, the Member States, the Commission, and also the Parliament, the Council, and the European Central Bank if the act the validity or interpretation of which is in dispute originates from one of them. On some occasions, also states (other than the Member States) which are parties to the Agreement on the European Economic Area and also to the EFTA Surveillance Authority referred to in that Agreement.

be 'stricter practical rules'.[190] The Brussels European Council of 21 and 22 June 2007 replied to this discussion paper by giving the Court the go-ahead to draft a formal proposal for an emergency preliminary ruling procedure based on the second option that had been put forward, where all Member States would keep their right to participate.

As a result, the new urgent procedure, now set out in Article 104b of the Rules of Procedure of the Court, allows all parties included in Article 23 of the same document to participate in the proceedings, but it distinguishes between those who may participate in the written stage of the procedure (parties to the main proceedings, the Member State of the court making the reference, the Commission and, if one of their measures is at issue, the Council and the Parliament) and those who may only attend a hearing at which they may submit oral observations (all other parties and, in particular, all other Member States).

Apart from the special arrangements on who may participate at what stage, the urgent preliminary ruling procedure seeks to achieve an accelerated handling of the case in two ways: firstly, by having a Chamber of five judges screening all cases falling within the AFSJ.[191] If the Chamber decides to allow a request for the urgent procedure, it will deliver a ruling after the hearing and after conveyance of the Advocate General's opinion in the course of its deliberations. Secondly, the process will be expedited by conducting the procedure and all necessary communications electronically.

The Court expects, thanks to this new procedure, to be able to deal with the most sensitive issues arising within the AFSJ far more swiftly, referring in its press release to 'situations where a person is deprived of his liberty and the answer to the question raised is decisive as to the assessment of the legal situation of the person detained or deprived of his liberty, or, in proceedings concerning parental authority or custody of children, where the jurisdiction under Community law of the court hearing the case depends on the answer to the question referred for a preliminary ruling'.[192]

---

[190] '[T]ranslation into all languages only of the questions referred for a preliminary ruling, setting of a shorter time-limit for replying than under the accelerated procedure, laying down a maximum length for observations or having no written observations, having no Advocate General's Opinion, although he would still be heard in the same way as under the accelerated procedure' Document 13272/06, 6.

[191] These five judges are designated for a period of twelve months.

[192] Information for the Press No 12/08, 3 March 2008 'A New Procedure in the Area of Freedom, Security and Justice: The Urgent Preliminary Ruling Procedure' http://curia.europa.eu/en/actu/communiques/cp08/info/cp080012en.pdf (accessed February 2009).

During 2007, the average duration of the standard preliminary reference procedure was 19 months.[193] This time went down to 16.8 months during 2008. Although this represents an all-time low in the past 20 years,[194] average duration remains considerable. The new procedure is thus to be welcomed in a field of law where time-sensitive issues are often at stake; indeed, the Court partly credits its introduction in March 2008 with the improvement in efficiency during the same year.

At the time of writing, the procedure has been used three times: it was used for the first time in *Inga Rinau*,[195] concerning the interpretation of the Brussels II Regulation; the ruling was delivered within eight weeks. The two other cases concerned the interpretation of the EAW Framework Decision.[196] In *Goicoechea*,[197] the process lasted six weeks. In *Leymann and Pustovarov*,[198] it lasted just under three months.

Although the procedure is indeed speedier, worries have arisen from the lack of publication, until recently, of any of the Advocate Generals' Opinions or *prises de position*.[199] Such policy would be hardly justifiable, since the Opinion of the Advocate General is often a needed source of reflection and a valuable tool for the understanding of a ruling that is, more often than not, tersely argued; at any rate, there have been indications that the Court has reached an internal decision to publish the Advocates General's contributions as a general rule, both within the urgent and the accelerated preliminary ruling procedure;[200] the Opinion of AG Sharpston in *Rinau* has indeed been published recently, some ten months after it was delivered.

---

[193]   P Koutrakos, 'Speeding up the Preliminary Reference Procedure—Fast but not too Fast' (2008) [33] ELR 617. See also the Court's 2007 Annual Report at: http://curia.europa.eu/en/instit/presentationfr/index.htm (accessed February 2009).

[194]   Information for the Press No 17/09, 19 February 2009 'Court of Justice–Statistics of Judicial Activity 2008' 1. Available at http://curia.europa.eu/en/actu/communiques/cp09/aff/cp090017en.pdf (accessed February 2009).

[195]   Case C-195/08 PPU *Rinau* [2008] ECR I-5271.

[196]   Council Framework Decision 2002/584/JHA of 13 June 2002 on the European arrest warrant and the surrender procedures between Member States, [2002] OJ L 190/1.

[197]   Case C-296/08 PPU *Goicoechea* [2008] ECR I-6307.

[198]   Case C-388/08 PPU *Leymann and Pustovarov* Judgment of 1 December 2008, nyr.

[199]   P Koutrakos, 'Speeding up the Preliminary Reference Procedure—Fast but not too Fast' (2008) 33 ELR 617, 618; see also the petition prepared by Dr Eleanor Spaventa, 11 September 2008, available at http://www.dur.ac.uk/resources/deli/ECJ-PPUprocedure2.doc (accessed March 2009). Similar concerns arose within the framework of the accelerated preliminary ruling procedure under Art 104a of the Rules of Procedure: D Chalmers, 'The Secret Delivery of Justice' (2008) 33 ELR 773, 774.

[200]   Lecture delivered by AG Sharpston within the Jean Monnet Seminar 'The Boundaries of EU Law after the Lisbon Treaty' 25 April 2009, Dubrovnik, Croatia.

Finally, it should be borne in mind that, at the time of submitting its proposal in 2006, the Court was operating under the assumption that either: (a) the Constitutional Treaty would be adopted, and so the judicial arrangements in the AFSJ would be those of the first pillar at present; or (b) in the absence of the Constitutional Treaty, the Commission's proposals on extending the standard first pillar arrangements on the jurisdiction of the Court to the whole of the AFSJ would be followed through.[201] In the absence of either of these wider reforms, the urgent preliminary reference procedure, although an improvement, is currently limited in its effects by the fact that not all national courts may ask for a preliminary ruling in the first place, something that would change with the ratification of the Lisbon Treaty.

2.3.2.3 Infringement Proceedings and Failure to Act

The Community control devices that apply to Title IV EC do not apply in the third pillar proper; there is no action for damages (as highlighted in *Segi*) or for failure to act, and instead of the Article 226 EC mechanism, Article 35(7) TEU sets out a procedure which resembles a public international law model of inter-state dispute settlement and which has, until the moment, never been used:[202]

Article 35(7) TEU
The Court of Justice shall have jurisdiction to rule on any dispute between Member States regarding the interpretation or the application of acts adopted under Article 34(2) whenever such dispute cannot be settled by the Council within six months of its being referred to the Council by one of its members. The Court shall also have jurisdiction to rule on any dispute between Member States and the Commission regarding the interpretation or the application of conventions established under Article 34(2)(d).

---

[201] Communication from the Commission to the European Council. A Citizens' Agenda: Delivering Results for Europe. Brussels, 10 May 2006. COM(2006) 211 final, 10; Communication from the Commission to the European Parliament, the Council, the European Parliament, the Council, the European Economic and Social Committee, the Committee of the Regions, and the Court of Justice of the European Communities: Adaptation of the Provisions of Title IV of the Treaty establishing the European Community relating to the jurisdiction of the Court of Justice with a view to ensuring more effective judicial protection. Brussels, 28 June 2006. COM(2006) 346 final.

[202] The same one already agreed for six pre-Amsterdan criminal, policing, or customs law conventions: S Peers, *EU Justice and Home Affairs Law* (OUP: Oxford, 2006) 41–2. For an overview of this dispute settlement procedure in the TEU: S Peers, 'Who's Judging the Watchmen: The Judicial System of the "Area of Freedom, Security and Justice" ' (1998) 17 YEL 337, 388–90.

Thus the Court has jurisdiction to rule on inter-state disputes, as well as on disputes between the Commission and a Member State regarding the interpretation or application of a convention; this is the 'equivalent' of Article 226 EC for this intergovernmental area. There are, of course, various differences between both mechanisms: Article 35(7) TEU covers only disputes on the interpretation or application of conventions, and not of any other measures;[203] furthermore, the TEU does not foresee the imposition of a penalty payment on the recalcitrant Member State—although this could in theory be specified in the text of a particular convention.

In general, the mechanism set out for this area in the TEU is much closer to the classic public international law model of settlement of international disputes, for various reasons. One of the features that set the Community supervisory mechanism apart from this classical model is that the Commission, an institution that is independent from the Member States, has the power to bring proceedings against a Member State because of any breach of EC law under Article 226 EC.[204] In *Commission v Italy*,[205] the Court strove to emphasize how this Community device is far removed from any classic public international law mechanism. By contrast, the role of the Commission is substantially diminished in the Article 35(7) TEU mechanism.

Equally, the TEU mechanism of inter-state supervision is weaker than its counterpart in the EC Treaty, Article 227. Even though the latter has hardly been used, Member States undertake, according to Article 292 EC, 'not to submit a dispute concerning the interpretation or application of this Treaty to any method of settlement other than those provided for therein'. This means that Member States can only bring their dispute before an international tribunal (other than the ECJ) if it relates to rights and obligations that do not flow from the EC Treaty.[206] Conversely, there is no

---

[203] According to Eeckhout, there may have been concerns that the Commission would otherwise use this procedure as a form of infringement action similar to that available within the first pillar: P Eeckhout, 'The European Court of Justice and the "Area of Freedom, Security and Justice": Challenges and Problems' in D O'Keeffe (ed), *Judicial Review in European Union Law: Liber Amicorum in Honour of Lord Slynn of Hadley* (Kluwer: London, 2000) 162.

[204] A Arnull, *The European Union and its Court of Justice* (2nd edn, OUP: Oxford, 2006) 34. On the obligation of the Commission, see A Evans, 'The Enforcement Procedure of Article 169 EEC: Commission's Discretion' (1979) 4 ELR 442.

[205] Case 39/72 *Commission v Italy* [1973] ECR 101 [24].

[206] As happened with a dispute between Ireland and the UK laid before the International Tribunal for the Law of the Sea (the *MOX Plant* case): see K Lenaerts and P Van Nuffel, *Constitutional Law of the European Union* (2nd edn, Sweet & Maxwell: London, 2005) 445.

such undertaking in the TEU—and thus the possibility of submitting an inter-state dispute to an international tribunal other than the ECJ, although outlandish and politically improbable, exists.[207] Of course, the unlikely use of this resort would fatally undermine the position of the ECJ as the guarantor of the Union's legal order.

Finally, Article 35(7) TEU makes it only possible to resort to adjudication when the diplomatic channel has been exhausted; the ECJ will step in only if the dispute cannot be settled by the Council of Ministers within six months.

2.3.2.4 Judicial Control of Third Pillar Bodies

Member States have not been willing to entrust the Commission with operational law-enforcement aspects; to the limited extent that they are willing to share any functions in this area (information exchange and coordination), such functions have normally been entrusted to agencies that remain decidedly intergovernmental in character.[208] Frontex is the first—and so far, only—agency of this type that has been created under the first pillar (Title IV EC);[209] Europol and Eurojust were created under the third one. Europol is a law enforcement organization created with the mission to improve the effectiveness and cooperation of the competent authorities in the Member States in preventing and combating international crime,[210] while Eurojust fosters the coordination of investigations and prosecutions between national judicial authorities.[211]

---

[207] This possibility is accepted by Denza—specifically, with regard to the International Court of Justice (ICJ)—who nevertheless considers it 'not a realistic option for most disputes given the time scale required for the ICJ to reach a decision'. E Denza, *The Intergovernmental Pillars of the European Union* (OUP: Oxford, 2002) 322.

[208] J Monar, 'Alternatives to the Community Method in EU Justice and Home Affairs' Summary of contribution to the CONNEX Workshop, Sciences Po, 29 November 2007 http://www.portedeurope.org/IMG/doc/Jorg_Monar.doc (accessed March 2009), 4.

[209] Council Regulation (EC) 2007/2004 of 26 October 2004 [2004] OJ L349/1. A general overview of this agency can be found in: V Mitsilegas, 'Border Security in the European Union: Towards Centralized Controls and Maximum Surveillance' in E Guild and F Geyer (eds), *Security versus Justice? Police and Judicial Cooperation in the European Union* (Ashgate: Aldershot, 2008).

[210] Convention on the establishment of a European Police Office (Europol Convention) [1995] OJ C316/2, with further reforms. A consolidated version is available on the official website of Europol: http://www.europol.europa.eu/legal/europol_convention_consolidated_version.pdf (accessed March 09).

[211] Council Decision 2002/187/JHA of 28 February 2002 setting up Eurojust with a view to reinforcing the fight against serious crime [2002] OJ L63/1.

The control of third pillar bodies is more problematic than that of first pillar ones.[212] The first case to bring this to the fore was *Spain v Eurojust*,[213] where the validity of several acts of Eurojust was challenged. The acts in question were seven calls for applications with a view to establishing a list of reserve temporary staff. Spain brought an action under Article 230 EC questioning the validity of parts of these acts, such as the fact that persons submitting their application in a language other than English had to nevertheless hand in some documents in English, and various points concerning candidates' qualifications in respect of knowledge of languages.

Eurojust is an independent body with legal personality which does not form part of the institutional framework of the European Union, as established in Article 5 TEU. Neither Article 230 EC nor its counterpart within the TEU, Article 35, allow an action to be brought against an act from this body.[214] Yet AG Poiares Maduro eloquently defended the need for the Court to ignore these considerations and review the validity of the acts at stake,[215] arguing that the principle of effective judicial supervision of authorities acting under Treaty provisions (as an expression of a general principle safeguarding respect for the law) should not be restricted in its application to the European Community—but should be applied in every area of European Union activity.[216] The Court did not heed the AG's

---

[212] On the judicial accountability of Frontex, see S Puntscher Riekmann, 'Security, Freedom and Accountability: Europol & Frontex' in E Guild and F Geyer (eds), *Security versus Justice? Police and Judicial Cooperation in the European Union* (Ashgate: Aldershot, 2008) 30–2; for a less optimistic view, see V Mitsilegas, 'Border Security in the European Union: Towards Centralized Controls and Maximum Surveillance' in E Guild and F Geyer (eds), *Security versus Justice? Police and Judicial Cooperation in the European Union* (Ashgate: Aldershot, 2008) 374–5. The Council Regulation that creates Frontex grants competence to the Court in cases of contractual and non-contractual liability (Art 19) and to review decisions on access to documents (Art 28). Further review of legality is not foreseen, but Craig argues convincingly for the review of all decisions of EC agencies that produce legal effects in relation to third parties, pursuant to the reasoning in *Les Verts:* P Craig, *EU Administrative Law* (OUP: Oxford, 2006) 164–8. Case 294/83 *Parti Écologiste 'Les Verts' v European Parliament* [1986] ECR 1339.

[213] Case C-160/03 *Spain v Eurojust* [2005] ECR I-2077.

[214] On the lack of control of Eurojust and the problems it creates, S Douglas-Scott, 'The Rule of Law in the European Union: Putting the Security into the EU's Area of Freedom Security and Justice' (2004) 29 ELR 219, 237–9.

[215] Even though Spain had sought review of these measures under an inapt heading, ie Art 230 EC, which can only encompass Community measures. AG Poiares Maduro prompted the Court to consider the validity of Eurojust's acts under Art 35 TEU instead (as measures adopted within the framework of the European Union). Opinion of AG Poiares Maduro in C-160/03 *Spain v Eurojust* [2005] ECR I-2077 [14].   [216] Opinon of AG Poiares Maduro in *Eurojust* [16].

urgings and simply declared the claim inadmissible under Article 230 EC because the challenged acts were not Community measures.[217] The Court considered that there was appropriate judicial control of Eurojust, since its staff are subject to the rules and regulations applicable to officials and other servants of the European Communities.[218] This means that the doors of the CFI are open to the candidates for the posts referred to in the contested calls for applications, but there is no chance for any other applicants (Member States in this case, but also Union institutions) to challenge these measures.[219] It is worth emphasizing that the Court did not sanction a lack of judicial protection, and in this it agreed with AG Maduro—rather, the ECJ denied the existence of such a lack.

It may be argued that this partial lack of control can be explained away by referring to the operational nature of Eurojust. This type of body generally has no legislative role or decision-making power: a foreseeable judicial control of its acts can thus be seen as superficial. *Spain v Eurojust*, however, shows that these assumptions can be proved wrong in some cases, however rare. More importantly, this justification will probably lose its force in the future, since Eurojust is likely to acquire further powers.[220]

As regards the judicial control of Europol, the situation is similar.[221] The ECJ has no competence to control its activities; presumably, such control was not deemed necessary at first because Europol has no executive powers and thus cannot carry out criminal investigations in a Member State in its own name: until now, its role has been limited to crime analysis, coordination, and information exchange.[222] Provided Member States make a declaration accepting its jurisdiction, the ECJ may give preliminary rulings on the interpretation of the Europol Convention, but cannot review

---

[217] Yet the AG's reasoning may have influenced later decisions, where the Court relied heavily on the principle of judicial protection and the rule of law (see ch 4).

[218] Following Art 30 of the Eurojust Decision: Council Decision 2002/187/JHA of 28 February 2002 setting up Eurojust with a view to reinforcing the fight against serious crime [2002] OJ L63/1.

[219] *Eurojust* [42].

[220] See for instance the proposals from Eurojust in Council of the European Union, 20 September 2007 Document 1307/07.

[221] For other types of accountability, see S Puntscher Riekmann, 'Security, Freedom and Accountability: Europol & Frontex' in E Guild and F Geyer (eds), *Security versus Justice? Police and Judicial Cooperation in the European Union* (Ashgate: Aldershot, 2008) 23–8.

[222] C Fijnaut, 'Police Co-operation and the Area of Freedom, Security and Justice' in N Walker (ed), *Europe's Area of Freedom, Security and Justice* (OUP: Oxford, 2004), 236; S Douglas-Scott, 'The Rule of Law in the European Union: Putting the Security into the EU's Area of Freedom Security and Justice' (2004) 29 ELR 219, 234–5.

Europol's activities.[223] Judicial control has been left to national legislation and courts: Declaration 7 on Article 30 TEU annexed to the Final Act of the Intergovernmental Conference of Amsterdam states that '(a)ction in the field of police cooperation under Article TEU, including activities of Europol, shall be subject to appropriate judicial review by the competent national authorities in accordance with rules applicable in each Member State'. Two main problems arise from this: first, there is no uniformity as to whether and in what way Europol activities are controlled across the Union, given that it is left up to national judiciaries; and second, not even those national judiciaries may be able to exercise control, because of the non-justiciable Protocol on privileges and immunities of Europol and its staff, which determines that Europol is immune from liability for 'unauthorized or incorrect data processing' and its officials are not liable for acts performed during the exercise of their duties.[224] And yet Europol has extensive powers to collect and store information on individuals—powers, in fact, that go beyond those needed to combat crime.[225] This is all the more worrying because of the lack of a coherent EU data protection regime.[226] Finally, some commentators have already warned about the fact that Europol is likely to acquire operational powers in the future:[227]

[223] According to the Protocol on the interpretation of the Europol Convention by the ECJ ([1996] OJ C299/2) and the Protocol on Privileges and Immunities of Europol Staff ([1997] OJ C221/1).

[224] The Europol Director may waive the immunity, but this decision is not subject to judicial review. The Protocol is to be reconsidered whenever Europol's functions are extended: Protocol on Privileges and Immunities of Europol Staff ([1997] OJ C221/1) Arts 2(1), 8(1)(a), 12 and 13. See S Peers, 'Who's Judging the Watchmen: The Judicial System of the "Area of Freedom, Security and Justice"' (1998) 17 YEL 337, 410–12 and 349.

[225] S Douglas-Scott, 'The Rule of Law in the European Union: Putting the Security into the EU's Area of Freedom Security and Justice' (2004) 29 ELR 219, 234. This author provides a very useful account of all instances of control of Europol, 234–7.

[226] For an in-depth study, see P De Hert, C Riehle, and V Papakonstantinou, 'Data Protection in the Third Pillar: Cautious Pessimism' in M Martin Crime (ed), *Rights and the EU: The Future of Police and Judicial Cooperation* (Justice: London, 2008) 121–94. On 27 November 2008, the Council adopted the Framework Decision 2008/977/JHA on the protection of personal data processed in the framework of police and judicial cooperation in criminal matters, intended to apply only to areas of the third pillar that do not have special sectorial measures on data protection. The standard of protection is below the EC regime of data protection (Directive EC 95/46/EC [1995] OJ L281/31).

[227] C Van den Wyngaert, 'Eurojust and the European Public Prosecutor' in N Walker (ed), *Europe's Area of Freedom, Security and Justice* (OUP: Oxford, 2004), 255–6. See also the Friends of the Presidency's Report on the Future of Europol. Brussels, 19 May 2006. 9184/1/06 REV 1. For a critical appraisal of the changes put forward in this report, see B Hayes, 'The Future of Europol: More Powers, Less Regulation, Precious Little Debate' (Statewatch Analysis 2006) http://www.statewatch.org/news/2006/oct/future-of-europol-analysis.pdf (accessed Nov 2006).

a change of this calibre would require not only national control but also, ideally, comprehensive judicial control at the European level.[228]

2.3.2.5 *The Jurisdiction of the ECJ to Police the Borders between Third and First Pillars*

According to Article 47 TEU, no encroachment upon the Community competences should result from the application of the procedures foreseen in the Treaty on European Union;[229] the Court of Justice is competent to ensure compliance with this provision, in accordance with Article 46 TEU.

It should be borne in mind that Article 47 TEU necessitates a procedural vehicle to be enforced: according to Article 46 TEU, the Court's powers in the EC Treaty apply to Article 47 TEU. This means that a direct action under Article 230 EC was the context within which the Court was first able to enforce Article 47 TEU (even though the Court had no powers under the TEU at the time).[230] After the entry into force of the Treaty of Amsterdam, where the Court was given limited powers within the third pillar under Article 35 TEU, the direct action foreseen in Article 35(6) TEU was used in subsequent cases.[231] The use of this *lex specialis* does not preclude the use of the *lex generalis* of the EC Treaty when necessary, typically when the latter offers an additional procedural venue that is not available within the TEU. In *Segi*, the CFI considered an action for damages brought by individuals under Articles 235 and 288 EC to the extent that such damages were allegedly caused by a breach of Article 47 TEU, even though there is no such action within the TEU.[232] This

---

[228] At the moment, the ECJ has only a very limited jurisdiction to interpret the provisions of the Europol Convention, as foreseen in one of its Protocols: [1996] OJ C299/1. Member States can decide the scope of the jurisdiction of the Court to give preliminary rulings (whether all national courts can refer a case, and whether some of them have a duty to do so).

[229] Art 47 TEU reads as follows: 'Subject to the provisions amending the Treaty establishing the European Economic Community with a view to establishing the European Community, the Treaty establishing the European Coal and Steel Community and the Treaty establishing the European Atomic Energy Community, and to these final provisions, nothing in this Treaty shall affect the Treaties establishing the European Communities or the subsequent Treaties and Acts modifying or supplementing them.'

[230] Case C-170/96 *Commission v Council (airport transit)* [1998] ECR I-02763.

[231] eg Cases C-176/03 *Commission v Council* [2005] ECR I-7879; C-440/05 *Commission v Council (ship-source pollution)* [2007] ECR I-9097.

[232] Case T-338/02 *Segi* [2004] ECR II-01647. The ECJ did not consider the issue afresh, but it agreed that the CFI had jurisdiction: C-355/04 P *Segi* [2007] ECR I-1657. See also Cases T-333/02 *Gestoras Pro Amnistía and others v Council*, unpublished, and C-354/04 *Gestoras Pro Amnistía and others v Council* [2007] ECR I-1579.

recourse to the EC Treaty has been more obvious when enforcing Article 47 TEU in the context of the CFSP, where no *lex specialis* is available: accordingly, not only has Article 230 EC been used (including by individuals), but also Article 241 EC (plea of illegality).[233] All this prompts two reflections: first, an individual must be able to challenge a third pillar measure directly under Article 230(4) EC because it should have been adopted under the first pillar, regardless of the fact that individuals may not bring actions for annulment within Title VI TEU. The same would apply to the European Parliament. And second, if all powers of the Court under the EC Treaty can be used to enforce Article 47 TEU (as per Article 46 TEU), it must be possible for national courts to ask for a preliminary ruling on the validity of third and second pillar measures, if they should have possibly been adopted under the EC Treaty.[234] Within the framework of the third pillar, this would be the case regardless of whether the Member State has accepted the jurisdiction of the Court under Article 35 TEU.

Furthermore, it could seem at first sight that the Court can only ensure that the intergovernmental pillars do not encroach upon the first one, but not the other way round. Indeed, this is the competence granted by Article 47 TEU. But it is worth remembering that in effect the Court can also ensure (and has in fact done so) that first pillar measures are not wrongly adopted in lieu of third pillar ones.[235] When doing this, the Court is exercising its general competence under Article 230(2) EC to ensure that a first pillar measure has been adopted on the correct legal basis.

In order to decide whether a certain measure could have been adopted under the first pillar, it seems the Court will apply its centre of gravity test. The Court may come to the conclusion that a measure could have been adopted under the first pillar because, either the measure's main aim falls within the first pillar, or the measure has two components (EC/third pillar) that are linked and equally important. In the first case, the preference for an EC legal basis would already seem the natural result of the Court's centre of gravity test. It is in the second case, when a measure has two equally

---

[233] In *ECOWAS*, the Commission used the direct action of Art 230 EC and the plea of illegality: Case C-91/05 *Commission v Council ('ECOWAS')* Judgment of 20 May 2008, nyr; in *OMPI* and *Selmani*, individuals were allowed to bring a direct action under Art 230 EC (insofar as it concerned Art 47 TEU): Case T 228/02 *Organisation des Modjahedines du Peuple d'Iran* [2006] ECR II-4665 and the Order in T-299/04 *Selmani* [2005] ECR II-20.

[234] R van Ooik, 'Cross-Pillar Litigation before the ECJ: Demarcation of Community and Union Competences' (2008) 4 EuConst 399, 405–6.

[235] Joined Cases C-317/04 and C-318/04 *Parliament v Council and Commission* [2006] ECR I-4721 (PNR Agreement).

central components, that a hierarchy rule becomes indispensable—since the centre of gravity test would dictate adoption under both legal bases, something that the Court does not accept when the legal bases are from separate legal orders (that is, EC and EU):[236] the Court's reading of Article 47 TEU provides such a hierarchy rule. Incidentally, in all cases decided until now by the Court that involved the use of Article 47 TEU to police the borders between third and first pillars, the Court found that the measure in dispute had only one main aim, pertaining to the EC pillar. The possibility of a measure having two equally important aims (EC/intergovernmental) has only materialized until now in the context of Article 47 litigation concerning the second pillar and the EC.[237]

Article 47 TEU has therefore been used by the Court as a delimitation rule that helps us decide between two equally valid legal bases. It has, however, been suggested in the literature that Article 47 TEU may have a secondary, wider function, in that it may allow the Court to ensure that a (properly adopted) third pillar measure does not breach the rules of the EC Treaty. In this case, the intergovernmental measure has passed the first test (legal basis), but it would be subject to a second one (compliance with other rules of the EC Treaty): if the TEU does not give the Council competence to adopt measures that should fall within the scope of the EC Treaty, the argument goes, it cannot logically give the Council competence to compel Member States to breach the EC Treaty.[238]

This wider understanding of the scope of Article 47 TEU is convincing, but two points may be made: first, that it may be virtually always possible for the Court to find that the aim of a certain provision of a third pillar measure that compels Member States to breach the EC Treaty comes

---

[236] Case C-91/05 *Commission v Council ('ECOWAS')* [2008] ECR I-3651 [76]. R van Ooik 'Cross-Pillar Litigation before the ECJ: Demarcation of Community and Union Competences' (2008) 4 EuConst 399, 413–18.   [237] *ECOWAS*, ibid.

[238] S Peers, 'Who's Judging the Watchmen: The Judicial System of the "Area of Freedom, Security and Justice" ' (1998) 17 YEL 337, 402. Peers puts forward the example of a properly adopted framework decision on money laundering that has the result of compelling Member States to breach Art 56 EC, which prohibits all restrictions on the movement of capital and on payments between the Member States and between Member States and third countries. Cremona suggests that this understanding of Art 47 TEU (as a rule of conflict between a rule of EU law and a rule of EC law rather than as a delimitation rule that concerns only the decision on legal basis) is possible in theory, but it has never been used by the Court: M Cremona, 'Coherence through Law: What difference will the Treaty of Lisbon make?' (2008) 3 Hamburg Rev of Social Sciences 11, 21–2.

within the scope of the latter and must thus be annulled.[239] And second, even if we do come across a situation where a provision breaches the EC Treaty but it cannot be claimed that it could have been adopted under it, a distinction should possibly be drawn between the obligation imposed by this provision on the Council—the obligation not to breach EC law when adopting EU law measures—and whether or not this obligation may be enforced by the Court. Whereas it seems clear that Article 47 TEU imposes such an obligation on the Council, an interpretation of this provision that allows the Court to conduct a substantive review of third or second pillar measures would only be possible to the extent that the Court has such powers under the TEU itself (rather than under the EC Treaty). The Court has interpreted Article 47 as a clause that allows it to resort to its EC powers to control EU measures, but only as far as checking their legal basis; this has always been justified by the need to preserve the distribution of competences and there is no indication that the Court would be willing to extend it any further. This means that while a control of third pillar measures for compliance with the EC Treaty is possible within the framework of Article 35 TEU, no such control can be realistically expected within the second pillar, where there are no procedural vehicles available to the Court.[240]

But let us now examine some of the cases in which the Court has had to apply Article 47 TEU, invariably to police the use of competences, within the framework of the third pillar: the first example was the *Airport Transit Visa* case,[241] where the Court confirmed that it was competent to define the boundaries between the first and third pillars. This particular case concerned a Council joint action regarding airport transit visas adopted under Article K.3 TEU; the Commission challenged this measure on the basis

---

[239] The provision could be annulled on its own, if it is severable from the rest of the measure. If both aims are inextricably linked, the whole measure must be annulled: Case C-440/05 *Commission v Council (ship-source pollution)* [2007] ECR I-9097. See on this point R van Ooik, 'Cross-Pillar Litigation before the ECJ: Demarcation of Community and Union Competences' (2008) 4 EuConst 399, 413–14. But cf J Heliskoski, 'Small Arms and Light Weapons within the Union's Pillar Structure: an Analysis of Art 47 of the EU Treaty' (2008) 33 ELR 898, 906–8. Regardless of whether splitting a measure is or is not possible, the threshold to consider that a measure should have been adopted under the EC pillar seems to be quite low: see Heliskoski, ibid, 908.

[240] This view seems more in keeping with the spirit of Title V TEU (CFSP), where it is obvious that the drafters of the Treaty wished for the Court to be excluded. A reading of Art 47 TEU as a provision that single-handedly grants the Court competence to review all CFSP measures for compliance with the EC Treaty seems a step too far.

[241] Case C-170/96 *Commission v Council (airport transit)* [1998] ECR I-02763.

that it should have been adopted under Article 100c EC. The Court examined the measure in order to determine whether it should have indeed been adopted under the EC Treaty; if this had been the case, the Court would have annulled the measure without further review.[242] The Court found that the act at stake could not possibly come within the scope of Article 100c EC, and was therefore upheld. More importantly, this benchmark decision gave a clear signal that the Court was willing to police the borders between first and third pillars in an active manner; equally, it hinted at the fact that even non-exclusive EC competences could preclude intergovernmental action in the same area,[243] something that was corroborated in later case-law.[244]

Later on, the Court used its competence under Article 47 TEU to review the adoption of criminal law measures within the third pillar, with surprising results. In *Commission v Council*,[245] the Commission sought the annulment of a framework decision concerning the enforcement of environmental law through the imposition of criminal liability. This measure had been adopted under the third pillar,[246] contrary to the Commission's contention that Article 175 EC should have been used instead. The Court proceeded to apply the same mechanism seen in the *Airport Transit Visa* case, this time coming to the conclusion that the action could have been taken under the first pillar; the use of a third pillar legal base was, therefore, precluded. Against the opposition of the intervening Member States, the Court famously stated in its bold judgment that:

As a general rule, neither criminal law nor the rules of criminal procedure fall within the Community's competence [...] However, the last-mentioned finding does not prevent the Community legislature, when the application of effective, proportionate and dissuasive criminal penalties by the competent national

---

[242] Ibid, [17]. On the contrary, AG Fennelly seemed to assume in his Opinion that, if the Court came to the conclusion that the measure fell within the scope of Art 100c EC, it would then be competent to review its substance for compliance with EC law: [46].

[243] P Eeckhout, *External Relations of the European Union: Legal and Constitutional Foundations* (OUP: Oxford, 2004) 148–50. To the contrary, some authors interpreted the Court's decision to mean that the visa competence of the Community was deemed exclusive: A Oliveira, 'Annotation to Case C170/96, *Commission of the European Communities v Council of the European Union*, Judgment of 12 May 1998, [1998] ECR I-2763' (1999) 99 CML Rev 149, 155. The Court avoided discussing the type of competence at stake in all cases of cross-pillar litigation until the *ECOWAS* case, concerning the second pillar: Case C-91/05 *Commission v Council ('ECOWAS')* [2008] ECR I-3651. [244] *ECOWAS*, ibid.

[245] Case C-176/03 *Commission v Council* [2005] ECR I-7879.

[246] Namely Arts 29, 31(e) and 34.2(b) TEU (pre-Nice).

authorities is an essential measure for combating serious environmental offences, from taking measures which relate to the criminal law of the Member States which it considers necessary in order to ensure that the rules which it lays down on environmental protection are fully effective.[247]

Thus the Court has arguably used Article 47 TEU to defend (or extend) the Community's competences to an extent few might have anticipated;[248] that is, criminal law becomes a matter for the EC legislature provided it can be connected adequately to the pursuit of environmental protection under the Court's rather ambiguous threshold test. In any case, the scope of the judgment is yet to be fully clarified: whereas many argue that the newly found criminal competence of the Community is, or should be, restricted to environmental law,[249] the Commission has taken a much broader interpretation, proposing to adopt criminal measures in the fields of money laundering and corruption, for example.[250] Article 47 TEU may have to be used again in the future to clarify this issue, at least in the absence of the Lisbon Treaty.[251] For the moment, the criminal competence of the EC in relation to environmental protection has been confirmed by the Court in the *ship-source pollution* case,[252] where the Commission sought and obtained the annulment of a third pillar framework decision on this basis.

So far these cases have concerned direct challenges to third pillar measures. But, as has already been pointed out, this is not the only procedural vehicle that can be used to enforce Article 47 TEU. Thus, in *Segi*, the CFI

---

[247] Case C-176/03 *Commission v Council* [2005] ECR I-7879 [47]–[48].

[248] For a fully fledged comment of this decision, see E Herlin-Karnell, '*Commission v Council*: Some Reflections on Criminal Law in the First Pillar' (2007) 13 Eur PL 69; C Tobler, 'Annotation to Case C-176/03, *Commission v Council* Judgment of the Grand Chamber of 13 September 2005, nyr' (2006) 43 CML Rev 835; EU Committee of the House of Lords, 'The Criminal Law Competence of the European Community. Report with Evidence' (42nd Report of Session 2005–6, HL Paper 227).

[249] At the informal meeting of the Justice and Home Affairs Council in Vienna on 12 to 14 January 2006, the representatives of the Member States apparently disputed the Commission's interpretation: Memorandum by R Plender. EU Committee of the House of Lords, 'The Criminal Law Competence of the European Community. Report with Evidence' (42nd Report of Session 2005–6, HL Paper 227) 9; see also the Memorandum by P Lachmann and C Thorning attached to the same report, 39.

[250] COM (2005) 583, 23 Nov 2005. In agreement, Memorandum by S Peers. EU Committee of the House of Lords, 'The Criminal Law Competence of the European Community: Report with Evidence' (42nd Report of Session 2005–6, HL Paper 227) 28.

[251] A Dawes and O Lynskey, 'The Ever-longer Arm of EC Law: The Extension of Community Competence into the Field of Criminal Law' (2008) 45 CML Rev 131; S Peers, 'The European Community's Criminal Law Competence: The Plot Thickens' (2008) 33 ELR 399.

[252] Case C-440/05 *Commission v Council (ship-source pollution)* [2007] ECR I-9097.

considered itself competent to entertain—and subsequently rejected—an action for damages caused by a breach of Article 47 TEU.[253]

Further first/third pillar litigation has taken place without involving Article 47 TEU, because the claim was that a first pillar instrument had been adopted where the Community had no competence to do so. In considering a conflict between the pillars from this perspective, the Court is examining whether the first pillar instrument was properly adopted, something it can do routinely under Article 230 EC. An example of this type of litigation has concerned the agreement between the European Community and the United States of America on the transfer of data on air travellers ('passenger name records' or PNR).[254] The European Parliament sought annulment of the (first pillar) agreement,[255] adopted under Article 95 EC. The Court obliged; the agreement concerned 'not data processing necessary for a supply of services, but data processing regarded as necessary for safeguarding public security and for law-enforcement purposes',[256] and was therefore outside the scope of Community law. A new PNR agreement has now been adopted under Articles 24 and 38 TEU, that is, under the third pillar.[257] A further example of this type of litigation arose when the

---

[253] Case T-338/02 *Segi* [2004] ECR II-01647. The ECJ did not consider the issue afresh, but it agreed that the CFI had jurisdiction: C-355/04 P *Segi* [2007] ECR I-1657. See also Cases T-333/02 *Gestoras Pro Amnistía and others v Council*, unpublished, and C-354/04 *Gestoras Pro Amnistía and others v Council* [2007] ECR I-1579.

[254] Joined Cases C-317/04 and C-318/04 *Parliament v Council and Commission* [2006] ECR I-4721.

[255] Council Decision 2004/496/EC of 17 May 2004 on the conclusion of an Agreement between the European Community and the United States of America on the processing and transfer of PNR data by Air Carriers to the United States Department of Homeland Security, Bureau of Customs and Border Protection [2004] OJ L183/83 and corrigendum at [2005] OJ 2005 L255/168. The European Parliament also sought annulment of the decision on the adequacy of this agreement: Commission Decision 2004/535/EC of 14 May 2004 on the adequate protection of personal data contained in the Passenger Name Records of air passengers transferred to the United States Bureau of Customs and Border Protection [2004] OJ L235/11.

[256] Joined Cases C-317/04 and C-318/04 *Parliament v Council and Commission* [2006] ECR I-4721 (PNR Agreement) [57]. Although the Court annulled the decision on adequacy of the agreement with the US, it limited the effect of this annulment: ibid, [73]. See also B Kunoy and A Dawes, 'Plate Tectonics in Luxembourg: The Ménage à Trois between EC Law, International Law and the European Convention on Human Rights Following the UN Sanctions Cases' (2009) 46 CML Rev 73, 86–8.

[257] Council Decision 2006/729/CFSP/JHA of 16 October 2006 on the signing, on behalf of the European Union, of an Agreement between the European Union and the United States of America on the processing and transfer of passenger name records (PNR) data by air carriers to the United States Department of Homeland Security: [2006] OJ L298/27.

Parliament challenged a first pillar Commission decision applying the EC's development policy legislation to fund anti-terrorist measures in the Phi-lipines. The Court annulled the decision in question.[258] In the latest case of this kind, Ireland challenged the legality of the Directive on Data Reten-tion,[259] adopted under Article 95 EC:[260] the Court found that the main aim of the measure was to aid the functioning of the single market, and it was therefore upheld.

It may be concluded from its case-law that the Court has played and is playing a very significant role in defining the boundaries between the first and third pillars, be it by way of Article 47 TEU when action has been undertaken within the third pillar, or by merely exercising its competence under Article 230(2) EC when action has been undertaken by the Com-munity. In practice, when policing the borders between third and first pillars, the Court has decided a majority of cases in favour of the EC—by arguing that the main aim of the measure at stake fell within the first pillar—but there have also been occasions where the Court has decided in favour of the third one.[261] The centre of gravity test is often highly sub-jective and the Court has a wide scope of discretion, making a bias in favour of the EC very likely. Ultimately, however, the problem seems to lie with the pillar structure, rather than with the Court itself. The Lisbon Treaty would solve this problem as far as the third pillar is concerned, since the normal rules on the adoption of measures under dual legal bases would apply. Yet the need to police the borders between 'integrated but separate legal orders'[262] would not disappear completely, and so the Court would still be called upon to continue performing a comparable role in the future, this time as regards the CFSP only.

---

[258] Case C-403/05 *European Parliament v Commission* [2007] ECR I-9045. For further examples of cross-pillar litigation, see S Peers, *EU Justice and Home Affairs Law* (OUP: Oxford, 2006) 72–7 and 510–23.

[259] Directive 2006/24/EC of the European Parliament and of the Council of 15 March 2006 on the retention of data generated or processed in connection with the provision of publicly available electronic communication services or of public communication networks and amending Directive 2002/58/EC [2006] OJ L105/54.

[260] Case C-301/06 *Ireland v Council and Parliament* Judgment of 10 February 2009, nyr.

[261] Case C-170/96 *Commission v Council (airport transit)* [1998] ECR I-02763; Joined Cases C-317/04 and C-318/04 *Parliament v Council and Commission* [2006] ECR I-4721.

[262] Joined Cases C-402/05 P and 415/05 P *Yassin Abdullah Kadi, Al Barakaat International Foundation v Council and Commission* [2008] ECR I-6351 [202].

2.4 Cherry-Picking: Institutional Ways to Fix Problems without the Constitutional Treaty

The ratification process of the Constitutional Treaty was on hold for more than two years.[263] Such standstill in the constitutional process was bound to spur a process of 'cherry-picking' or selection of those reforms that were most needed and could be brought about within the framework of the current treaties.[264] Unsurprisingly therefore, in the interim between the failure of the Constitutional Treaty and the signature of the Lisbon Treaty, the European Court of Justice and the Commission signalled in different ways their intention to get to grips with much needed reforms in the Area of Freedom, Security and Justice.

2.4.1 The Court's Case-Law

Instances where the Court has adopted a progressive approach to constitutional problems that presented themselves in the third pillar have already been discussed in this chapter. On a more general level, the Court's arguable readiness to cherry-pick concerns the Charter of Fundamental Rights, due to become binding at the same time as the Constitutional Treaty in which it was included.

The CFI did not hesitate to refer to the Charter quite early on in its case-law;[265] neither did several Advocates General.[266] The ECJ, on the other hand, was reluctant to refer to this document until 2006, when dealing with the European Parliament's challenge to the EC directive on the right to family reunification.[267] The Parliament contended that the measure breached the right to family life and invoked Article 7 of the Charter; the Court

---

[263] After the French and the Dutch rejected it in referenda held in May and June 2005, respectively. The Constitutional Treaty had been ratified by 16 of the 27 Member States by the time the ratification process was put on hold. The Treaty needed to be ratified by all signatory countries in order to enter into force.

[264] A Hinarejos, 'Judicial Control of CFSP in the Constitution: A Cherry Worth Picking?' (2006) 25 YEL 363, 363–93.

[265] Famously, if not for the first time, in Case T-177/01 *Jégo-Quéré v Commission* [2002] ECR II-2365.

[266] For instance AG Tizzano in Case C-173/99 *BECTU v Secretary of State for Trade and Industry* [2001] ECR-I 4881; AG Jacobs in C-50/00 *Unión de Pequeños Agricultores v Council* [2002] ECR I-6677; AG Stix-Hackl in Case C-60/00 *Mary Carpenter v Secretary of State for the Home Department* [2002] ECR I-06279; AG Geelhoed in Case C-413/99 *Baumbast* [2002] ECR I-7091.

[267] Council Directive 2003/86/EC [2003] OJ L251/12; Case C-540/03 *European Parliament v Council* [2006] ECR I-5769.

disagreed, but it nevertheless discussed and admitted the significance of the Charter.[268] Further mentions have ensued, remarkably also in high-profile cases with a connection to the intergovernmental pillars and, in general, the legal system of the EU:[269] in *Advocaten*, the Court referred to Articles 49, 20, and 21 of the Charter (the principle of the legality of criminal offences and penalties and the principle of equality and non-discrimination);[270] in *Kadi*, the Court referred to Article 47 of the same document (the principle of effective judicial protection).[271] We can only speculate as to the reasons for the Court's change of heart but it is, again, quite telling that it only referred to the Charter once it had become clear that the Constitutional Treaty was not likely to be ratified. It may be that the Court was waiting for the Charter to become binding through the proper constitutional mechanism; once this mechanism came to a halt, the Court may have decided to move the constitutional process forward of its own accord; after all, the Court has acted in an adventurous manner in the past, in the absence of impetus from Treaty revision or legislative initiatives.[272]

2.4.2 The Commission's Proposals

For its part, the Commission stated that 'the EU should use existing Treaties more effectively [...], without pre-empting the Constitutional Treaty'[273] and put together an agenda of necessary reforms that could be achieved within the current framework of the treaties. The problems caused by the current restrictions in the jurisdiction of the ECJ were to be tackled through two different proposals that were, ultimately, unsuccessful.

2.4.2.1 First Proposal: The Transfer of the Third Pillar

In its communication to the European Council 'A Citizens' Agenda: Delivering Results to Europe',[274] the Commission highlighted the need for

---

[268] Ibid, [38]. This was made easier by the fact that the directive itself referred to the Charter in its preamble.

[269] For subsequent first pillar examples, see Cases C-411/04 P *Salzgitter Mannesmann v Commission* [2007] ECR I-959; C-432/05 *Unibet* [2007] ECR I-2271.

[270] Case C-303/05 *Advocaten voor de Wereld* [2007] ECR I-3633 [46].

[271] Joined Cases C-402/05 P and 415/05 P *Yassin Abdullah Kadi, Al Barakaat International Foundation v Council and Commission* [2008] ECR I-6351 [335].

[272] As it was the case from the entry into force of the EEC Treaty until the breakdown of the Luxembourg Compromise in the early eighties: see A Arnull, *The European Union and its Court of Justice* (2nd edn, OUP: Oxford, 2006) 639–42.

[273] Communication from the Commission to the European Council. A Citizens' Agenda: Delivering Results for Europe. Brussels, 10 May 2006. COM(2006) 211 final, 10.   [274] Ibid.

action and announced its intention to make a formal proposal to transfer all or part of the third pillar to the first one. This would be done using the mechanism set out in Article 42 TEU:

The Council, acting unanimously on the initiative of the Commission or a Member State, and after consulting the European Parliament, may decide that action in areas referred to in Article 29 shall fall under Title IV of the Treaty establishing the European Community, and at the same time determine the relevant voting conditions relating to it. It shall recommend the Member States to adopt that decision in accordance with their respective constitutional requirements.

Several issues arose from the proposed reform: first, a transfer was never likely to be easy given the necessity of a unanimous decision of the Council. Second, it would have to be approved by different national procedures, depending on the legislation of each Member State; it was not likely to be a speedy process either.[275] Finally, the transfer could only be into Title IV of the EC Treaty, according to Article 42 TEU. Apart from this, the Commission's agenda was not very specific: the transfer could affect the whole of the third pillar or only part of it. Equally, the transfer could be 'total'— in that no special conditions for the transferred areas were imposed—or the Council's decision to operate this change could introduce new settings affecting the areas formerly within the third pillar. Of the different possible outcomes, one would have been absolutely unacceptable, namely the transfer of the third pillar into Title IV of the EC Treaty while the restrictions of Article 68 EC continued to apply. In that case, all the measures adopted in the AFSJ would have been measures of Community law, but the jurisdiction of the Court to give preliminary rulings would still be curtailed because of Article 68 EC. Only courts of last resort would be able to ask the ECJ for a preliminary ruling, and the Court would not be able to rule on measures based on Article 62(1) EC and 'relating to the maintenance of law and order and the safeguarding of internal security'.[276] The

---

[275] For an in-depth analysis of the proposed reform, see S Peers, 'Transferring the Third Pillar' (Statewatch Analysis 2006) http://www.statewatch.org/news/2006/may/analysis-3rd-pill-transfer-may-2006.pdf (accessed August 2006).

[276] Arguably, this exception affects only the competence of the Court to give preliminary rulings and thus its competence to review these measures under Art 230 EC (direct review) would remain unaffected. The Commission seems to take a more extensive view of the exception: see Communication from the Commission to the European Parliament, the Council, the European Economic and Social Committee, the Committee of the Regions, and the Court of Justice of the European Communities: Adaptation of the Provisions of Title IV of the Treaty establishing the European Community relating to the jurisdiction of the Court of Justice with a view to ensuring more effective judicial protection. Brussels, 28 June 2006. COM(2006) 346 final, 6.

Commission, however, was aware of this undesirable outcome—one which would only aggravate the problem—and consequently issued a complementary proposal to reform the jurisdiction of the Court within Title IV EC.

2.4.2.2 Second Proposal: Abolishing Article 68 EC

The Commission also issued a formal proposal concerning the jurisdiction of the Court within Title IV of the EC Treaty,[277] arguing for the elimination of the restrictions contained in Article 68, (1) and (2) EC. On the one hand, argued the Commission, all national courts should be able to ask for a preliminary reference in this area—anything else being a danger for the consistency of interpretation of Community law and offering a less than satisfactory way of redress for individuals wishing to challenge the validity of a Community measure indirectly. On the other hand, the Commission also argued, the Court should have full jurisdiction to review Council measures connected with the removal of controls on the movement of persons across internal borders 'relating to the maintenance of law and order and the safeguarding of internal security'.

This reform would have taken place under Article 67(2) EC, which requires the Council, at the end of a transitional period of five years since the entry into force of the Treaty of Amsterdam, to take a decision 'with a view to adapting the provisions concerning the jurisdiction of the Court of Justice' within Title IV EC. The Commission noted in the Introduction to this Communication that 'the transitional period expired on 1 May 2004 and that the Council has not launched work to fulfil this legal obligation'. The Council did use the remit of Article 67(2) EC to extend the application of the co-decision procedure in 2004,[278] but remained silent as regards the jurisdiction of the Court despite the protests of the Commission and the European Parliament.[279] Indeed, the wording chosen by the Commission in its proposal ('the Council has not launched work to fulfil this legal obligation') seemed to hint at its intention to bring an action for failure to

---

[277] Ibid, COM(2006) 346 final.

[278] Council Decision 2004/927/EC of 22 December [2004], OJ L396/45.

[279] Communication from the Commission to the European Parliament, the Council, the European Parliament, the Council, the European Economic and Social Committee, the Committee of the regions, and the Court of Justice of the European Communities: Adaptation of the Provisions of Title IV of the Treaty establishing the European Community relating to the jurisdiction of the Court of Justice with a view to ensuring more effective judicial protection. Brussels, 28 June 2006. COM(2006) 346 final 2, fn 2.

act against the Council under Article 2(32) EC, were its proposal to be ignored.

Article 67(2) EC requires the Council to 'act unanimously on a proposal from the Commission or on the initiative of a Member State and after consulting the European Parliament'. As opposed to the procedure set out in Article 42 TEU and detailed above, no national approval is necessary, and thus the reform could have been completed more quickly—provided the necessary political will had been at hand, since the decision would have had to be adopted unanimously. As was pointed out earlier, however, neither of the Commission's proposals was taken up by the Council: instead, an agreement on a wider Treaty reform was eventually reached in the shape of the then-called Reform Treaty.

2.4.3 The Reform/Lisbon Treaty

Up to now, this section has discussed some of the very concrete institutional initiatives that saw the light during the interim between the blockage and then failure of the Constitutional Treaty and the agreement on the need for a new Treaty. It has already been mentioned throughout this monograph that the result of the latter agreement, the Lisbon Treaty, is still awaiting ratification. It seems however necessary to include a few lines on the process leading to this new Treaty, especially since this section deals with the institutional 'cherry-picking' that has been taking place— those proposals for reform that several institutions put forward after the demise of the Constitutional Treaty. In fact, the Lisbon Treaty could be presented as another 'cherry-picking' exercise, if far more general in its scope, and hopefully successful, than the rest.

In the wake of the failure of the Constitutional Treaty, and following the conclusions of the Presidency of the Brussels European Council meeting of 21 and 22 June 2007, an Intergovernmental Conference convened on 23 July to draft the text of a new Treaty. The Member States reached a political agreement on the draft Reform Treaty during the informal meeting of the Heads of State and Government being held in Lisbon on 18 and 19 October 2007; the Treaty was officially signed in Lisbon on 13 December 2007 and was subsequently renamed the Lisbon Treaty.

In what seems like an attempt to stir away from past mistakes, the new Treaty eschews all 'constitutional' terminology. The formal distinction between the pillars will cease to exist, in that the Union will be a single entity with full legal personality and the Community method will apply across the board, with the exception of the Common Foreign and Security Policy, where special arrangements should be kept. Nevertheless, the current Treaties will not be unified in a single document, but rather only modified and partially renamed: the TEU will remain the Treaty on European Union, whereas the EC Treaty shall be the Treaty on the Functioning of the European Union. Generally, as regards judicial control in the AFSJ, the Lisbon Treaty has followed the arrangements contained in the Constitutional Treaty. The very short period of time granted to the IGC to do their job meant that judicial arrangements, fairly unproblematic from a geopolitical point of view (at least in comparison to issues such as the voting system in Council), were understandably not the subject of new, *tabula rasa* discussions, but were rather straightforwardly 'transplanted' from the Constitutional Treaty.

The Lisbon Treaty was, in principle, supposed to be ratified by all Member States by the end of 2008, but it was rejected in a referendum in Ireland in June of that year. As of May 2009, the Treaty has obtained parliamentary approval in all other Member States, although ratification is being delayed in Germany, Poland, and the Czech Republic. For its part, the Irish government decided in December 2008 to hold a second referendum, set to be a turning point in the ratification process, before the end of 2009. Although it is impossible to foresee the conclusion of this very problematic process, it is my assumption that, even if the Lisbon Treaty is not ratified in its present form, it can be used as a blueprint for the future reform of the jurisdiction of the Court of Justice.

2.5 The Jurisdiction of the ECJ under the Lisbon Treaty

Should the Lisbon Treaty be ratified,[280] it will bring about significant changes in the 'appearance' of the Area of Freedom, Security and Justice. Since there will be no intergovernmental third pillar anymore, neither will

---

[280] Treaty of Lisbon amending the Treaty on European Union and the Treaty establishing the European Community, [2007] OJ C 306/1, 17 December 2007. The consolidated version is used throughout this chapter: Consolidated versions of the Treaty on European Union and the Treaty on the Functioning of the European Union, [2008] OJ C 115/1, 9 May 2008. The Lisbon Treaty is not a substantive Treaty: it reforms—without turning them into a single document—the TEU and the EC Treaty, renaming the latter Treaty on the Functioning of the European Union or TFEU. For that reason, references to the Lisbon Treaty will appear as 'Art X TEU (after LT)' or 'Art X TFEU'.

there be a distinction between police and judicial cooperation in criminal matters (Title VI TEU), on the one hand, and the rest of AFSJ matters (Title IV EC), on the other. Both 'blocks' will be again reunited under a common heading, this time in the TFEU (Title V, Part Three). Consequently, for the purposes of this study, it will not be necessary from now on to distinguish between restrictions placed upon the jurisdiction of the Court when dealing with the communitarized provisions and when dealing with the third pillar proper. Rather, the following pages will deal with the Area of Freedom, Security and Justice as a whole.

This section will map out the pattern of judicial control in matters of the AFSJ envisaged in the Lisbon Treaty. First, however, it is necessary to bear in mind that, should the Treaty be ratified, change will not be immediate; a series of transitional measures have been included in a Protocol (No 36) annexed to the Treaty to that effect. According to Article 10 of the said Protocol, police and judicial cooperation measures that are already in place before the Treaty enters into force will still be reviewed by the ECJ under the pre-Lisbon arrangements currently in force in Title VI TEU. This will last five years and is acceptable as long as the legal effects of these pre-Lisbon third pillar measures also remain unaltered during that time—which, it is submitted, is the interpretation that should be given to Article 9 of the same Protocol.[281] Finally, it is worth remembering that the urgent preliminary ruling procedure, studied in Section 2.3.2.2, would continue to be available in the AFSJ after the ratification of the Lisbon Treaty.

This section will now explore the main avenues of judicial control that, should the Lisbon Treaty be ratified, will apply immediately to all new measures produced in the AFSJ, as well as to those third pillar measures already in place, after a period of five years.

2.5.1 Direct Review of AFSJ Measures

The direct review of measures that the Court can currently undertake under Article 230 EC is contemplated in Article 263 TFEU in similar

---

[281] Art 9, Protocol No. 36 on Transitional Measures annexed to the Lisbon Treaty: 'The legal effects of the acts of the institutions, bodies, offices and agencies of the Union adopted on the basis of the Treaty on European Union prior to the entry into force of the Treaty of Lisbon shall be preserved until those acts are repealed, annulled or amended in implementation of the Treaties. The same shall apply to agreements concluded between Member States on the basis of the Treaty on European Union.'

terms. The Court can thus annul a Union measure 'on grounds of lack of competence, infringement of an essential procedural requirement, infringement of the Treaties or of any rule of law relating to their application, or misuse of powers'.

There is no specific limitation on what types of AFSJ measures may be reviewed in this manner; Article 263(1) TEU states, in general terms, that the Court may control the legality 'of legislative acts, of acts of the Council, of the Commission and of the European Central Bank, other than recommendations and opinions, and of acts of the European Parliament and of the European Council intended to produce legal effects vis-à-vis third parties. It shall also review the legality of acts of bodies, offices or agencies of the Union intended to produce legal effects vis-à-vis third parties'. Similarly, there is no restriction on the possible applicants, only the general rules contained in Article 263(2–4) TFEU. This means that an AFSJ measure can be challenged by the Commission, the Council, the European Parliament, or a Member State.[282] Alternatively, a natural or legal person can also bring such challenge forward if the rules of standing—as specified in Article 263(4) TFEU—are complied with.

In this way, the Lisbon Treaty does away with the restrictive approach to direct review of the current Title VI TEU. It will be remembered that, initially, Article 35(6) TEU allowed only for the direct review of framework decisions and decisions, although it has later been interpreted by the Court to include common positions that have effects on third parties also.[283] Equally, it is not possible for individuals to challenge an AFSJ measure directly at the moment, a limitation that disappears in the Lisbon Treaty.

2.5.1.1 *Standing for Individuals against AFSJ Measures*

At present, Article 230(4) EC sets out the requirements of direct and individual concern for an individual wishing to challenge the validity of an EC law measure directly. The Court of Justice has interpreted these requirements in a famously strict fashion,[284] drawing criticism and

---

[282] Also by the Court of Auditors, by the European Central Bank and by the Committee of the Regions for the purpose of protecting their prerogatives (Art 263 TFEU).

[283] Case C-355/04 P *Segi* [2007] ECR I-1657.

[284] See eg Cases C-50/00 *Unión de Pequeños Agricultores v Council* [2002] ECR I-6677; C-263/02 *Commission v Jégo-Quéré* [2004] ECR I-03425.

spurring a long discussion on the matter.[285] Rather than challenging an EC law measure directly, individuals are supposed to do it indirectly through the preliminary reference procedure; this would normally involve challenging the validity of the national implementing measures before a national court. This may not be possible, however, when the EC law measure is self-executing and national implementation is therefore non-existent.

The Lisbon Treaty seeks to address this shortcoming by setting out different tests. Article 263(4) TFEU establishes that an individual may 'institute proceedings against an act addressed to that person or which is of direct and individual concern to them, and against a regulatory act which is of direct concern to them and does not entail implementing measures'.

'Regulatory acts' could be taken to mean 'all Union acts of general application', an interpretation that would drastically widen the access of individuals to the Court. It seems, however, that the Convention had something different in mind when originally drafting this provision for its inclusion in the Constitutional Treaty. Both this document and its successor, the Lisbon Treaty, distinguish elsewhere between legislative and non-legislative acts,[286] and it seems clear from the preparatory works that

---

[285] The very restricted access granted by Art 230(4) has been the subject of an ongoing discussion on the suitability of some changes in the Court's attitude towards individuals. Most scholars have argued for a relaxation of these requirements. For a non-exhaustive account of this discussion, compare A Albors-Llorens, *Private Parties in European Community Law: Challenging Community Measures* (Clarendon Press: Oxford, 1996); A Albors-Llorens, 'The Standing of Private Parties to Challenge Community Measures: Has the European Court Missed the Boat?' (2003) 62 CML Rev 72; P Craig, 'Legality, Standing and Substantive Review in Community Law' (1994) 14 OJLS 507; M Hedemann-Robinson, 'Article 173 EC, General Community Measures and Locus Standi for Private Persons: Still a Cause for Individual Concern?' (1996) 2 European Public Law 127; P Nihoul, 'La Recevabilité des recours en annulation introduits par un particulier à l'encontre d'un acte communautaire de portée générale' (1994) 30 Revue Trimestrielle de Droit Européen 171; F Ragolle, 'Access to Justice for Private Applicants in the Community Legal Order: Recent (R)evolutions' (2003) 28 ELR 90; JA Usher, 'Direct and Individual Concern: An Effective Remedy or a Conventional Solution?' (2003) 28 ELR 575; A Arnull, *The European Union and its Court of Justice* (2nd edn, OUP: Oxford, 2006) 69–94; A Ward, *Judicial Review and the Rights of Private Parties in EU Law* (OUP: Oxford, 2007).

[286] Arts 290 and 297 TFEU refer to 'non-legislative acts', whereas Arts 263(4) and 207 TFEU refer to 'regulatory acts'.

the Convention seemed to use 'regulatory acts' in the sense of 'non-legislative acts of general application'. [287]

As regards the specific application of Article 263(4) TFEU to the third pillar, it is necessary to bear in mind that all binding Union measures—directives, regulations, and decisions—could be adopted in this area. All these measures may be legislative or non-legislative (regulatory, in the language of Article 263(4) TFEU), depending on whether they are adopted following the legislative procedure referred to in Article 289 TFEU.[288] The only one of these measures which may have a formal addressee is the decision, according to Article 288 TFEU.

It has already been pointed out earlier that the choice of legislative or non-legislative instruments to be adopted under different headings of the Treaty may seem random at times. This questionable choice has, however, important consequences for the standing of individuals who wish to challenge these measures.[289] Within the AFSJ in particular, the choice has been almost exclusively legislative acts. The vast majority of legal bases in Title V Part Three TFEU ('AFSJ Title') that foresee the adoption of measures on a substantive matter establish that this should be done through the legislative procedure, be it ordinary or special.

The adoption of non-legislative acts is foreseen in order to implement legislative ones (eg Article 75 TFEU, on preventing and combating terrorism and related activities, or, it may be assumed, whenever it is deemed necessary even if not explicitly foreseen under the particular legal basis in the Treaty; these acts are foreseen generally under Article 291 TFEU) and

---

[287] It seems that the distinction between legislative and regulatory acts was used for the first time in CONV 572/03, 10 March 2003, and CONV 575/03, 10 March 2003. Throughout the ensuing discussion, the term 'regulatory act' seems to be used as a synonym for 'non-legislative act of general application'. For an overview of the terminology in the preparatory works, see J Bering Liisberg, 'The EU Constitutional Treaty and its Distinction between Legislative and Non-legislative Acts: Oranges into Apples?' Jean Monnet Working Paper 01/06 http://www.jeanmonnetprogram.org/papers/06/060101.html (accessed January 2009), 37–9.

[288] It is worth noting here that Art 289 TFEU refers both to an ordinary legislative procedure (co-decision, further regulated in Art 294 TFEU in the same terms as the current Art 251 EC) and to special legislative procedures where the Treaty so provides. These special legislative procedures would require the Council to act with the participation of the European Parliament, or the European Parliament to act with the participation of the Council. In the first case, the Council may be required to obtain the Parliament's consent or only to consult with it.

[289] Either because their scope and subject-matter do not justify the distinction or because the non-legislative procedure established in some cases by the Treaty is indistinguishable from the special legislative procedure that foresees only consultation with the European Parliament. For this and other problems created by the legislative/non-legislative distinction, see M Dougan, 'The Treaty of Lisbon 2007: Winning Minds, Not Hearts' (2008) 45 CML Rev 617, 647–8.

delegated acts adopted by the Commission following authorization contained in a legislative act (again, not explicitly foreseen in Title V, but
generally in Article 290 TFEU). Finally, there are a few further legal bases
in the AFSJ Title which foresee the adoption of non-legislative acts that
are neither delegated nor implementing acts: Article 70, on laying down
arrangements to evaluate the implementation of Union policies; Article 74,
on ensuring administrative cooperation;[290] Article 78(3), on the adoption
of temporary measures to deal with a sudden inflow of third-country
nationals, and Article 86(4), allowing the Council to extend the powers of
the European Public Prosecutor's Office.[291]

The predominant use of legislative instruments in the AFSJ Title means
that it will still be almost impossible for individuals to challenge the
majority of AFSJ measures directly. It is, however, welcome that the legal
basis to adopt restrictive economic measures against natural or legal persons, groups, or non-state entities in order to prevent and combat terrorism (Article 75 TFEU) differentiates between, on the one hand, the
competence of the Council to define such 'a framework of administrative
measures with regard to capital movements and payments, such as the
freezing of funds, financial assets or economic gains' and, on the other
hand, the Council's obligation 'to adopt measures to implement the framework referred to in the first paragraph'. Whereas the Council would
define the general framework through legislative regulations, its implementation would take place through non-legislative acts. This separation,
at least, ensures that individuals are able to access the ECJ to challenge the
Union implementing measures directly.

As regards the rest of the AFSJ headings, individuals' direct access to the
ECJ will depend on whether implementing or delegated measures are at
hand. This is, of course, assuming that the Court interprets the term
'regulatory act' within Article 263(4) TFEU in the same sense as the
Convention seems to have done ('non-legislative instruments of general

---

[290] The Treaty does not consider the procedure for the adoption of measures under this
heading legislative, although, from a formal point of view, it is undistinguishable from the special
legislative procedure that foresees consultation with the European Parliament.

[291] There are three further legal bases which foresee that the Council may decide to subject
certain aspects of family law to an ordinary legislative procedure rather than a special one (Art 81
(3) TFEU) and that the Council may decide to regulate very specific aspects of criminal procedure or criminal law through the legislative procedure, although not explicitly foreseen in the
Treaty (Art 82(2) and 83(1) TFEU). In all three cases, the Council's decision is a non-legislative
act. The result, however, is merely to allow the substantive area at stake to be regulated through
a legislative act.

application'). Hopes have been voiced in the literature that the Court may feel able to distance itself from the Convention's apparent intentions, because of the failure of the Constitutional Treaty and the long and protracted process between the Convention's work and the (eventual) ratification of the Lisbon Treaty.[292] Although desirable, it seems unlikely that the Court would feel inclined to such liberality in its interpretation of the standing test in the future, when it has been so consistently strict until now.

2.5.2 *Indirect Review of AFSJ Measures*

The Court can currently control the legality of measures indirectly through the preliminary ruling procedure foreseen in Article 2(34) EC. Within the framework of the Lisbon Treaty, the same mechanism would be available under Article 267 TFEU.

It has already been pointed out earlier that the preliminary reference procedure is, at present, limited within the AFSJ in various ways. In terms of procedural limitations, the Lisbon Treaty fares well when compared to the EC and EU Treaties. Within Title IV EC, Article 6(8) EC makes this mechanism available only to national courts of last resort and, within the third pillar proper, Article 35 TEU makes the jurisdiction of the Court voluntary and variable in extension. On the contrary, the Lisbon Treaty does not impose a special, limited form of the preliminary ruling mechanism in the AFSJ (although the urgent preliminary ruling procedure would continue to be available in this area).[293] The general rules contained in Article 267 TFEU apply fully, doing away with the problems highlighted earlier and fostering the equality and uniformity of Union law.

Restrictions *ratione materiae* are nevertheless still present in the Lisbon Treaty. Following the same pattern we have seen in the EC and EU Treaties, the Lisbon Treaty contains restrictions that relate to the maintenance of law and order and the safeguarding of internal security. It has been shown that Member States have tried to assuage their concerns and preserve their autonomy in this area by consistently introducing two different kinds of provisions: general clauses clarifying the separation of competences between the EC/EU and themselves, and more specific

---

[292] M Dougan, 'The Treaty of Lisbon 2007: Winning Minds, Not Hearts' (2008) 45 CML Rev 617, 649.

[293] The urgent preliminary ruling procedure is set out in Art 104b of the Rules of Procedure of the Court and would remain unchanged by the Lisbon Treaty. See Section 2.3.2.2.

provisions that explicitly limit the jurisdiction of the Court of Justice. The Lisbon Treaty is not an exception.

To start with, the drafters of the Treaty were not content with introducing a general clause clarifying the division of competences in this area between the Union and the Member States within the framework of the AFSJ. They also introduced a general clause among the Common Provisions of the TEU that is applicable across the board: Article 4(2) TEU (after LT) states that the Union shall respect the Member States' essential state functions, 'including ensuring the territorial integrity of the State, maintaining law and order and safeguarding national security', before adding that, in particular, 'national security remains the sole responsibility of each Member State'.

Within Title IV, Part Three TFEU (hereafter 'AFSJ Title'), the pattern is similar to that of the current TEU: there is a general clause (Article 72 TFEU) and a provision restricting the jurisdiction of the ECJ within a particular area within the AFSJ. Let us start with the first one: the Lisbon Treaty maintains the general clause that we currently find under Articles 64 (1) EC and 33 TEU in the guise of Article 72 TFEU: 'This Title [AFSJ Title] shall not affect the responsibilities incumbent upon Member States with regard to the maintenance of law and order and the safeguarding of internal security'.

Similarly to the earlier discussion on Articles 64(1) EC and 33 TEU, it is possible to take different points of view as regards the nature of Article 72 TFEU. On the one hand, it is possible to argue that this is a derogation from Union law similar to current derogations from Community law in other areas (such as public health, public security, and public policy in the realm of the common market). This situation could therefore be considered equivalent to that found in the *ERT* and *Familiapress* cases,[294] where the ECJ found that Member States were under its control for compatibility with the general principles of EC law when derogating from the latter. The question would then be to what extent the Court would be willing to extend the *ERT* doctrine to the whole of Union law, across the board. In any case, from this point of view on the nature of Article 72 TFEU, it would be in the Court's hand to decide whether and to what extent to scrutinize Member States' actions.

---

[294] Cases C-260/89 *ERT/DEP* [1991] ECR I-2925; C-368/95 *Vereinigte Familiapress Zeitungsverlags- und vertriebs GmbH/Bauer Verlag* [1997] ECR I-3689.

On the other hand, Article 72 TFEU can be interpreted differently: not as a derogation from Union law comparable to the EC derogations from the law of the single market, but as a provision that tells us where the limits of Union legislative competence lie. The practical result, however, is not likely to differ greatly. As I argued in relation to Article 64(1) EC, the Court has made it clear that it is willing to control, at least to a certain extent, national action that is undertaken in a field of national competence but which nevertheless interferes with, at least, certain rules of the Treaty. As a result, even if adopting this second reading of Article 72 TFEU, the Court would be able to check national action covered by this provision in some situations: although it is initially outside the scope of EU law, it may be 'brought back in' if a breach occurs. Due to the sensitivity of the subject-matter, the control exercised by the Court would, in any case, include a review of proportionality of the national action (that is, whether the breach of the Treaty rule was necessary and appropriate); but even if Article 72 TFEU were treated as a derogation, it is doubtful that the Court would be willing to exercise an extensive control (for example, for compliance with human rights standards). The review of proportionality would be less strict than in other cases, in accordance with the broad discretion exercised by national governments in the field at stake.[295]

So far, we have studied the effects of the general clause of Article 72 TFEU on the whole of the AFSJ. There is, however, an additional, specific restriction to the jurisdiction of the Court that operates within a particular field of the AFSJ. Article 276 TFEU states that, within Chapters 4 and 5 of the AFSJ Title (the chapters that deal with judicial cooperation in criminal maters and police cooperation, respectively) the Court shall have 'no jurisdiction to review the validity or proportionality of operations carried out by the police or other law-enforcement services of a Member State or the exercise of the responsibilities incumbent upon Member States with regard

---

[295] Tridimas has noted that, although the standard of scrutiny is less rigorous, the Court is prepared to review proportionality even when issues of national security are at stake: T Tridimas, *The General Principles of EU Law* (2nd edn, OUP: Oxford, 2006) 229. For example, in *Albore* the ECJ expected Italy to prove the existence of 'real, specific, and serious risks which could not be countered by less restrictive procedures' C-423/98 *Alfredo Albore* [2000] ECR I-5965 [22]. Although the proportionality test was defined in strict terms, it was left for national courts to apply. In several cases involving public policy derogations, the final decision on the proportionality of the national action has been left to the national courts: Cases 222/84 *Johnston v Chief Constable of the Royal Ulster Constabulary* [1986] ECR 1651; C-367/89 *Criminal Proceedings against Richardt* [1991] ECR I-4621; 72/83 *Campus Oil* [1984] ECR 2727. On this point, see also S Peers, 'National Security and European Law' (1996) 16 YEL 363, 392.

to the maintenance of law and order and the safeguarding of internal security'. This provision follows in the footsteps of Articles 68(2) EC and 35(5) TEU, in that it is a specific restriction to the jurisdiction of the Court of Justice. As regards its scope, however, Article 276 TFEU covers the same instances of national action covered by Article 35(5) TEU at present (judicial cooperation in criminal matters, police cooperation), but not those covered by Articles 68(2) EC. Thus, Article 276 TFEU does not catch the reintroduction of Schengen internal borders (the practical effect of the current Article 68(2) EC).[296] Further, contrary to the restrictions contained in Articles 68(2) EC, and 35(5) TEU, Article 276 TFEU affects not only the Court's capacity to give preliminary rulings, but also to decide on infringement proceedings.[297]

Indeed, some may say that Article 276 TFEU may only affect the competence of the Court to deal with infringement actions, since this is the only way in which the Court formally controls national action, the subject-matter of Article 276 TFEU. As has already been pointed out, the ECJ does not have jurisdiction to interpret or consider the validity of national measures when giving a preliminary ruling; all it does is interpret and spell out the requirements of Union/Community law. Arguably, this could deprive the exception of Article 276 TFEU of practical significance as regards the preliminary ruling procedure.[298] The distribution of competences hinted at in this Article could be simply understood as a reminder of the general principle of distribution of competences between the ECJ and the national courts that underlies the Union's judicial architecture. It is nevertheless true that the way in which the preliminary ruling procedure works in practice is very often far from the principle of separation of competences. The Court, however, commonly tries to preserve this

---

[296] This reintroduction would not take place under the heading of Chapters 4 or 5 of the AFSJ Title, but under Art 77 TEU (Chapter 2).

[297] It is however possible to argue that Art 68(2) EC does not only affect the preliminary reference procedure: the Commission seems to believe that Art 68(2) EC excludes any kind of jurisdiction—not only the competence to give preliminary rulings. This can be inferred from the Communication from the Commission to the European Parliament, the Council, the European Economic and Social Committee, the Committee of the Regions and the Court of Justice of the European Communities: Adaptation of the Provisions of Title IV of the Treaty establishing the European Community relating to the jurisdiction of the Court of Justice with a view to ensuring more effective judicial protection. Brussels, 28 June 2006. COM(2006) 346 final, 6.

[298] The view taken by A Arnull, *The European Union and its Court of Justice* (2nd edn, OUP: Oxford, 2006) 136. Were one to adopt this view, it would still be necessary to acknowledge the effects of the exception on infringement proceedings (where the Court does scrutinize national rules directly).

'fiction'. From this understanding it can be argued that, just as with the current Article 35(5) TEU, Article 276 TFEU may have an effect on the Court's behaviour when providing preliminary rulings, in that it may feel the need to tread more carefully than normally in this area, due to the existence of an added safeguard or reminder as to the boundaries of its jurisdiction. Article 276 TFEU, in sum, is likely to affect not only the Court's competence to decide in infringement proceedings, but also its competence to give preliminary rulings when prompted by national courts.[299]

As regards the national action it catches, Article 276 TFEU is identical to Article 35(5) TEU, and thus the discussion on the problems caused by the latter provision apply wholly to this section. As regards the first part of Article 276 TFEU, the more specific exception concerning operations carried out by the police or law-enforcement services, the only difference when compared to the current Article 35(5) TEU is that, within the framework of the Lisbon Treaty, we may be more likely to come across situations where the national law-enforcement services are carrying out an EU measure directly. It is difficult to imagine this sort of scenario in practice; should it ever arise at all, however, it will be in the post-Lisbon scenario, where directly applicable, self-executing measures are more likely to be adopted than within the framework of the current TEU. Finally, contrary to Article 35(5) TEU, Article 276 TFEU has the effect of precluding not only indirect control, but also direct control of national police action in infringement proceedings; when asked by the Commission to rule on whether a Member State has breached EU law, all the Court can do is check whether the national action is indeed caught by the first paragraph of Article 276 TFEU. If it is, there is no possibility of further review—at least in theory.

Let us now turn to the second, more general claim of Article 276 TFEU, regarding Member States' law and order and internal security responsibilities, and which mirrors the general clause contained in Article 72 TFEU. It has already been argued in the previous section that this clause, like Articles 64(1) EC and 33 TEU, can be interpreted as a derogation from EU law or as a provision that lays the limits of EU legislative competence. Regardless of what reading is adopted, the Court has made it clear that it is

---

[299] See also the oral evidence given by AG Jacobs on this point in EU Committee of the House of Lords, 'The Future Role of the European Court of Justice: Report with Evidence' (6th Report of Session 2003–4. HL Paper 47) 36.

willing to control, at least to a certain extent, national action that is undertaken in a field of national competence but which nevertheless interferes with a rule of the Treaty. This possibility is however excluded within Chapters 4 and 5 of the AFSJ Title by Article 276 TFEU, with the result that the Court would not be competent in any case to exercise either direct or indirect control of this type of national action.

Article 276 TFEU has thus the exact same scope and likely rationale as the current Article 35(5) TEU: in Maastricht, the drafters of the Treaty may have tried to prevent the Court from treating the 'law and order' provision of Article 35(5) TEU exactly as it had treated other general clauses laying down the limits of EU law: as liable to be brought within the scope of the Treaties and therefore scrutinized to a certain extent.[300] In Lisbon, the Member States may have felt the need to maintain this safe-guard in light of the fact that the Court, since Maastricht, has continued in its approach to the control of Member States' action taken within their fields of exclusive competence: in this sort of situation, the Court has been willing to apply EC rules to Member States' decisions, at least as long as it is not convinced that such decisions concern a fundamental policy choice.[301] Thus it is not only that the Member States fear that they may see some of their decisions in a matter such as internal security reviewed; it is also the case that they cannot foresee in what particular instances such review will take place, since the line drawn in *Dory* is hardly watertight.[302] Against this backdrop, Article 276 TFEU acts as an added safeguard, a hard and fast rule ensuring that, at least within the areas of judicial cooperation in criminal matters and police cooperation (Chapters 4 and 5, AFSJ Title), this sort of national action continues to be safe from review, regardless of whether it breaches EU rules and of whether it deals or not with a funda-mental policy choice.

In general, the problems arising from Article 276 TFEU are the same ones to arise from Article 35(5) TEU; they are likely to seem, however, more acute in the context of a homogeneous and 'stronger' Union, where the third pillar is no more an intergovernmental forum but a fully 'com-munitarized' policy. In this new setting, one would expect the Court of

---

[300] Cases C-265/95 *Commission v France ('Spanish Strawberries')* [1997] ECR I-6959; C-124/95 *The Queen, ex parte Centro-Com Srl v HM Treasury and Bank of England* ECR [1997] I-81.

[301] eg Cases C-285/98 *Tanja Kreil v Bundesrepublik Deutschland* [2000] ECR I-69; C-273/97 *Angela Maria Sirdar v The Army Board and Secretary of State for Defence* [1999] ECR I-7403; C-186/01 *Alexander Dory v Bundesrepublik Deutschland* [2003] ECR I-2479.

[302] Case C-186/01 *Alexander Dory v Bundesrepublik Deutschland* [2003] ECR I-2479.

Justice to hold Member States to their EU law commitments and to ensure that actions carried out by its agents conform to an EU-wide standard of protection of fundamental rights.

It seems unfortunate that the ECJ will not be able to review the actions of its agents, neither directly nor indirectly. Further, whenever Member States claim to be exercising their responsibility to maintain law and order and internal security, they may be able to breach Union law without the ECJ being able to act upon it. National courts may, however, be in a position to control national action in both instances.[303] The separation of competences underlying the judicial system of the Union finds an obvious expression in an area that is uncomfortably close to the core of national sovereignty. Although problematic in some respects, this separation of competences seems unavoidable. If this arrangement is going to work, however, the actors involved have to collaborate fully and exercise self-restraint. The Court of Justice has to be allowed some leeway: it has to be able to discharge its duty as interpreter of EU law, even if this means, in some instances, framing its preliminary rulings by reference to national action that is caught by Article 276 TFEU. At the same time, the Court should always strive to leave the application of the proportionality test to the national court.[304] National courts, on their part, should strive to review national action for compliance not only with national law, but also with EU law.

Finally, it may be useful to remember that the draft Constitutional Treaty contained an almost identical clause to Article 276 TFEU, albeit with the final proviso 'where such action is a matter of national law'.[305] At the time, this tail-piece was considered confusing and superfluous and was subsequently removed from the definite version of the Constitutional Treaty.[306] This proviso would have indeed been superfluous as regards the 'the Member States' responsibility to maintain law and order and internal security', obviously a matter of national law as already established elsewhere (Articles 4(2) TEU (after LT) and 72 TFEU). However, as regards

---

[303] Depending on whether, and to what extent, national law foresees such control.

[304] As done, for example, in Case C-423/98 *Alfredo Albore* [2000] ECR I-5965, concerning national security. For further references, see n 295.

[305] Art III-283, Draft Treaty establishing a Constitution for Europe CONV 850/03.

[306] Art III-377, Treaty establishing a Constitution for Europe [2004] OJ C310/01. See EU Committee of the House of Lords, 'The Future Role of the European Court of Justice: Report with Evidence' (6th Report of Session 2003–4, HL Paper 47) 37, plus oral evidence submitted by AG Jacobs (p 36) and P Craig (p 12–13) on this particular point.

'operations carried out by the police or other law-enforcement services of a Member State', it would have been desirable for the deleted proviso to remain part of what is now Article 276 TFEU. This would have ensured that the Court is competent to review such operations when they have their origin in EU law, avoiding some of the potential pitfalls highlighted in this section. At any rate, it remains to be seen how the Court chooses to deal with Article 276 TFEU in future case-law, if the Lisbon Treaty comes into force.

2.5.3 Policing the Borders between the AFSJ and other Policies

We have seen earlier that the ECJ is currently competent, pursuant to Article 47 TEU, to ensure that the intergovernmental pillars do not encroach upon any competence belonging to the Community, and how this competence has been exercised in relation to the third pillar. Within the Lisbon Treaty, Article 40 TEU (after LT) can be said to have a comparable—although not identical—purpose. This provision has two parts: the first one establishes that the implementation of the CFSP may not affect any of the other competences of the Union (which includes, of course, the AFSJ). The second part establishes that the implementation of all other Union competences may not affect the CFSP. In a case of conflict between a plausible legal basis in the AFSJ and in the CFSP, it is not totally clear whether Article 40 TEU (after LT) establishes the priority of the AFSJ over the CFSP in the same terms as the current Article 47 TEU establishes the priority of the EC Treaty. The case-law of the Court of Justice has consistently established the priority of a plausible EC legal basis over an intergovernmental one,[307] and it seems logical that, once the Community method applies to the AFSJ, it will also be accorded priority over CFSP. It is unclear, however, whether the second part of Article 40 TEU (after LT), an innovation with regard to the present Article 47 TEU, would have any deterring effects in this respect.

But what of cases where the competence dispute is not between the AFSJ and the CFSP, but between the AFSJ and other Union policies? There is no longer a distinct rule giving priority to the first pillar over the third one or, within the framework of the Lisbon Treaty, giving priority to all other competences contained in Articles 3–6 TFEU over the AFSJ when a measure has two equally central aims or components. Such a rule of priority would be superfluous, given that the third pillar and the EC pillar

[307] Case C-91/05 *Commission v Council ('ECOWAS')* [2008] ECR I-3651. See Section 3.3.1.

are no longer separate legal orders. Direct review of all AFSJ measures will be possible on grounds of lack of competence, and the Court will merely apply its 'centre of gravity' test, developed in intra-Community competence disputes,[308] to determine what the main aim and/or component of a measure is. If the main aim of an AFSJ measure falls in fact within the scope of a different legal basis, it will be annulled. If two different aims can be considered equally central to the measure, then it will be possible for it to be adopted both under an AFSJ legal bases and under a formerly first pillar one: although this does not seem to be possible at the moment,[309] it should no longer be a problem once both legal bases are part of the same legal system, and as long as they do not entail different decision-making procedures.[310] Given that a dual basis is possible, it would seem no longer necessary to have a rule of priority such as the one contained in the current Article 47 TEU, as far as non-CFSP Union policies are concerned.

2.5.4 Infringement Proceedings, Failure to Act, Damages

The depillarization envisaged by the Lisbon Treaty and the consequent extension of the Community method—and thus of the normal pattern of judicial control—means that, within the AFSJ, the Court would be called upon to perform all the functions we have come to expect in the first pillar. The Court would thus be competent to deal with infringement proceedings, actions for failure to act, or actions for damages.[311]

---

[308] See Case C-300/89 *Commission v Council ('Titanium Dioxide')* [1991] ECR I-2867; H Cullen and A Charlesworth 'Diplomacy by other Means: The Use of Legal Basis Litigation as a Political Strategy by the European Parliament and Member States' (1999) 36 CML Rev 1234. The test has already been used in cross-pillar litigation: see eg Cases C-176/03 *Commission v Council* [2005] ECR I-7879 [45]; C-91/05 *Commission v Council ('ECOWAS')* [2008] ECR I-3651 [60], [73], [75].

[309] The fact that the pillars constitute separate legal orders seems to be the reason why it was not possible to adopt the measure at stake in *ECOWAS* both under a CFSP and an EC legal basis, and the same would apply when trying to adopt a measure under a third pillar legal basis and an EC one: C-91/05 *Commission v Council ('ECOWAS')* Judgment of 20 May 2008, nyr. R van Ooik, 'Cross-Pillar Litigation before the ECJ: Demarcation of Community and Union Competences' (2008) 4 EuConst 399, 413–18. For a different overview of the application of Art 47 TEU, see J Heliskoski, 'Small Arms and Light Weapons within the Union's Pillar Structure: an Analysis of Article 47 of the EU Treaty' (2008) 33 ELR 898.

[310] Case C-300/89 *Commission v Council ('Titanium Dioxide')* [1991] ECR I-2867 [17]–[21].

[311] It should be recalled that the change will affect third pillar measures that are adopted after the entry into force of the Lisbon Treaty immediately, but it will only affect pre-Lisbon third pillar measures that remain in effect after five years: Art 10, Protocol No. 36 on Transitional Measures annexed to the Lisbon Treaty.

Within the framework of the Lisbon Treaty, if a Member State fails to fulfil its obligations in the AFSJ, the Commission may bring infringement proceedings against it. This is the common mechanism that applies across the board, meaning that there is no longer a *lex specialis* for this area, as is the case in the current TEU. Account needs to be taken, nonetheless, of the restrictions contained in Articles 72 and 276 TFEU (on the maintenance of law and order and the safeguarding of internal security), discussed earlier in this chapter in relation to the Court's jurisdiction to give preliminary rulings. Regardless of whether Article 72 TFEU is considered as a derogation from EU law or as an indication as to whether the limits of EU law lie, Article 276 TFEU suggests that the Court may not be able to engage in any kind of control of the Member State action at stake (not even as to proportionality), once it is satisfied that such action comes within the scope of this provision. Of course, it remains to be seen how the Court deals with this restriction in future case-law.

It is in Article 226 TFEU that we can find infringement proceedings, which can be brought by the Commission against a state at fault:[312]

If the Commission considers that a Member State has failed to fulfil an obligation under the Constitution, it shall deliver a reasoned opinion on the matter after giving the State concerned the opportunity to submit its observations.

If the State concerned does not comply with the opinion within the period laid down by the Commission, the latter may bring the matter before the Court of Justice of the European Union.

The full-blown extension of the supervisory powers of the Commission to the third pillar is of no little importance. As we have seen before, the Commission is the independent third party with a duty to ensure compliance with the Treaty and bring disobedient states to justice if necessary; this is a supervisory mechanism that has proved efficient in the past.[313] Article 227 TFEU, in turn, deals with infringement proceedings brought by one Member State against another one. The procedure has not changed either and follows the letter of the current Article 227 EC.[314]

Even though the two mechanisms are left untouched, the Lisbon Treaty introduces some changes on the procedure for the imposition of sanctions, currently to be found under Article 228 EC. The first change affects one of

---

[312] Article 226 EC at present; this was Article III-360 in the Constitutional Treaty.

[313] In 2005, 2,653 procedures were initiated; the number had decreased slightly from 2,993 in 2004. XXIIIrd Report on Monitoring the Application of Community Law COM (2006) 416, 3.

[314] Art III-361 in the Constitutional Treaty.

the administrative stages of the procedure for the imposition of penalties on a recalcitrant Member State: Article 228(2) TFEU makes it unnecessary for the Commission to issue a second reasoned opinion if the state has already been found by the Court to be in breach of its obligations.[315] The second change can be found in Article 228(3) TFEU:

> When the Commission brings a case before the Court of Justice of the European Union pursuant to Article 226 on the grounds that the Member State concerned has failed to fulfil its obligation to notify measures transposing a directive adopted under a legislative procedure, it may, when it deems appropriate, specify the amount of the lump sum or penalty payment to be paid by the Member State concerned which it considers appropriate in the circumstances.

The introduction of these changes means that, if the infringement proceedings are being brought against a state because of lack of notification of the measures implementing a legislative directive, the Commission does not have to go through the 'normal' procedure, with its two different phases: the first one, where the Court decides whether the state is in breach of its duty or not; and the second one, where, only if the state does not take steps to remedy the breach, the Commission can ask the Court to impose a penalty and suggest a sum. In this case, the Commission can ask the Court directly to impose a penalty on the state if it finds that it is in breach of its duty.[316]

As regards actions for failure to act, the equivalent of the current Article 232 EC is to be found in Article 265 TFEU. The procedure remains generally the same; the only significant change is that, whereas the current EC provision makes it possible to bring this action against the European Parliament, the Council, the Commission, and the European Central Bank, the TFEU or post-Lisbon provision sets out a more comprehensive list

---

[315] These provisions have been taken from the Constitutional Treaty without changes. For a general overview of the effect of the Constitutional Treaty on the infringement procedure, see also A Arnull, *The European Union and its Court of Justice* (2nd edn, OUP: Oxford, 2006) 51–2.

[316] The text of this provision remains the same since the Constitutional Treaty (Art III-362 (3)), if referring to 'failure to notify measures implementing a European framework law'. Arnull rightly pointed out that this provision was oddly worded in that it referred to the failure to notify measures implementing a European framework law, when there was no general duty imposed on Member States to notify such measures. Such duty could only be laid down by a specific European framework law, and it seemed rather peculiar that a special, harsher way of dealing with disobedience should be created for these few cases. It seems more likely that the provision referred in reality to the situation where a Member State had merely failed to implement a European framework law (Arnull ibid, 51–2). The same reasoning could now be applied to Art 228 TFEU and the 'failure to notify measures implementing a directive'.

which includes the European Council and all 'bodies, offices and agencies of the Union'.

Finally, the non-contractual liability of the Union for the actions of its institutions and servants is foreseen in the Lisbon Treaty (Article 340 TFEU) in the same terms as the current Article 288 EC; further, Article 260 TFEU (the equivalent of the current Article 235 EC) spells outs the competence of the Court to award damages. The situation at stake in *Segi*, where the CFI and the Court of Justice had to corroborate the lack of an action for damages in the third pillar,[317] would be rectified with this welcome extension. Of special relevance is the extension of non-contractual liability to the actions of bodies created under the current third pillar, to be discussed in the next section.

2.5.5 *Judicial Control of AFSJ Bodies*

We have already seen how the Member States have been weary of entrusting any law enforcement functions to the Commission, and have instead sought to cooperate in the third pillar through a series of operational support agencies. These agencies have no legislative role or decision-making power, but rather have limited information exchange and coordination functions.[318] It is only against this background that the ECJ's decision in *Spain v Eurojust* can be explained. This case also proved, however, that there may be situations, however uncommon, in which these agencies produce decisions that affect individuals.

More importantly, the role of these agencies is likely to evolve in the future; Member States may rely on them in the future for more than mere support or coordination. Furthermore, the Lisbon Treaty seems to allow these agencies to play a bigger part than they do at present. Eurojust, for example, could go from proposing to national authorities the initiation of investigations to being able to 'initiate criminal investigations' directly.[319] Formal acts of judicial procedure will nevertheless continue to be carried out by national authorities, and a legislative regulation will lay down

---

[317] Cases T-338/02 *Segi* [2004] ECR II-01647; C-355/04 P *Segi* [2007] ECR I-1657.

[318] J Monar, 'Alternatives to the Community Method in EU Justice and Home Affairs' Summary of contribution to the CONNEX Workshop, Sciences Po, 29 November 2007 http://www.portedeurope.org/IMG/doc/Jorg_Monar.doc (accessed March 2009).

[319] Art 85.1(a) TFEU. See further EU Committee of the House of Lords, 'Judicial Co-operation in the European Union: The Role of Eurojust. Report with Evidence' (23rd Report of Session 2003–4, HL Paper 138) 33.

procedures for the scrutiny of the activities of Eurojust by the European and national parliaments.[320]

In the case of Europol, judicial control of its activities has not been deemed necessary until now because this body has no executive powers and so cannot carry out criminal investigations in a Member State in its own name.[321] The Lisbon Treaty would seem to give Europol, however, a wider mandate. The current Article 30(2) TEU foresees that Europol may 'facilitate and support the preparation, [...] encourage the coordination and carrying out of specific investigations', 'ask the competent authorities of the Member States to conduct and coordinate their investigations' and 'promote liaison arrangements'. On the other hand, Article 88(2) TFEU goes further by referring to the 'coordination, organisation and implementation of investigative and operational action'. The fact that Europol may become operational and not only managerial in nature does not come as a surprise.[322] It does, however, prompt questions as to the arrangements that will have to be laid down in the future to monitor its activities. According to Article 88(2) TFEU, a legislative regulation must determine Europol's 'structure, operation, field of action and tasks'; just like in the case of Eurojust, such regulation must also 'lay down the procedures for scrutiny of Europol's activities by the European Parliament, together with national Parliaments'.

The Lisbon Treaty thus foresees parliamentary control of both Eurojust and Europol. But what of judicial control? Article 230 TFEU widens the scope of the action for annulment: the ECJ 'is to review the legality of acts

---

[320] Art 85(1)–(2) TFEU.

[321] C Fijnaut, 'Police Co-operation and the Area of Freedom, Security and Justice' in N Walker (ed), *Europe's Area of Freedom, Security and Justice* (OUP: Oxford, 2004) 236. The most obvious worry given the present mandate of Europol is data protection. In this respect, each Member State is liable for any damage caused to an individual as a result of legal or factual errors in data stored or processed within Europol. Only the Member State in which the event that caused damage occurred may be the subject of an action for compensation by the injured party (Art 38, Europol Convention: Council Act of 26 July 1995 drawing up the Convention on the establishment of a European Police Office [1995] OJ C316/01).

[322] See eg C Van den Wyngaert, 'Eurojust and the European Public Prosecutor' in N Walker (ed), *Europe's Area of Freedom, Security and Justice* (OUP: Oxford, 2004), 255–6; it was also foreseen in the Friends of the Presidency's Report on the Future of Europol. Brussels, 19 May 2006. 9184/1/06 REV 1. For a critical appraisal of the changes put forward in this report, see B Hayes, 'The Future of Europol: More Powers, Less Regulation, Precious Little Debate' (Statewatch Analysis 2006) http://www.statewatch.org/news/2006/oct/future-of-europol-analysis.pdf (accessed November 2006).

of bodies, offices or agencies of the Union intended to produce legal effects vis-à-vis third parties'. To the extent that current third pillar agencies may be able adopt acts that have legal effects on individuals in the future, these acts could be reviewed by the Court.

This would undoubtedly cover similar situations to that encountered in *Spain v Eurojust*. It is not clear, however, whether the Court would allow an individual to challenge the validity of a Eurojust decision to initiate criminal investigations, or whether such a decision would only be considered a preparatory measure.[323]

As regards Europol, its activities would be covered by Article 230 TFEU to the extent that there is an act with legal effects that may be challenged. And yet, the wider mandate given to Europol in the Lisbon Treaty make this body likely to develop more operational powers; if this were so, its activities would not necessarily entail adoption of measures intended to produce legal effects vis-à-vis third parties, but rather purely executive police action—which could not be subsumed under Article 230 TFEU. Judicial control would then take place under two different guises: on the one hand, the Court would have to deal with actions for damages brought against the Union under Article 340 TFEU (the equivalent of the current Article 288 EC). An individual may thus obtain damages if the Union is found to be liable for the actions of Europol or any of its staff, in the performance of their duties.[324] If the Union is not liable for the actions of a Europol officer, he or she may be liable under national law. The Europol Convention establishes, however, the immunity of Europol officials 'for acts performed during the exercise of their duties'.[325] More generally, the Protocol on Privileges and Immunities of the European Union refers to the Union's officials' and other servants' immunity from liability for acts

---

[323] The latter was the position adopted by the CFI when asked to review a comparable OLAF decision. OLAF's acts and omissions are subject to review by the EU Courts in the same way as other acts and omissions of the Commission, but the CFI has been reluctant to accept jurisdiction to protect the fundamental rights of individuals who were being investigated, before an investigation was finished: T-215/02 *Gomez-Reino v Commission* Order of the President of the Court, 17 October 2002.

[324] The ECJ has given a narrow interpretation to the expression 'in the performance of their duties': Case 9/69 *Sayag v Leduc* [1969] ECR 329. On the relationship between this expression and the immunity of officials 'for acts performed during the exercise of their duties': H Schermers and C Swaak, 'Official Acts of Community Servants and Article 215(4) EC' in T Heukels and A McDonnell (eds), *The Action for Damages in Community Law* (Kluwer: The Hague, 1997).

[325] Protocol on Privileges and Immunities of Europol Staff [1997] OJ C221/1, Arts 2(1), 8(1)(a), 12, and 13.

performed 'in their official capacity'.[326] An institution is nevertheless required to waive the immunity of one of its officials, if such waiver is not contrary to the interests of the Union.[327]

In sum, the Lisbon Treaty foresees a much-needed extension of the judicial control of third pillar bodies. The two most important agencies created by the Member States in this area, Eurojust and Europol, are likely to outgrow their current, merely supportive roles. It is therefore an improvement that the control of their acts is foreseen under Article 230 TFEU, and that the Union may be found liable for their activities under Article 340 TFEU. Non-contractual liability is especially welcome in the case of Europol, where operational action (rather than the production of legal acts) may become a concern in the future.

2.6 Final Remarks

The jurisdiction of the Court in the Area of Freedom, Security and Justice has extended throughout the years and the different Treaty reforms, and is set to extend further if the Lisbon Treaty is ratified. Should ratification not take place, the reforms studied in this chapter are still likely to be implemented in the future and they can, in any case, be used as a blueprint for discussion on the future outlines of the Court's jurisdiction.

This chapter has sought to present a thorough account of the current and future extension of judicial control in the AFSJ. Judicial control is, however, inextricably linked to the nature of the measures produced in a certain area. Accordingly, the nature and legal effects of AFSJ acts has been examined. It has been argued that third pillar measures are not at present directly applicable, directly effective, or indeed should be accorded primacy over national law. The change from public international to Union law within the framework of the Lisbon Treaty changes the nature and legal effects of these measures substantially, as the chapter further shows. Should the Lisbon Treaty fail to secure ratification by all the Member States, it may be argued that the current state of uncertainty as to the status of third

---

[326] Art 11 of Protocol No 7 on Privileges and Immunities of the European Union, attached to the consolidated versions of the Treaty on European Union and the Treaty on the Functioning of the European Union [2008] OJ C115/01.

[327] Art 17, ibid. The Europol Protocol on Privileges and Immunities currently states that the Director of Europol should decide on the waiver of immunity; this decision is not subject to judicial control. The Protocol is to be reconsidered whenever Europol's functions are extended.

pillar may lead national courts and/or the ECJ granting these measures primacy over national law. In the absence of a wider reform (especially of the arrangements for judicial control), this development is likely to be problematic.

The study of the present jurisdiction of the Court in the AFSJ has highlighted the procedural and substantive restrictions imposed both within Title IV EC and Title VI TEU. The Lisbon Treaty goes a long way to improve these arrangements, leaving only one restriction standing (on action undertaken by national law enforcement services and national action intended to safeguard law and order and national security) and unifying the system of judicial control across the current first and the third pillars. Abnormalities such as the impossibility to review common positions, already tackled to some extent by the Court in its case-law, disappear. The chapter has further enquired as to the scope of the restriction that remains in the Lisbon Treaty; although its contours are unclear and will need to be defined in the future, this exception is not far-reaching enough to detract from the general conclusion that the envisaged extension of the Court's jurisdiction in the AFSJ is all-embracing and set to become a milestone in the constitutional evolution of the Union.

The role that the Court is playing in the current intergovernmental pillars as well as its future role, both following a Treaty reform and in the absence thereof, will be analysed in the final chapter of this monograph.

Judicial Control in the Common Foreign and Security Policy

3.1 Introduction

Although its origins lie with the European Political Cooperation (1970), the Common Foreign and Security Policy (CFSP) itself was introduced at Maastricht as Title V of the TEU, or the second pillar of the EU. Despite important changes made by the Treaty of Amsterdam, the second pillar has remained wholly intergovernmental in nature and generally outside the scope of the powers of the EU courts. The reluctance of the Member States to grant powers to the Court of Justice in this area results from the range of competences at stake: these are not only extremely sensitive, but also of a nature such that judicial control and supervision may be difficult: foreign and security policy is rarely implemented by strong and permanent legislative instruments.[1] The Union's CFSP counts among its objectives, according to Article 11 TEU, the safeguarding of the Union's common values and fundamental interests, the strengthening of its security and of international security more generally, the preservation of peace, the promotion of international cooperation, and the promotion of democracy, the rule of law, and human rights.

The intergovernmental pillars of the European Union are areas in continuous evolution. Although we should not make over-hasty assumptions of 'depillarization', it is clear that this evolution seems to be towards a more deeply institutionalized cooperation. This is obvious within the third pillar,

---

[1] E Denza, *The Intergovernmental Pillars of the European Union* (OUP: Oxford, 2002) 312; MG Garbagnati-Ketvel, 'The Jurisdiction of the European Court of Justice in Respect of the Common Foreign and Security Policy' (2006) 55 ICLQ 77, 79–82.

where *Pupino*,[2] for example, seems to be part of a slow trend of approximation to the logic of the Community pillar. Although infinitely less pronounced, a shift of perspective may be said to be taking place in the realm of the second pillar also. That is arguably why the governments of the Member States have shown themselves ready to integrate all three pillars into the same unitary structure in the Lisbon Treaty. Yet this does not necessarily mean that, in the short or even medium term, the CFSP is set to attain the same status as the AFSJ or other Union policies: the proximity of foreign policy and defence to the core of the Member States' sovereignty and national identity means that unanimity will remain as the decision-making procedure in this area, and that judicial oversight at EU level will continue to be extremely restricted. In short, there is a clear natural limit to the level of integration that the Union is likely to aim for, at least for the foreseeable future.

This chapter will critically assess the role that the Court of Justice is given within Common Foreign and Security Policy in the TEU and in the Lisbon Treaty.[3] Within the current framework, the Court of Justice has virtually no jurisdiction in CSFP matters. It has nevertheless exercised control over EC measures that implemented CFSP measures and over common positions that were adopted both under the second and the third pillars. Additionally, the Court has discharged 'peripheral' duties such as policing the borders between the second and the first pillars or enforcing the right of access to documents. All of these relatively recent

---

[2] C-105/03 *Criminal Proceedings against Maria Pupino* [2005] ECR I-5285. For a full account of the significance of this judgment, see M Fletcher, 'Extending "Indirect Effect" to the Third Pillar: The Significance of Pupino' (2005) 30 ELR 862; J Spencer, 'Child Witnesses and the European Union' (2005) 64 CLJ 569; E Spaventa, 'Opening Pandora's Box: Some Reflections on the Constitutional Effects of the Decision in Pupino' (2007) 3 EuConst 5; E Spaventa, 'Remembrance of Principles Lost: On Fundamental Rights, the Third Pillar and the Scope of Union Law' (2006) 25 YEL 153; S Peers, 'Salvation outside the Church: Judicial Protection in the Third Pillar after the Pupino and Segi Judgments' (2007) 44 CML Rev 885. For further discussion, see also S Prechal, 'Direct Effect, Indirect Effect, Supremacy and the Evolving Constitution of the European Union' in C Barnard (ed), *The Fundamentals of EU Law Revisited* (OUP: Oxford, 2007).

[3] For earlier analysis of the role given to the Court in CFSP matters in the Treaty establishing a Constitution for Europe, see A Arnull, 'From Bit Part to Starring Role? The Court of Justice and Europe's Constitutional Treaty' (2005) 24 YEL 1; T Tridimas, 'The European Court of Justice and the Draft Constitution: A Supreme Court for the Union?' in T Tridimas and P Nebbia (eds), *European Union Law for the Twenty-First Century: Rethinking the New Legal Order* (Hart: Oxford, 2004); MG Garbagnati-Ketvel, 'The Jurisdiction of the European Court of Justice in Respect of the Common Foreign and Security Policy' (2006) 55 ICLQ 77; A Hinarejos, 'Judicial Control of CFSP in the Constitution: A Cherry Worth Picking?' (2006) 25 YEL 363.

developments, the focus of the first part of this chapter, reveal a constitutional court striving to play an active role in all areas of the legal system, albeit within the very restricted limits set by the current Treaty.

The second part of this chapter will focus on the reform envisaged in the Lisbon Treaty. If the latter is ratified, the current second pillar will form part of the reorganized and overarching structure of the European Union, an entity with full legal personality: this was already foreseen in the Constitutional Treaty, and has been kept on as one of the basic premisses of the Lisbon Treaty. Just as with the AFSJ, this rearrangement will bring with it changes relating to the nature of the measures taken pursuant to this policy, given that as a general observation a number of features of the current Community method will be extended to apply across the fields formerly covered by the three distinct pillars. This extension of the Community method, however, does not include judicial review within the CFSP; the jurisdiction of the Court of Justice is still excluded, save for some exceptions. This chapter will consider the scope of these exceptions: it will determine how far reaching they are, in order to understand better the role that the Court will be called upon to fulfil in the area of CFSP if the Lisbon Treaty is ratified.

The last section will reflect on the shortcomings of the Court's jurisdiction and the effects this will have on its role as a constitutional court of the Union and on the future of the CFSP itself. Comparisons will be made between the role of the Court of Justice and that of national courts. Finally, the last section will explore the consequences that the Court's limited powers may have for its relationship with national constitutional courts and the European Court of Human Rights.

3.2 The Nature of CFSP Measures

3.2.1 At Present

According to Article 12 TEU, the Union can adopt joint actions and common positions in order to implement its Common Foreign and Security Policy. Joint actions are defined in Article 14 TEU as measures that address specific situations where operational action by the Union is required. They 'lay down their objectives, scope, the means to be made available to the Union, if necessary their duration, and the conditions for their implementation'.[4] Common positions, on the other hand, are very vaguely defined in Article 15 TEU: they define 'the approach of the Union to a particular matter of a geographical or thematic nature', and are binding on the Member States by virtue of the duty of loyal cooperation.[5]

It has already been argued throughout this book that, as a general observation, these measures are best considered as public international law measures. They are not directly applicable as a matter of EU law, since neither the Treaty nor the ECJ have stated a claim in this regard; similarly, they lack direct effect and supremacy. It is also unlikely that they could have the necessary level of detail to be self-executing (in the sense of achieving their aim without further implementation), since the Treaty describes them as very general measures that need implementation. They could be self-executing in the sense that they could be applied by a court as a standard of legality, but this is, of course, only in theory; in practice we would need either direct effect or primacy as a precondition for this application.

Since Maastricht, joint actions and common positions have binding force under international law.[6] They are not part of the legal system of the EC and cannot be challenged within it; as we shall see later, the TEU does not foresee general judicial control of these measures within the EU legal system either.[7] To the extent, however, that these CFSP measures require the adoption of measures binding on third parties, such measures have to be adopted by the states themselves or by the Community. The EC has traditionally adopted such implementing measures under Articles 60 and

---

[4] On the legal effects of joint actions, A Dashwood, 'The Law and Practice of CFSP Joint Actions' in M Cremona and B de Witte (eds), *EU Foreign Relations Law: Constitutional Fundamentals* (Hart: Oxford, 2008) 54–6. For further discussion of the legal effects of all CFSP instruments, ibid, 54–60. On how CFSP acts restrict Member States, C Hillion and R Wessel, 'Restraining External Competences of EU Member States under CFSP' in M Cremona and B de Witte (eds), *EU Foreign Relations Law: Constitutional Fundamentals* (Hart: Oxford, 2008).

[5] The ECJ has clarified that these measures are generally not supposed to produce legal effects in relation to third parties; if they do, they are reviewable under Art 35 TEU: C-355/04 P *Segi* [2007] ECR I-1657 [52]–[56]. It was in the same case that the Court confirmed that common positions are binding on the Member States by virtue of the duty of loyal cooperation, [52].

[6] cf E Denza, *The Intergovernmental Pillars of the European Union* (OUP: Oxford, 2002) 311.

[7] But see Section 3.31 on Art 47 TEU. Further, Hillion and Wessel have argued for a reading of the principle of loyal cooperation which would allow the ECJ to make Member States comply with their CFSP obligations: C Hillion and R Wessel, 'Restraining External Competences of EU Member States under CFSP' in M Cremona and B de Witte (eds), *EU Foreign Relations Law: Constitutional Fundamentals* (Hart: Oxford, 2008).

301 EC.[8] What is truly significant from the point of view of judicial control is that these EC implementing measures can be challenged through the normal Community venues: in fact, the most noteworthy developments in CFSP in recent years have resulted from the challenge of EC measures that implemented CFSP ones. This will be dealt with in depth in Section 3.3.2.

On the other hand, CFSP measures themselves—viewed as measures of public international law—may be subject to challenge by national courts, if national law so allows. National courts may be competent to consider whether the national government acted legitimately when agreeing to the adoption of such measure; in that sense, they could analyse the measure itself in order to determine whether it is consistent with the national constitution and with fundamental rights standards. Whether (or which) national courts have this jurisdiction would be a matter of domestic law.

3.2.2 CFSP Measures after the Lisbon Treaty

The formal disappearance of the pillars in the Lisbon Treaty brings with it an important phenomenon: the difference between EU and EC law disappears; thus we have no more, on the one hand, a corpus of measures adopted under the intergovernmental pillars which are, ultimately, measures of public international law and, on the other hand, measures of EC law which have 'stronger' features. Nevertheless, the CFSP continues to be a distinct policy with unique features.

Article 25 TEU (after LT) states that the CFSP shall be implemented through 'decisions', instead of common positions and joint actions as it is done currently. Decisions, in the general framework of the Lisbon Treaty, can be either legislative or non-legislative instruments. In the case of the CFSP, however, they can never be of a legislative nature, according to Article 31 TEU (after LT).[9] Decisions may be implemented by other

---

[8] JA Usher, 'Direct and Individual Concern: An Effective Remedy or a Conventional Solution?' (2003) 28 ELR 575, 593; M Cremona, F Francioni, and S Poli, 'Challenging EU Counter-Terrorism Measures through the Courts' EUI Working Paper (forthcoming). Art 308 EC has also been used as a 'complementary' legal basis: see Cases T-315/01 *Yassin Abdullah Kadi v Council and Commission* [2005] ECR II-3649 [64]–[135] and T-306/01 *Yusuf and Al Barakaat International Foundation v Council and Commission* [2005] ECR II-3533 [125]–[171]; ECJ *Kadi* [2008] ECR I-6351 [158]–[236].

[9] Art 31.1 TEU (after LT) also states that decisions shall be taken generally by the European Council and the Council unanimously, except in cases foreseen in its second paragraph.

decisions. Further, Article 288 TFEU establishes generally that all Union decisions are binding in their entirety; if a decision has a formal addressee, it shall be binding on them only. The Treaty remains silent as to the direct applicability, direct or indirect effect of these measures. The assumption is, of course, that all features of current EC law would apply to Union law within the framework of the LT. If these features are conditional on certain criteria, the default should be that such criteria remain the same. We can thus assume, for example, that CFSP decisions would have (at least as a matter of theory) primacy over national law, since this is bound to become a feature of all Union law.[10] By the same token, one can also assume that these measures would be directly applicable in the sense that they would become the 'law of the land' as soon as they are binding, and Member States would have no claim as to how they enter their domestic legal system.[11]

In general, the fact that CFSP measures cease to be binding under international law only and become binding Union law ('Union law' being the post-Lisbon equivalent of the current EC law) is of great significance. Not only from the point of view of the 'stronger' effects that these measures acquire, but also from the point of view of judicial control. It has been pointed out earlier that, at least as a matter of theory, national courts may be competent to control the legality of EU law measures, viewed as measures of public international law, using national standards. Once the evolution from public international law to (post-Lisbon) Union law takes place, it will be necessary to take two possible changes into account: first, that CFSP measures will have primacy over national law, at least in theory. This would preclude their review against national standards. And second, it remains to be seen whether the *Foto-Frost* principle applies in this area,[12] as it will do in the rest of Union activity.[13] Its application would preclude national courts from ruling a CFSP measure invalid, making the ECJ the only court that can exercise control over such measures. Since, as it will become clear from the following sections, the role of the ECJ is very

---

[10] The extension of primacy was made explicit in the Constitutional Treaty (Art I-6) and is implicit in the case of the LT.

[11] For further discussion on the extension of the features of EC law, see also Chapter 2.

[12] Case 314/85 *Foto-Frost v Hauptzollamt Lübeck-Ost* [1987] ECR 04199.

[13] The application of *Foto-Frost* would seem the default approach, in the absence of powerful reasons against it. It was explicitly stated in the Constitutional Treaty that the case-law of the ECJ would have continuity (Art IV-438); in the Lisbon Treaty, this seems implicit.

limited in this area and there is no complete system of remedies,[14] it seems more logical for the *Foto-Frost* principle not to apply.

The fact that national courts may review CFSP measures in the absence of *Foto-Frost* would still leave open the question of the primacy of such measures over national law and its effects: if national courts reviewed CFSP measures using EU and not national standards, for example, they would still be acting in accordance with the principle of primacy. In practice, although Union law may make a theoretical claim as to the primacy of CFSP measures over national law, the ECJ would not be able to enforce it.[15] This means that it would be up to national courts to decide to what extent CFSP measures are accorded primacy over measures of national law within their Member State, since the ECJ would not be there to impose on national courts (or remind them of) their *Simmenthal* duty within the framework of the preliminary ruling procedure.[16]

3.3 The Jurisdiction of the ECJ in CFSP at Present

Although the Court is competent to deal with cases where Community policies have touched upon Member States' external powers,[17] the Member States have been reluctant to allow the EU judiciary to play a significant role in the CFSP. As a result, the courts have only dealt with CFSP matters in a tangential manner: notably, in *Svenska Journalistförbundet*,[18] the CFI held that the citizens' right of access to documents applied to the intergovernmental pillars, a statement that was confirmed as regards CFSP

---

[14] Hillion and Wessel have, however, argued for a reading of the principle of loyal cooperation which would allow the ECJ to make Member States comply with their CFSP obligations: C Hillion and R Wessel, 'Restraining External Competences of EU Member States under CFSP' in M Cremona and B de Witte (eds), *EU Foreign Relations Law: Constitutional Fundamentals* (Hart: Oxford, 2008).

[15] Similarly, AG Bot has argued in his Opinion in *Kozlowski* that the principle of primacy applies, in theory, in the third pillar, but that there are no mechanisms to enforce it apart from indirect effect or the duty of conform interpretation: Opinion of AG Bot in Case C-66/08 *Kozlowski* [2008] ECR I-6041[115] and ff. The Court did not address the issue.

[16] On primacy and CFSP measures after the Lisbon Treaty, see also Sections 3.4.1 and 3.5.3.

[17] For an extensive study of this impact and the litigation it has caused, A Dashwood and C Hillion (eds), *The General Law of EC External Relations* (Sweet & Maxwell: Oxford, 2000); P Eeckhout, *External Relations of the European Union: Legal and Constitutional Foundations* (OUP: Oxford, 2004); P Koutrakos, *EU International Relations Law* (Hart: Oxford, 2006).

[18] Case T-174/95 *Svenska Journalistförbundet v Council* [1998] ECR II-2289 [81].

documents specifically in *Hautala*.[19] More importantly, the Court is competent to police the borders between the EC and the intergovernmental pillars and it recently exercised this function in relation to the second pillar for the first time, as we will see in the next section. The fact that the Court has only these 'peripheral' powers in the second pillar[20] means that it has only been able to exercise a substantive review of action undertaken in the field of foreign and security policy to the extent that such action has been implemented by the Community, which will be the focus of section (b).

3.3.1 Policing the Boundaries

The extension of the Court's jurisdiction to police the boundaries between the EC and the intergovernmental pillars under Article 47 TEU has already been examined in Section 2.3.2.5. The ECJ has had the opportunity to police the boundaries between the second and the first pillar on one occasion:[21] in the *ECOWAS* case,[22] the Commission challenged the validity of a CFSP Council decision that implemented a joint action supporting the moratorium on small arms and light weapons in West Africa because it should have been adopted under the EC Treaty as

---

[19] Case T-14/98 *Hautala v Council* [1999] ECR II-2489 [42]. The ECJ upheld the CFI's ruling on appeal; at this point the jurisdiction of the Court was no longer contested: C-353/99 P *Council v Hautala* [2001] ECR I-9565. More recently, see Joined Cases T-110/03, T-150/03, T-405/03 *Sison v Council* [2005] ECR II-1429 and C-266/05 P *Sison v Council* [2007] ECR I-1233.

[20] See also eg Case T-231/04 *Greece v Commission* on jurisdiction over CFSP spending, now on appeal: Case C-203/07 P *Greece v Commission* [2007] ECR I-63.

[21] The CFI had already allowed individuals to challenge a CFSP common position directly for breach of Art 47 TEU. The challenges were unsuccessful: Case T 228/02 *Organisation des Modjahedines du Peuple d'Iran* [2006] ECR II-4665 and the Order in T-299/04 *Selmani* [2005] ECR II-20. The earlier cases T-349/99 *Miskovic*; T-350/99 *Karic* were discontinued after the Council amended the measure at stake (a Council Decision imposing a visa ban on the applicants). MG Garbagnati-Ketvel, 'The Jurisdiction of the European Court of Justice in Respect of the Common Foreign and Security Policy' (2006) 55 ICLQ 77, 88.

[22] Case C-91/05 *Commission v Council* ('*ECOWAS*') [2008] ECR I-3651 See also P Koutrakos, 'Development and Foreign Policy: Where to Draw the Line between the Pillars?' (2008) 33 ELR 289. The problematic link between security and development can also be seen in the Philippines Border Management Case, C-403/05 *European Parliament v Commission* [2007] ECR I-9045: for a full comment, M Cremona, 'Case C-403/05, European Parliament v Commission (Philippines Border Management Project), Judgment of the Grand Chamber of 23 October 2007 [2007] ECR I-9045'; (2008) 45 CML Rev 1727. For a general analysis of delimitation of competences involving CFSP matters, see also P Koutrakos, 'Legal Basis and Delimitation of Competences' in M Cremona and B de Witte (eds), *EU Foreign Relations Law: Constitutional Fundamentals* (Hart: Oxford, 2008).

development aid.[23] The Commission also used the plea of illegality to ask the Court to declare illegal, and thus inapplicable, the CFSP joint action itself.[24] Departing from AG Mengozzi's Opinion, the Court annulled the CFSP Council Decision; it did not consider it necessary to go into the plea of illegality of the joint action that the decision was implementing, since the decision had to be annulled because of its own defects.[25]

The case is illuminating for several reasons; first, it was the first case of cross-pillar litigation between second and first pillar before the ECJ. Second, the case illustrates to what extent the Court will apply its 'centre of gravity' test to this sort of cross-pillar litigation, and the role that Article 47 TEU is bound to have within this framework. And finally, it was the first time the Court addressed the issue of the type of EC competence that triggers the application of Article 47 TEU. Let us examine all these issues in turn.

This was the first opportunity for the Court to police Article 47 TEU within the second pillar; to do so, it necessarily had to resort to its EC Treaty powers, as foreseen in Article 46 TEU. This meant that the procedural vehicles used were Articles 230 EC, or action for the annulment of the CFSP decision, and 241 EC, or plea of illegality against the joint action. Two Member States argued that the Court had no jurisdiction to rule on a plea of illegality brought against a CFSP measure. The Court considered itself competent to rule on such a plea to the extent that it concerned a possible breach of Article 47 EU: in general, the Court has considered that all of its EC Treaty powers can be exercised in order to enforce Article 47 TEU, be it within the second or the third pillar. In *Segi*, the CFI considered an action for damages brought by individuals under Articles 235 and 288 EC to the extent that such damages were allegedly caused by a breach of Article 47 TEU, even though there is no such action within the TEU.[26] In *OMPI* and *Selmani*, individuals were allowed to bring a direct action under Article 230(4) EC against a CFSP common position,

---

[23] Council Decision 2004/833/CFSP of 2 December 2004 implementing Joint Action 2002/589/CFSP with a view to a European Union contribution to ECOWAS in the framework of the Moratorium on Small Arms and Light Weapons [2004] OJ L359/65.

[24] Council Joint Action 2002/589/CFSP of 12 July 2002 on the European Union's contribution to combating the destabilizing accumulation and spread of small arms and light weapons and repealing Joint Action 1999/34/CFSP [2002] OJ L191/1.   [25] *ECOWAS* [111].

[26] Case T-338/02 *Segi* [2004] ECR II-01647. The ECJ did not consider the issue afresh, but it agreed that the CFI had jurisdiction: C-355/04 P *Segi* [2007] ECR I-1657. See also Cases T-333/02 *Gestoras Pro Amnistía and others v Council*, unpublished, and C-354/04 *Gestoras Pro Amnistía and others v Council* [2007] ECR I-1579.

on grounds of breach of Article 47 TEU only.[27] It would be in keeping with this approach to allow all national courts to ask for a preliminary ruling on the validity of third and second pillar measures, if they should have possibly been adopted under the EC Treaty.[28]

As regards the substance of the case, the Court applied, as far as possible, its classic EC pillar test to find the proper legal basis of the measure. Within the first pillar, the Court applies an objective test according to which the main/component of a measure determines its legal basis. There may be an incidental aim, but that does not justify adding a second legal basis: this is only legitimate where the measure truly has two equally central aims.[29] Until *ECOWAS*, the Court had found in the third pillar/EC pillar litigation cases that the main purpose of the measure at stake lied within EC law, and thus an EC legal basis had to be used. In *ECOWAS*, the Court came for the first time to the conclusion that the CFSP decision at issue had two equally central aims or components, and that they could not be dissociated (otherwise it is possible the measure could have been split between two different legal bases). Within the first pillar, the solution would have been to attribute a dual legal basis to the measure. In *ECO-WAS*, however, the Court rejected the possibility of adopting a measure on a CFSP/first pillar legal basis simultaneously, presumably because these are still separated legal orders.[30] It was at this point that the 'hierarchy rule' of Article 47 TEU was applied by the Court: once it had determined that both pillars could have been used, a conflict rule that establishes preference for one over the other became necessary.

Finally, *ECOWAS* was also clarifying as to the type of EC competence that triggers the application of Article 47 TEU. In prior cross-pillar

---

[27] Case T 228/02 *Organisation des Modjahedines du Peuple d'Iran* [2006] ECR II-4665 and the Order in T-299/04 *Selmani* [2005] ECR II-20.

[28] R van Ooik, 'Cross-Pillar Litigation before the ECJ: Demarcation of Community and Union Competences' (2008) 4 EuConst 399, 405–6.

[29] See Case C-300/89 *Commission v Council* ('*Titanium Dioxide*') [1991] ECR I-2867; even if there are two equally central aims, it is not possible to use two legal bases if they would entail the application of incompatible decision-making procedures: ibid, [17]–[21]. H Cullen and A Charlesworth, 'Diplomacy by other Means: The Use of Legal Basis Litigation as a Political Strategy by the European Parliament and Member States' (1999) 36 CML Rev 1234. The test was already used in the context of cross-pillar litigation in Case C-176/03 *Commission v Council* [2005] ECR I-7879 [45].

[30] *ECOWAS* [76]. R van Ooik, 'Cross-Pillar Litigation before the ECJ: Demarcation of Community and Union Competences' (2008) 4 EuConst 399, 413–18. For a different overview of the application of Art 47 TEU, see J Heliskoski, 'Small Arms and Light Weapons within the Union's Pillar Structure: An Analysis of Article 47 of the EU Treaty' (2008) 33 ELR 898.

litigation involving the third pillar, the Court had not addressed the issue directly. In *ECOWAS*, the Court made it clear that the nature of the EC competence being encroached upon is of no relevance for the purposes of the application of Article 47 TEU.[31]

As a general observation, Article 47 TEU has proved to be a valuable tool for the Court, which has shown itself very willing to police the borders between the intergovernmental pillars and the EC Treaty actively. To this purpose, the Court has used its EC Treaty powers when necessary, often in the face of Member States' opposition. The Court can hardly be criticized for this, since Article 46(f) TEU is unequivocal in this respect. A different question is whether Article 47 TEU could be potentially widened to allow the Court to review the compliance of (properly adopted) CFSP measures with the EC Treaty.[32] Although the wording of Article 47 TEU may lend itself to this wider interpretation,[33] a substantive review of third or second pillar measures should only be possible to the extent that the Court has such powers under the TEU itself (rather than under the EC Treaty). The Court has interpreted Article 47 as a clause that allows it to resort to its EC powers to control EU measures, but only as far as checking their legal basis; this has always been justified by the need to preserve the distribution of competences and there is no indication that the Court would be willing to extend it any further. This means that while a control of third pillar measures for compliance with the EC Treaty may be possible within the framework of Article 35 TEU, no such control can be realistically expected within the second pillar, where there are no procedural vehicles available to

---

[31] *ECOWAS* [63].

[32] eg S Peers, 'Who's Judging the Watchmen: The Judicial System of the "Area of Freedom, Security and Justice"' (1998) 17 YEL 337, 402. Peers puts forward the example of a properly adopted framework decision on money laundering that has the result of compelling Member States to breach Art 56 EC, which prohibits all restrictions on the movement of capital and on payments between the Member States and between Member States and third countries.

[33] 'Nothing in this treaty will affect the EC treaty' may be read to subordinate all measures based on the TEU to all substantive rules of the EC Treaty. Also, a parallel could be drawn between checking CFSP measures for compliance with EC rules and the Court's record of ensuring that Member States act in accordance with certain EC rules even when discharging their exclusive competences (eg Case C-124/95 *The Queen, ex parte Centro-Com Srl v HM Treasury and Bank of England* ECR [1997] I-81). On this point, see also M Koskenniemi, 'International Law Aspects of the Common Foreign and Security Policy' in M Koskenniemi (ed), *International Law Aspects of the European Union* (Kluber Law International: The Hague, 1998) 36–42.

the Court.[34] Anything else would be arguably contrary to the logic and the spirit of Title V TEU (CFSP).

3.3.2 *Review of CFSP Measures*

The TEU does not contemplate the review, be it direct or indirect, of joint actions and common positions. A chapter on the judicial review of CFSP measures, strictly speaking, would therefore be extremely short or, rather, non-existent. And yet the ECJ has played a role in this area: firstly, the Court has interpreted Article 35 TEU to allow it to review common positions directly if they have legal effects on third parties, although it is unclear if this would extend to 'purely' CFSP common positions.[35] But secondly and more importantly, the Court has controlled the legality of EC legislation implementing CFSP measures in a number of cases which are of relevance for this study: although the measures at stake before the ECJ were first pillar measures, controlling them goes a long way towards controlling the way in which CFSP powers are generally exercised. This section will start by focusing on such instances of review.

For some time now, anti-terrorism measures with a 'foreign' element or connection have been adopted within the CFSP. In many cases, the Courts of the European Union have been called upon to review the legality of such measures and/or their implementation, and they have been able to offer different levels of judicial protection according to the particular circumstances of the case. The cases where individuals have turned to the Court because they were affected by measures in this area concern, once again, the adoption of 'terror lists'—in this case drafted under the second pillar because of their predominant foreign-policy dimension. Even though in these cases the Court did not review second pillar measures, but rather

---

[34] This view seems more in keeping with the spirit of Title V TEU (CFSP), where it is obvious that the drafters of the Treaty wished for the Court to be excluded. A reading of Art 47 TEU as a provision that single-handedly grants the Court competence to review all CFSP measures for compliance with the EC Treaty seems a step too far. Furthermore, the implementation of properly adopted CFSP measures that breach EC law could always be challenged at EU level (either through Art 230 EC in the case of EC measures, or through infringement proceedings in the case of direct national implementation).

[35] In *Segi* and *Gestoras pro Amnistía* the common position at stake had been adopted under both the second and the third pillars. Further, the Court treated the common position as a third pillar measure to the extent that it affected the applicants. It is thus impossible to know for certain if the conclusion of the Court in this case would apply to a purely CFSP common position, but it seems improbable.

their EC implementation, these decisions concern judicial protection within the general realm of the Union's CFSP. Before we review these cases, it should perhaps be recalled that the listing at stake in these cases may have been done by the Union autonomously, or it may be the mere transposition of a list drafted at UN level.[36] Both strings of cases have different implications. On a different note, the decisions of the CFI and the ECJ on cases involving UN lists also merit discussion to the extent that they signify opposite understandings of the autonomy of the EU legal order and of the role of constitutional review within the latter.

First in this thread are the CFI judgments in *Kadi* and *Yusuf*.[37] At stake was an EC regulation adopted on the basis of Articles 60, 301, and 308 EC to implement a CFSP common position which in turn implemented UN Security Council Resolution 1373/2000,[38] a measure which seeks to impose financial sanctions on terrorist organizations and individuals listed in it.[39]

The European Union has been implementing UN sanctions against individuals for years, even though there is no specific legal basis for this in the Treaties. The EC Treaty allows for the adoption of economic sanctions against third countries when the Union adopts a CFSP common position or joint action that provides for it. Typically, then, this kind of sanction has been possible through cross-pillar action: first the Union adopts a second pillar common position, then the Community gives effect to it by adopting a regulation.[40]

---

[36] On this distinction, see S Bartelt and H Zeitler, '"Intelligente Sanktionen" zur Terrorismusbekämpfung in der EU' (2003) 23 Europäische Zeitschrift für Wirtschaftsrecht 712; I Cameron, 'European Union Anti-Terrorist Blacklisting' (2004) 4 HRLRev 225.

[37] Cases T-315/01 *Yassin Abdullah Kadi v Council and Commission* [2005] ECR II-3649 and T-306/01 *Yusuf and Al Barakaat International Foundation v Council and Commission* [2005] ECR II-3533. An earlier version of the following analysis of these judgments was included in A Hinarejos, 'Recent Human Rights Developments in the EU Courts: The Charter of Fundamental Rights, the European Arrest Warrant and Terror Lists' (2007) 7 HRLRev 793.

[38] Common Position 2001/154/CFSP concerning additional restrictive measures against the Taliban and amending Common Position 96/746/CFSP [2001] OJ L57/1.

[39] Council Regulation (EC) 881/2002 of 27 May 2002 imposing certain specific restrictive measures directed against certain persons and entities associated with Usama bin Laden, the Al-Qaeda network and the Taliban, and repealing Regulation (EC) No 467/2001 [2002] OJ L139/9. The list annexed to this regulation is regularly reviewed by the Commission, on the basis of updating by the Sanctions Committee: most recently at the time of the judgment, Commission Regulation (EC) 1378/2005 of 22 August 2005 amending for the 52nd time Council Regulation (EC) 881/2002 [2002] OJ L219/27.

[40] Under Arts 60 and 301 CE: JA Usher, 'Direct and Individual Concern: An effective Remedy or a conventional Solution?' (2003) 28 ELR 575, 593; M Nettesheim, 'UN Sanctions against Individuals: A Challenge to the Architecture of European Union Governance' (2007) 44 CML Rev 567, 571.

This mechanism—with slight changes—is now being used to impose economic sanctions on individuals named in 'terror lists'.[41] In the case of *Kadi* and *Yusuf*, the list was a mere reproduction of a list compiled by the UN (rather than autonomously within the Union), a fact that prompted a more general debate on the relationship between EC and international law.

Kadi and Yusuf had been named in the 'terror list' annexed to the UN resolution and later to the EC regulation. Accordingly, they sought the annulment of the latter before the CFI under Article 230(4) EC, alleging, among other things,[42] a breach of their fundamental rights—in particular, the right to the use of their property and the right to a fair hearing. The judgment of the CFI in this case and the ECJ's judgment in the appeal have generated a vast amount of commentary in the literature. The present discussion will therefore be limited to the reasons these courts put forward in order to deny or assert their jurisdiction, and to their views on the autonomy of the EU legal order, to the extent that it determines the role to be played by the EU courts. The intricate discussion in both instances on the suitability of Articles 60, 301, and 308 EC as joint legal bases is, therefore, beyond the scope of this section.[43]

The CFI started by mapping out the relationship between UN and EU law so as to determine the scope of its competence to review a regulation that merely transposed a UN Security Council resolution. In order to do this, the Court started by considering international law (the Vienna Convention and the UN Charter) and then focusing on EC law.

---

[41] With the addition of Art 308 EC as a further legal basis. Art 308 EC permits the Community to adopt any action necessary to achieve a legitimate aim of the Community. Both the CFI and the ECJ agreed that the use of Art 308 EC was legitimate in this context, albeit for different reasons: CFI *Kadi* [87]–[135]; ECJ *Kadi* [158]–[236].

[42] They also claimed, firstly, that there was no competence for the adoption of the regulation at stake, since there is no specific legal base in the treaties for the adoption of sanctions against individuals and Arts 60, 301, and 308 EC cannot be used for this purpose. Secondly, they alleged that the regulation breached Art 249 EC, the article that describes regulations as instruments of general application. The regulation at stake prescribed individual sanctions and had therefore, according to the applicants, no general application. The Court rejected both claims.

[43] On the discussion of the use of Arts 60, 301, and 308 EC as legal basis, see: D Halberstam and E Stein, 'The United Nations, the European Union, and the King of Sweden: Economic Sanctions and Individual Rights in a Plural World Order' (2009) 46 CML Rev 13, 35–42; A Gattini, 'Annotation: Joined Cases C-402/05 P & 415/05 P, *Yassin Abdullah Kadi, Al Barakaat International Foundation v Council and Commission*, judgment of the Grand Chamber 2008, nyr' (2009) 46 CML Rev 213, 218–21, 223–4; T Tridimas and JA Gutierrez-Fons, 'EU Law, International Law, and Economic Sanctions Against Terrorism: The Judiciary in Distress?' (2009) 32 Fordham Int LJ 660, 664–79; M Cremona, F Francioni, and S Poli, 'Challenging EU Counter-Terrorism Measures through the Courts' EUI Working Paper (forthcoming).

According to the CFI, states can neither rely on their national law nor on other international treaties in order to avoid fulfilling their obligations under the UN Charter.[44] Article 103 UN Charter establishes that said obligations—which include those derived from Security Council resolutions—prevail over the EU and EC Treaties.[45] Although the EC itself is not a party to the UN Charter and is not directly bound by it, the CFI came to the conclusion that the Community is indirectly bound to the same obligations imposed by the UN Charter on Member States as a matter of EC law, that is, by virtue of Articles 307 and 297 EC.[46] Although the Community is not a signatory to the Charter, 'in so far as under the EC Treaty the Community has assumed powers previously exercised by Member States in the area governed by the Charter of the United Nations, the provisions of that Charter have the effect of binding the Community'.[47]

Once the CFI had asserted that the Community is bound by UN Charter obligations (including obligations arising from Security Council resolutions) because of functional succession, it followed that it was not in a position to review the validity of such a resolution according to EU law standards. Accordingly, it refused to review a Community regulation that merely implemented a UN Security Council resolution—without the

[44] Art 27 of the Vienna Convention on the Law of Treaties and Art 103 of the UN Charter, respectively.

[45] 'In the event of a conflict between the obligations of the Members of the United Nations under the present Charter and their obligations under any other international agreement, their obligations under the present Charter shall prevail.'

[46] Art 307 EC: 'The rights and obligations arising from agreements concluded before 1 January 1958 or, for acceding States, before the date of their accession, between one or more Member States on the one hand, and one or more third countries on the other, shall not be affected by the provisions of this Treaty. To the extent that such agreements are not compatible with this Treaty, the Member State or States concerned shall take all appropriate steps to eliminate the incompatibilities established. Member States shall, where necessary, assist each other to this end and shall, where appropriate, adopt a common attitude. [...]' Art 297 EC: 'Member States shall consult each other with a view to taking together the steps needed to prevent the functioning of the common market being affected by measures which a Member State may be called upon to take in the event of serious internal disturbances affecting the maintenance of law and order, in the event of war, serious international tension constituting a threat of war, or in order to carry out obligations it has accepted for the purpose of maintaining peace and international security.' CFI *Kadi* [192]–[204]. See C Tomuschat, 'Annotation to Yusuf and Kadi' (2007) 43 CML Rev 537, 542.

[47] CFI *Kadi* [253]. To this end, the CFI relies extensively by analogy on *International Fruit*, where the ECJ had to rule on whether the Community was bound by the GATT: In [245], [246], [250], [251], [253]. Case 21/72 *International Fruit Company and others/Produktschap voor Groenten en Fruit* [1972] ECR 1219.

exercise of any discretion—according to the general principles of Community law (in particular those regarding the protection of fundamental rights). In its view, doing so would amount to reviewing the UN Security Council resolution itself.[48] As a result, the CFI believed it had only limited competence in this case.[49] But this did not mean that no review could take place; the Court's limited competence still allowed it to review the validity of this regulation in light of *jus cogens*.[50] The Court did not articulate its reasons for limiting the standard of review in this way, in what seems to be an effort to preserve the 'political prerogative' of the Security Council:[51] the Court stated that checking the appropriateness and proportionality of the Security Council resolution, even indirectly, would amount to encroaching upon the Security Council's prerogative to determine the existence of a threat to international peace and security and how to deal with it.[52] Thus the lowering of the standard of review would seem an attempt to respect the prerogative of the Security Council to decide what is, essentially, a political question.

It is in light of this standard of protection of fundamental rights that the CFI set out to examine the applicants' claims. As regards the alleged breach of the right to property, the CFI argued that the freezing of funds did not submit the person affected to inhumane or degrading treatment, since the regulation allowed for derogations in the case of basic and extraordinary expenses.[53] Moreover, according to the Court, only an arbitrary deprivation of property can be considered a breach of the right to property protected by *jus cogens*;[54] the deprivation at issue could not be considered arbitrary, inappropriate, or disproportionate.[55]

The Court then moved on to consider the second claim, on the breach to the right to be heard: the applicants contended that they had not been

[48] CFI *Kadi* [266].

[49] Ibid, [269].

[50] 'International law thus permits the inference that there exists one limit to the principle that resolutions of the Security Council have binding effect: namely, that they must observe the fundamental peremptory provisions of *jus cogens*. If they fail to do so, however improbable that may be, they would bind neither the Member States of the United Nations nor, in consequence, the Community.' CFI *Kadi* [281]. For a general overview of the concept of *jus cogens*, see eg A Orakeshevili, *Peremptory Norms in International Law* (OUP: Oxford, 2006).

[51] S Griller, 'International Law, Human Rights and the European Community's Autonomous Legal Order: Notes on the European Court of Justice Decision in Kadi' (2008) 4 EuConst 528, 539–40.   [52] CFI *Kadi* [284].

[53] Ibid, [290]–[291].

[54] Because of Art 17(2) of the Universal Declaration, which states that '[n]o one shall be arbitrarily deprived of his property'.   [55] CFI *Kadi* [293]–[302].

informed of the reasons or justification for the sanction, nor were they given the opportunity to be heard during its adoption. On this point the Court distinguished between the applicants' rights to be heard by the UN organs—prior to their inclusion in the list—and by the Community institutions, prior to the adoption of the regulation. In the first case, the Court could not find any rule of *jus cogens* which would oblige the UN Sanctions Committee to hear the applicants prior to their inclusion in the list; furthermore, the purpose of the measure could have been defeated by alerting the persons at an early stage, and, finally, individuals may later rely on their state to request the Sanctions Committee to remove them from the list. In the second case (right to be heard before the Community Institutions), the Court conceded that 'the right to a fair hearing is, in all proceedings initiated against a person which are liable to culminate in a measure adversely affecting that person, a fundamental principle of Community law'.[56] This, however, cannot apply where the Community institutions exercise absolutely no discretion—exactly the situation at hand.

Finally, the Court had to deal with the applicants' right to an effective judicial remedy, and it held that its assessment of the regulation with regard to the UN resolution it implemented from the viewpoint of procedural and substantive appropriateness, internal consistency and proportionality, plus the review of the contents of the regulation that the Court carried out in light of *jus cogens*, was sufficient to uphold this right. There was a *lacuna* in judicial protection in that there was no judicial remedy against the Security Council resolution available to the applicants, but this, in the view of the Court, did not amount to a breach of their fundamental rights since the right of access to courts is not absolute, and its limitation in the circumstances of the case was justified: 'the applicants' interest in having a court hear their case on its merits [was] not enough to outweigh the essential public interest in the maintenance of international peace and security.'[57] In the absence of an international court with jurisdiction to review these measures, the Court went on to say, the fact that individuals can resort to their Government to get their case reviewed before the Sanctions Committee is a reasonable method of affording adequate protection of the applicants' fundamental rights, as recognized by *jus cogens*.[58]

---

[56] CFI *Kadi* [325]. This applies in principle to a regulation if it is of direct and individual concern to the applicants.   [57] Ibid, [344].
[58] Ibid, [345].

In later case-law dealing with the transposition of UN lists, the CFI has reiterated its position as regards the sufficiency of diplomatic protection.[59] The Court had already pointed out in *Yusuf* and *Kadi* that individuals should avail themselves of judicial remedies provided by national law if their right to request removal from the list has been breached by national authorities;[60] this was repeated again in *Hassan* and *Ayadi*,[61] where the CFI also stated that Member States have an obligation to protect their affected citizens through the diplomatic mechanism offered by the UN system, and sought to flesh out this obligation.[62] This way of attempting to fill a gap in judicial protection by developing and imposing a new obligation on Member States is reminiscent of the approach taken by the ECJ to the matter of access to a court for individuals who cannot challenge general instruments of EC law directly.[63] Needless to say, this solution does not seem without difficulties: as a matter of principle, it is debatable whether a diplomatic mechanism can substitute judicial protection. It is also unclear whether it can be effective.[64]

The way in which the CFI dealt with Community measures that implement UN sanctions seems unsatisfactory because it allows for the existence of a gap in the system of judicial protection. The European Community operates within a system of multi-level governance, in which many competences of the nation-state have been 'sourced out' to different levels of supranational cooperation. This is a long process of adjustment

---

[59] Cases T-253/02 *Ayadi v Council* [2006] ECR II-2139; T-49/04 *Hassan v Council and Commission* [2006] ECR II-52. Case T-318/01 *Othman v Council and Commission*, pending, also concerns implementation of a UN list. See also Case T-362/04 *Minin v Commission* [2007] ECR II-2003. The appeals in *Ayadi* and *Hassan* are now pending before the ECJ: Cases C-403/06 P *Ayadi v Council*, pending; C-399/06 P *Hassan v Council and Commission*, pending. On the implementation of UN listings, see also the preliminary ruling in Case C-117/06 *Möllendorf and Möllendorf-Niehuus* [2007] ECR I-8361.

[60] CFI *Kadi* [270]; *Yusuf* [317].

[61] T-49/04 *Hassan v Council and Commission* [2006] ECR II-52 [122]–[123]; T-253/02 *Ayadi v Council* [2006] ECR II-2139 [150].   [62] *Hassan*, ibid, [114]–[118]; *Ayadi*, ibid, [144]–[148].

[63] Under Article 230(4) EC, the ECJ continues to apply a very restrictive test to grant standing to individuals, and this can in turn lead to a gap in judicial protection. The ECJ dealt with this in *UPA* by imposing an obligation on Member States to make it easier for individuals to challenge EC legislation indirectly before national courts: Case C-50/00 P *UPA v Council* [2002] ECR I-6677. M Nettesheim, 'UN Sanctions against Individuals: A Challenge to the Architecture of European Union Governance' (2007) 44 CML Rev 567, 574–5.

[64] B Kunoy and A Dawes, 'Plate Tectonics in Luxembourg: The Ménage à Trois between EC Law, International Law and the European Convention on Human Rights Following the UN Sanctions Cases' (2009) 46 CML Rev 73, 94–6.

that creates problems of overlap and synchronization, and requires rules of conflict resolution. As Nettesheim eloquently has put it, conflict arises 'when the evolution of differing public powers does not coincide with the simultaneous evolution of standards regarding the protection of human rights and corresponding mechanisms of legal protection'.[65] In *Yusuf, Kadi*, and *Ayadi* the CFI had to face such a conflict, in that it had to deal with measures produced at a different level of governance—a level without a system of protection of fundamental rights equivalent to that of the EC. Unsurprisingly, criticisms were levelled at various aspects of the CFI's decision,[66] from its understanding of the way in which the EC is bound by UN Charter obligations to the consequences this had on the scope of jurisdiction of the Court and the way the review was conducted: the 'functional succession' argument used by the CFI to conclude that the EC was under a positive obligation to implement the Security Council resolution does not seem fully convincing,[67] and even if agreeing that the EC is bound by the Security Council resolution to the same extent that its Member States are,[68] it is debatable whether the CFI had to limit its jurisdiction the way it did.

A first possible critique concerns the fact that the Court sought to apply a very low international standard of legality, that is, the CFI's reading of *jus cogens*—something that may be read as a *sui generis* application of the

[65] M Nettesheim, 'UN Sanctions against Individuals: A Challenge to the Architecture of European Union Governance' (2007) 44 CML Rev 567.

[66] See eg P Eeckhout, 'Community Terrorism Listings, Fundamental Rights, and UN Security Council Resolutions: In Search of the Right Fit' (2007) 3 EuConst 183; Nettesheim, ibid. 567. For a more favourable review of the judgment, see eg E Spaventa, 'Fundamental What? The Difficult Relationship between Foreign Policy and Fundamental Rights' in M Cremona and B de Witte (eds), *EU Foreign Relations Law: Constitutional Fundamentals* (Hart: Oxford, 2008) 238–42.

[67] CFI *Kadi* [253]. To this end, the CFI relies extensively by analogy on *International Fruit*, where the ECJ had to rule on whether the Community was bound by the GATT: In [245], [246], [250], [251], [253]. Case 21/72 *International Fruit Company and others/Produktschap voor Groenten en Fruit* [1972] ECR 1219. Yet the analogy cannot be complete: Member States had totally surrendered the competences covered by the GATT, something that has not happened as regards the competences covered by the UN Charter. See also D Halberstam and E Stein, 'The United Nations, the European Union, and the King of Sweden: Economic Sanctions and Individual Rights in a Plural World Order' (2009) 46 CML Rev 13, 48 with further references on functional succession in this area.

[68] On the different underlying assumptions, see also C Tomuschat, 'Annotation to Yusuf and Kadi' (2007) 43 CML Rev 537, 543.

political questions doctrine.[69] A second and more general critique concerns the fact that the Court sought to apply international standards of legality only, skewing domestic ones. Public international law instruments do not have a claim as to how they penetrate a domestic legal system;[70] this depends on the domestic legal system itself.[71] Typically as well, public international law instruments bind the domestic polity—but when applying such an instrument, the national court is not under a national law obligation to ignore the domestic constitution if there is a conflict between them.[72] Of course, the national court may cause the international responsibility of the state to arise,[73] but it is not under a direct obligation to apply the international instrument that conflicts with the national constitution, and in practice nobody would expect it to do so.[74] The CFI chose, however, not to deal in this way with the conflict between EC and international law.

[69] The Court lowers the standards in an attempt to protect the political prerogative of the Security Council. In doing so, however, the CFI fails to distinguish between a political decision (the existence of a threat to peace and security and how to deal with it) and a legal one (the respect for the constitutional limits set to that political decision): S Griller, 'International Law, Human Rights and the European Community's Autonomous Legal Order: Notes on the European Court of Justice Decision in Kadi' (2008) 4 EuConst 528, 539–40. For an examination of the standard of *jus cogens* used by the CFI see also: T Tridimas and JA Gutierrez-Fons, 'EU Law, International Law, and Economic Sanctions Against Terrorism: The Judiciary in Distress?' (2009) 32 Fordham Int LJ 660, 689–98; C Tomuschat, 'Annotation to Yusuf and Kadi' (2007) 43 CML Rev 537, 547–51.

[70] The CFI referred to the EC legal order as the domestic legal system: eg CFI *Kadi* [178], [180].

[71] For a non-comprehensive overview of the relationship between international and domestic law, A Cassesse, 'Modern Constitutions and International Law' 192 1985-III Hague Recueil des Cours 331; F Jacobs and S Roberts (eds), *The Effects of Treaties in Domestic Law* (Sweet and Maxwell: London, 1987); T Buergenthal, 'Self-executing and Non Self-executing Treaties in National and International Law' 235 1992-IV Hague Recueil des Cours 303.

[72] It is worth remembering how the Polish constitutional court annulled the national law that implemented an EU law measure (the EAW framework decision) because it did not accord with its constitution (albeit delaying the effects of the judgment so that the legislature could solve the conflict by amending the constitution in the meantime). The latitude given by the framework decision to the national legislator did not allow for a constitutional implementation in any case; the case is therefore comparable to the present, where the EC legislator had no discretion to change the content of the UN resolution in any way. See Section 2.2.2.6; Trybunal Konstytucyjny (Polish Constitutional Court), Judgment of 27 April 2005, No. P 1/05 [2006] 1 CMLR 36.

[73] M Claes, *The National Courts' Mandate in the European Constitution* (Hart: Oxford, 2006) 167–8.

[74] This is the duty imposed upon national courts that deal with a conflict between national and EC law, also called the *Simmenthal* duty.

It seems that (arguably mistakenly) the CFI viewed the primacy of public international law in the same way as the primacy of EC law: as an obligation imposed directly on national courts, the so-called *Simmenthal* duty or obligation to disapply national law that conflicts with EC law.[75] That is why it referred to *Internationale Handelsgesellschaft*,[76] where the ECJ stressed that Community law cannot be reviewed for compatibility with national fundamental rights standards. Two objections can be raised: first, it can be argued that the UN law–EC law relationship should not be compared to the EC law–national law relationship, but to the EU law–national law one. EC law has stronger features that distinguish it from orthodox public international law. Second, by the time of *Internationale Handelsgesellschaft* the EC legal system had accepted fundamental rights as a general principle of law and was prepared to protect them.[77] It was therefore reasonable to ask the domestic legal systems to relinquish their control in favour of a system with an equivalent mechanism of protection of fundamental rights—something not present in this case.

On their part, Advocate General Maduro and the ECJ took a radically different approach to the relationship between EC and international law in the appeal.[78] AG Maduro emphasized the autonomy and separateness of the EC legal order, 'a municipal order of transnational dimensions' with its own constitutional charter.[79] He conceded that 'the application and interpretation of Community law is [...] guided by the presumption that the Community wants to honour its international commitments',[80] but he

---

[75] On the contrary, the ECJ—despite its use of monist terminology—has always made sure that international law acts pass thorough controls before being allowed applicability within the EU legal system. M Nettesheim, 'UN Sanctions against Individuals: A Challenge to the Architecture of European Union Governance' (2007) 44 CML Rev 567, 582. For a general overview of the legal effects of international law instruments within the EU legal system, P Eeckhout, *External Relations of the European Union: Legal and Constitutional Foundations* (OUP: Oxford, 2004) 274–344.

[76] Case 11/70 *Internationale Handelsgesellschaft mbH v Einfuhr- und Vorratstelle für Getreide und Futtermittel* [1970] ECR 1125.

[77] C Tomuschat, 'Annotation to Yusuf and Kadi' (2007) 43 CML Rev 537, 544.

[78] Appeals were brought by Mr Kadi and the Al-Barakaat foundation: Joined Cases C-402/05 P and 415/05 P *Yassin Abdullah Kadi, Al Barakaat International Foundation v Council and Commission* [2008] ECR I-6351. Mr Yusuf withdrew his claim after being removed from the UN list in the meantime: A Gattini, 'Annotation: Joined Cases C-402/05 P & 415/05 P, *Yassin Abdullah Kadi, Al Barakaat International Foundation v Council and Commission*, judgment of the Grand Chamber 2008, nyr' (2009) 46 CML Rev 213, 216.   [79] Opinion of AG Maduro in *Kadi* [21].

[80] Ibid, [22].

took a decidedly dualist approach to how these international obligations take effect within the EC legal order: 'The relationship between international law and the Community legal order is governed by the Community legal order itself, and international law can permeate that legal order only under the conditions set by the constitutional principles of the Community'.[81] Ultimately, AG Maduro urged the Court to act as a national constitutional court by safeguarding the integrity of the domestic constitutional framework: since there was nothing in the EC legal order that granted immunity to Security Council resolutions, the measure at stake had to be reviewed for compliance with EC standards of fundamental rights. Of special note is AG Maduro's explicit rejection of the political questions doctrine in this context.[82]

The Court of Justice followed the Advocate General's dualist approach, choosing to emphasize the autonomy of the EC legal order and asserting its role as gate-keeper. AG Maduro seemed to have assumed that the EC was in fact bound by Article 103 of the UN Charter, but did not discuss the point further than mentioning the fact that this may cause the international responsibility of the EC to arise;[83] the ECJ, on its part, did not engage directly with the rank or significance of the international norms at stake, and simply acknowledged the fact that the EC is traditionally open to international law.[84] It also denied categorically that an international agreement could affect the allocation of powers fixed by the Treaties, or the autonomy of the EC legal system.[85] Further, within the EC legal order,

---

[81] Ibid, [24].

[82] Ibid, [34]. AG Maduro cited the dissenting opinion of J Murphy in the *Korematsu* case (US Supreme Court): 'Like other claims conflicting with the asserted constitutional rights of the individual, [that] claim must subject itself to the judicial process of having its reasonableness determined and its conflicts with other interests reconciled. What are the allowable limits of [discretion], and whether or not they have been overstepped in a particular case, are judicial questions.' United States Supreme Court, *Korematsu v United States*, 323 US 214, 233–4 (1944) (Murphy J, dissenting).   [83] Opinion of AG Maduro in *Kadi* [39].

[84] G De Búrca, 'The European Court of Justice and the International Legal Order after Kadi' Jean Monnet Working Paper 01/09 http://www.jeanmonnetprogram.org/papers/09/090101. html (accessed March 2009), 34. The Court did briefly acknowledge the significance of UN Security Council resolutions, and stated that their reasons and objectives should be taken into account when interpreting the EC measures that implement them: ECJ *Kadi* [294], [296].

[85] ECJ *Kadi* [282]. The Court counterfactually referred to 'the place that obligations under the Charter of the United Nations would occupy in the hierarchy of norms within the Community legal order if those obligations were to be classified in that hierarchy' [305]: by virtue of Art 300 (7) EC, UN Charter obligations would rank higher than secondary EC law, but lower than the EC Treaties and the general principles of EC law [306]–[308].

Articles 307 and 297 EC cannot 'be understood to authorise any deroga-tion from the principles of liberty, democracy and respect for human rights and fundamental freedoms enshrined in Article 6(1) EU as a foundation of the Union'.[86] The Court argued that reviewing an EC measure imple-menting a Security Council resolution would not amount to reviewing the Security Council resolution itself, and that even annulling the EC measure would not affect the primacy of the UN resolution as a matter of interna-tional law.[87] Having thus drawn a clear line between the effects of UN resolutions as a matter of international law, on the one hand, and on their effects within the EC legal order, on the other, it set out to review the Council regulation for compliance with EC standards. The measure was found to have breached the right of defence, in particular the right to be heard, and the right to judicial review. It was therefore annulled, insofar as it concerned the applicants.[88]

In a display of 'constitutional confidence',[89] the approach taken by the Court of Justice is that of a domestic constitutional court that sees itself as gate-keeper of the domestic legal order.[90] Whereas the Court has always played the role of guarantor of 'the constitutional framework created by the Treaty' internally,[91] *Kadi* may be read as the Court's way of showing that it

---

[86] ECJ *Kadi* [303]. Ziegler points out a possible hierarchy between derogable and non-derogable constitutional principles of the EU; the former would include the market freedoms: K Ziegler, 'Strengthening the Rule of Law, but Fragmenting International Law: The Kadi Deci-sion of the ECJ from the Perspective of Human Rights' (2009) 9 HRLRev 288.

[87] ECJ *Kadi* [288].

[88] Although the effects of the judgment were delayed by three months, so as to allow the EC Council to remedy the breach. The Commission decided, after hearing representations from both applicants, that it was justified to include them again on the list: EC Regulation 1190/2008 of 28 November 2008 [2008] OJ L322/25. On the effects of the annulment: T Tridimas and JA Gutierrez-Fons, 'EU Law, International Law, and Economic Sanctions against Terrorism: The Judiciary in Distress?' (2009) 32 Fordham Int LJ 660, 702–5.

[89] An expression used by T Tridimas and JA Gutierrez-Fons, ibid.

[90] Halberstam and Stein point out that this is not the first time the Court acts as a domestic court, since it has often considered the applicability of international law within the EC legal order (eg Case 104/81 *Hauptzollamt Mainz v CA Kupferberg Cie KG a.A.* [1982] ECR 3641), but that 'the clarity with which the Advocate General and the Grand Chamber defend the primacy of the European legal order vis-à-vis international law is remarkable nonetheless': D Hal-berstam and E Stein, 'The United Nations, the European Union, and the King of Sweden: Economic Sanctions and Individual Rights in a Plural World Order' (2009) 46 CML Rev 13, 47.

[91] Opinion of AG Maduro in *Kadi* [24]. He cites, *inter alia*, Opinion 2/94 [1996] ECR I-1759 [30], [34]–[35].

is willing or able to perform the same function against external interferences. In so doing, it has been compared to the US Supreme Court,
which has recently resisted the interference of international norms with the
US system of criminal justice.[92]

The Court's zeal has of course attracted the criticisms of many commentators who would have preferred the Court to act as a gate-keeper that
applies international law standards of legality as well, rather than only
internal ones: after all, the Court of Justice is in a privileged position to
engage with the international legal order in a responsible manner, contributing to the development of the international rule of law.[93] Although it
would have been desirable for the ECJ to additionally assert that the
Security Council's practices were not consistent with international human
rights law either, this might have been too much to expect at a time when
the Union's legal order is still in the process of asserting its autonomy: the
Court was accordingly more intent on emphasizing such autonomy in its
judgment.

Incidentally, the judgment does not clarify whether the Court would
consider a *Solange*-type of arrangement in the future (something explicitly
proposed by AG Maduro),[94] if the UN system could guarantee an
equivalent level of protection to that of the EC legal order. While the
Court seems to exclude this, it may be that we should not take such
exclusion at face value: again, the Court may have found it necessary to
assert the external autonomy of the legal order in the strongest terms
possible—especially to 'correct' the CFI's take on the matter—but this

---

[92] *Medellin v Texas* 552 US 128 s Ct 1346 (2008); *Sanchez-Llamas v Oregon* 548 US 331 (2006);
Breard v Greene 523 US 371 (1998). Also, the US Supreme Court has long sustained the view that
the Bill of Rights takes precedence over any international treaty: *Reid v Covert* 354 US 1, 15–
16 (1957).

[93] eg D Halberstam and E Stein, 'The United Nations, the European Union, and the King of
Sweden: Economic Sanctions and Individual Rights in a Plural World Order' (2009) 46 CML
Rev 13; A Gattini, 'Annotation: Joined Cases C-402/05 P & 415/05 P, Yassin Abdullah Kadi, Al
Barakaat International Foundation v Council and Commission, judgment of the Grand Cham-
ber 2008, nyr' (2009) 46 CML Rev 213; G De Búrca, 'The European Court of Justice and the
International Legal Order after Kadi' Jean Monnet Working Paper 01/09 http://www.jean-
monnetprogram.org/papers/09/090101.html (accessed March 2009).

[94] Opinion of AG Maduro in *Kadi* [54]: 'Had there been a genuine and effective mechanism of
judicial control by an independent tribunal at the level of the United Nations, then this might
have released the Community from the obligation to provide for judicial control of implementing measures that apply within the Community legal order. However, no such mechanism
currently exists.'

could change once such autonomy is well settled.[95] At any rate, the Court was anxious to emphasize its role as the constitutional/supreme court of an autonomous and new legal order against that of other international courts such as the European Court of Human Rights, upholder of a classic international agreement.[96] And finally, the Court of Justice also seems to take a stance against the use of the political questions doctrine to exclude this sort of anti-terrorism legislation from judicial control,[97] insisting in its refusal to relinquish its position as guarantor of the constitutional framework of the Community.

Although the Court may have left itself open to criticism because of its inward-looking stance and the conflicting obligations that Member States now face,[98] the judgment does represent an improvement in terms of judicial protection and the need to build a coherent legal system based on the rule of law. The CFI's approach, on the contrary, may have led to a possible reprimand by the European Court of Human Rights.[99] As we will now see, it also would have led to an unjustifiably unequal treatment of cases where economic sanctions against individuals are the result of the implementation of a UN list, on the one hand, and where the sanctions follow autonomous listing at Union level, on the other.

Cases where the applicants are included in a list that is the result of autonomous drafting at Union level have also been arriving in a steady flow before the EU courts. The crucial distinction is that, in the absence of UN listing such as the one at stake in *Yusuf* and *Kadi*, the CFI has treated them as reviewable against EC human rights standards, considerably higher than

---

[95] This is, however, a medium- to long-term observation; the Court's stance is not likely to change in the pending cases of *Ayadi* and *Hassan*, which involved UN listing as well and were decided by the CFI on the same grounds as *Yusuf* and *Kadi*: Cases C-403/06 P *Ayadi v Council*, pending; C-399/06 P *Hassan v Council and Commission*, pending.

[96] The ECJ engaged with the ECtHR's case-law on the same issue, while making it clear that the legal premisses at stake differed widely: *Kadi* [310]–[314] and [315]–[318]. B Kunoy and A Dawes, 'Plate Tectonics in Luxembourg: The Ménage à Trois between EC Law, International Law and the European Convention on Human Rights Following the UN Sanctions Cases' (2009) 46 CML Rev 73, 78–80. On the ECtHR's approach to the UN Charter: T Tridimas and JA Gutierrez-Fons, 'EU Law, International Law, and Economic Sanctions against Terrorism: The Judiciary in Distress?' (2009) 32 Fordham Int LJ 660, 685–9.

[97] An issue explicitly addressed by AG Maduro in his Opinion, [33]–[35].

[98] As a result of *Kadi*, Member States can neither implement the UN Security Council Resolution through the EC nor on their own, to the extent that such domestic implementation falls within the scope of EC law. Whereas the Court did not mention this, AG Maduro did so explicitly in his Opinion [30], [39].

[99] A Hinarejos, 'Bosphorus v Ireland and the Protection of Fundamental Rights in Europe' (2006) 31 ELR 251, with further references.

jus cogens standards. In *Organisation des Modjahedines du Peuple d'Iran (OMPI)*,[100] the CFI had to review an EC Council decision that contained an autonomous list that was comparable in all other respects to the one at stake in *Yusuf* and *Kadi*. This was the first case where the CFI annulled a Community measure freezing an individual's assets,[101] and it did so after stating, in a very nuanced analysis, that the EC rights to a fair hearing, to a fair trial, and to effective judicial protection are, as a matter of principle, fully applicable.[102] The Court went on to clarify that the Council's wide discretion in this field means that judicial review must be 'restricted to checking that the rules governing procedure and the statement of reasons have been complied with, that the facts are materially accurate, and that there has been no manifest error of assessment of the facts or misuse of power';[103] the measure did not meet the test.[104] Several other cases followed: in *Al-Aqsa, Sison, Kongra-Gel*, and *PKK*,[105] the CFI annulled the EC measure at stake because of a breach of defence rights and the right to

[100] Case T 228/02 *Organisation des Modjahedines du Peuple d'Iran* [2006] ECR II-4665 ('*OMPI*').

[101] Almost a year earlier, the CFI had dismissed the action in *PKK* because of lack of standing. This was appealed successfully before the ECJ and when the matter came back to the CFI (this time already after *OMPI*), the latter annulled the EC measure at stake: T-229/02 *PKK and KNK v Council* [2005] ECR II-539 (Order); C-229/05 P *PKK and KNK v Council* [2007] ECR I-439; T-229/02 *PKK and KNK v Council* [2008] ECR II-45.

[102] *OMPI* [91]–[111]. The Court distinguished this case from *Yusuf* and *Kadi*: *OMPI* [99]–[108].   [103] *OMPI* [159].

[104] The measure breached the right to a hearing, the duty to state reasons, and the right to judicial review: *OMPI* [165]. See generally C Eckes, 'Annotation to Case T-228/02, Organisation des Modjahedines du peuple d'Iran v Council and UK (OMPI), Judgment of the Court of First Instance (Second Chamber) of 12 December 2006' (2007) 44 CML Rev 1117. For an in-depth analysis of the CFI's application of the right to a hearing, duty to state reasons and the right to judicial protection: T Tridimas and JA Gutierrez-Fons, 'EU Law, International Law, and Economic Sanctions against Terrorism: The Judiciary in Distress?' (2009) 32 Fordham Int LJ 660, 709–20.

[105] Cases T-327/03 *Sitchting Al-Aqsa v Council* [2007] ECR II-79; T-47/03 *Jose Maria Sison* [2007] ECR II-73; T-229/02 *PKK and KNK v Council* [2008] ECR II-45; T-253/04 *Kongra-Gel and Others v Council* [2008] ECR II-46. Eckes and Spaventa have expressed concern as to the limited scope of review. The scope of defence rights and of judicial review varies depending on whether an initial decision on listing or a decision on continuing to include a name on the list is at stake. In any event, the substantive review of reasons for the initial inclusion is a matter left to national courts: C Eckes, 'Sanctions against Individuals: Fighting Terrorism within the European Legal Order' (2008) 4 EuConst 205, 213–18; E Spaventa, 'Fundamental What? The Difficult Relationship between Foreign Policy and Fundamental Rights' in M Cremona and B de Witte (eds), *EU Foreign Relations Law: Constitutional Fundamentals* (Hart: Oxford, 2008) 248–51. See also T Tridimas and JA Gutierrez-Fons, 'EU Law, International Law, and Economic Sanctions against Terrorism: The Judiciary in Distress?' (2009) 32 Fordham Int LJ 660, 711 and ff.

judicial review (albeit not granting any damages when asked to do so). It should be borne in mind that all of these applicants were relisted after the judgments in subsequent Council Decisions,[106] and some of them have brought new actions before the CFI to challenge the new measure.[107] The first batch of successful challenges was not, however, without consequence, since they led to a number of changes in the Union's sanctioning practices.[108]

Finally, all cases discussed until now concerned a challenge to the EC implementation of a CFSP common position. By contrast, the CFI was also asked in *Selmani* and *OMPI* to review the validity of such a common position directly. Unsurprisingly, the Court only deemed itself competent to check whether a CFSP common position should have been adopted under the EC Treaty (that is, the limited scope of Article 47 TEU). Since the measure had been properly adopted under the CFSP, no further review followed. It has been mentioned before that the TEU does not contemplate the review of common positions, be they adopted under the second or third pillar: neither directly, through an action for annulment, nor indirectly, by giving a preliminary ruling to a national court that is dealing

---

[106] Council Decision 2007/868/EC of 20 December 2007 implementing Art 2(3) of Regulation (EC) No 2580/2001 on specific restrictive measures directed against certain persons and entities with a view to combating terrorism and repealing Decision 2007/445/EC [2007] OJ L340/100; Council Decision 2008/583/EC of 15 July 2008 implementing Art 2(3) of Regulation (EC) No 2580/2001 on specific restrictive measures directed against certain persons and entities with a view to combating terrorism and repealing Decision 2007/868/EC [2008] OJ L188/21; the latest one is Council Decision 2009/62/EC of 26 January 2009 implementing Art 2(3) of Regulation (EC) No 2580/2001 on specific restrictive measures directed against certain persons and entities with a view to combating terrorism and repealing Decision 2008/583/EC [2009] OJ L23/25. The latest Council Decision (January 2009) has finally delisted OMPI; all other applicants are still listed.

[107] A new action brought by OMPI was dismissed in part by the CFI: Case T-256/07 *People's Mojahedin Organization of Iran v Council* Judgment of 23 October 2008. The appeal is now pending before the ECJ: C-576/08 P *People's Mojahedin Organization of Iran v Council*, pending. The latest action brought by OMPI (T-284/08 *People's Mojahedin Organization of Iran v Council* Judgment of 4 December 2008, nyr) was successful in finally making the Council delist OMPI (see n 106). See also the new actions brought by Al-Aqsa and Sison: T-348/07 *Al-Aqsa v Council*, pending; T-341/07 *Sison v Council*, pending.

[108] On these changes: C Eckes, 'Sanctions against Individuals: Fighting Terrorism within the European Legal Order' (2008) 4 EuConst 205, 206–7, 218–20. For the specific safeguards that have been introduced, see also Notice for the attention of the persons, groups and entities on the list provided for in Art 2(3) of Council Regulation EC No. 2580/2001 on specific restrictive measures directed against certain persons and entities with a view to combating terrorism [2007] OJ C144/01; Council Document 10826/07 on the fight against the financing of terrorism: implementation of common position 2001/931/CFSP of 21 June 2007 [17] and ff.

with the common position and seeks guidance on its validity. It therefore came as no surprise at the time that the CFI refused to review directly the common position at issue, or that it did not offer an alternative remedy. The CFI had already come to a similar conclusion in *Segi*,[109] where another common position (this time adopted jointly under second and third pillar legal bases) with an annexed list of terrorist organizations had been at stake.

The CFI's decision in *Segi* was, however, appealed before the European Court of Justice after the CFI had decided on *Selmani* and *OMPI*.[110] The ECJ took a different approach to the reviewability of common positions, pointing the applicants towards an alternative remedy and extending judicial control in the intergovernmental pillars of the Union.[111] But the Court considered that the common position at stake was a third pillar measure insofar as it affected the applicant, and it is thus doubtful that the solution adopted by the Court in *Segi* (the extension of Article 35 TEU to cover the indirect review of common positions that affect the rights of third parties) would be applicable to the second pillar also.[112]

3.4 The Jurisdiction of the ECJ Under the Lisbon Treaty

Although the Lisbon Treaty integrates the CFSP into the general structure of the Union to a certain extent, it does not extend fully fledged judicial control to this area. The Court is granted some additional powers to control the validity of sanctions against individuals but it is not set to become a central player in the CFSP, unlike in the AFSJ. There is, if anything, a difference of approach to the limited role of the Court in the CFSP: on the one hand, the general rule within Title V TEU is that the Court has no role to play, and Article 47 TEU (the 'policing the borders' provision) is a clear exception. On the other hand, the Lisbon Treaty places the CFSP within the same general framework of Union policies, and part

---

[109] Case T-338/02 *Segi and others v Council* [2004] ECR II-1647.

[110] Cases C-355/04 P *Segi* [2007] ECR I-1657; T 228/02 *Organisation des Modjahedines du Peuple d'Iran* [2006] ECR II-4665 and the Order in T-299/04 *Selmani* [2005] ECR II-20.

[111] See Section 2.3.2.1.

[112] See further C Hillion and R Wessel, 'Restraining External Competences of EU Member States under CFSP' in M Cremona and B de Witte (eds), *EU Foreign Relations Law: Constitutional Fundamentals* (Hart: Oxford, 2008) 90–1.

of this general framework is that the Court has full competence. This is not the case within the CFSP because of an explicit exception in the Treaty:[113]

Article 275 TFEU

The Court of Justice of the European Union shall not have jurisdiction with respect to the provisions relating to the common foreign and security policy nor with respect to acts adopted on the basis of those provisions.

However, the Court shall have jurisdiction to monitor compliance with Article 40 of the Treaty on European Union and to rule on proceedings, brought in accordance with the conditions laid down in the fourth paragraph of Article 263 of this Treaty, reviewing the legality of decisions providing for restrictive measures against natural or legal persons adopted by the Council on the basis of Chapter 2 of Title V of the Treaty on European Union.

A shift of perspective may thus take place: the lack of ECJ jurisdiction, currently a general rule, is framed as an explicit exception within the framework of the Lisbon Treaty, where judicial control is otherwise all-pervasive. Although this shift may have limited practical effects, it is also possible that the Court will feel enabled to interpret the 'CFSP exception' narrowly. Be that as it may, the following sections will reflect on the different aspects of the Court's jurisdiction under the Lisbon Treaty, starting with the questions of whether the Court is in a position to enforce the primacy of CFSP measures and how it will police the borders between the CFSP and other policies. Sections 3.4.3 and 3.4.4 will consider the Court's competence to review restrictive measures against individuals and international agreements, respectively.

3.4.1 Primacy

We have already seen how one of the main effects of the envisaged reform is that primacy is arguably extended to the whole of Union law. A different matter is whether the ECJ has the jurisdiction to guarantee that this principle is upheld within the CFSP.

Article 275 LT precludes the jurisdiction of the Court 'with respect to the provisions relating to the common foreign and security policy [and] with respect to acts adopted on the basis of those provisions'. The 'exceptions to the exception' concern only the Court's duty to police the borders of the CFSP and to control restrictive measures against individuals.

---

[113] The contents of Art 275 TFEU are also echoed, albeit in more general terms, in Art 24 TEU.

Although primacy, as a theoretical claim, would be extended to CFSP measures, it seems that the ECJ would not be able to enforce it in practice: that is, if a national court is faced with a conflict between a CFSP measure and a measure of national law, it will not be able to ask for a preliminary ruling because the ECJ is not competent to interpret the CFSP measure.[114] Two main consequences arise from this: first, it will be up to national courts to decide to what extent CFSP measures are accorded primacy over measures of national law within their Member State, since the ECJ will not be there to impose or remind national courts of their *Simmenthal* duty within the framework of the preliminary ruling procedure. And second, different national courts are bound to take different approaches to the primacy of CFSP measures, resulting in fragmentation of the way Union law is applied across the Member States.

Within the framework of an earlier discussion on the same issue, this time as regulated in the failed Constitutional Treaty, it was argued in the literature that primacy should not be deemed to apply in the CFSP in the absence of a preliminary ruling procedure.[115] The same argument could indeed be extended to the Lisbon Treaty. Yet it seems that we should rather distinguish between primacy as a theoretical claim of the EU legal order, on the one hand, and the practical effects of primacy, generally ensured by the ECJ within the framework of the preliminary reference procedure. The CFSP would have the first one, but not the second one. This may lead to unsatisfactory results such as the fragmentation of EU law, but this has been a feature of the CFSP until now, and one that is likely to remain for the near future. On the whole, the fact that primacy (as a theoretical claim of EU law) applies to CFSP measures within the framework of the Lisbon Treaty may not necessarily have a great impact on the

---

[114] Although it was possible to make the contrary argument in relation to the forebear of the Lisbon Treaty, the Constitutional Treaty, where Art III-376 left room to argue that the Court was, in theory, competent to give guidance in these situations. Of course, in practice it would have been difficult (if not impossible) for the Court to give guidance on the issue of primacy of CFSP measures without overstepping the limits of its jurisdiction. For a fuller argument (now only of historical interest), see A Hinarejos, 'Judicial Control of CFSP in the Constitution: A Cherry Worth Picking?' (2006) 25 YEL 363, 368–9.

[115] EU Committee of the House of Lords, 'The Future Role of the European Court of Justice. Report with Evidence' (6th Report of Session 2003–4, HL Paper 47) 16; Editorial, 'The CFSP under the EU Constitutional Treaty: Issues of Depillarization' (2005) 42 CML Rev 325, 326–7. On the contrary, Denza assumed that Art I-6 applied to CFSP: E Denza, 'Common Foreign Policy and Single Foreign Policy' in T Tridimas and P Nebbia (eds), *European Union Law for the Twenty-First Century: Rethinking the New Legal Order* (Hart: Oxford, 2004), 267–8.

practical effects and status that CFSP measures have at the moment, in the absence of mechanisms to enforce such a claim.[116]

3.4.2 Policing the Borders

Article 275 TFEU foresees, as an 'exception to the exception' that the Court shall be able to police Article 40 TEU (after LT), which reads as follows:

> The implementation of the common foreign and security policy shall not affect the application of the procedures and the extent of the powers of the institutions laid down by the Treaties for the exercise of the Union competences referred to in Articles 3 to 6 of the Treaty on the Functioning of the European Union.
> Similarly, the implementation of the policies listed in those Articles shall not affect the application of the procedures and the extent of the powers of the institutions laid down by the Treaties for the exercise of the Union competences under this Chapter [CFSP].

This provision is the successor of Article 47 TEU,[117] whereby the ECJ currently polices the borders between the intergovernmental pillars and the competences of the Community. There are some differences between these provisions: the first one is that, contrary to its counterpart in the Lisbon Treaty, Article 47 TEU could be understood to give power to the Court to check the compliance of (properly adopted) CFSP measures with the EC Treaty, an argument that has been studied in more depth in a previous section.[118] This is because Article 47 TEU merely states that 'nothing in this Treaty shall affect the Treaties establishing the European Communities', whereas Article 40 TEU (after LT) refers specifically to 'the application of the procedures and the extent of the powers of the institutions' laid down in the TEU and the TFEU. It has been argued that, within the CFSP, the current Article 47 TEU should not be read as single-handedly granting the Court competence to review CFSP measures for compliance with EC rules in the absence of any review mechanism in the area; in any case, this possibility would now be precluded in the Lisbon Treaty.

The second difference is that, within the framework of the Lisbon Treaty, the borders would be set between the CFSP and all other Union policies,

---

[116] Similarly, AG Bot has argued in his Opinion in *Kozlowski* that the principle of primacy applies, in theory, in the third pillar, but that there are no mechanisms to enforce it apart from indirect effect or the duty of conform interpretation: Opinion of AG Bot in Case C-66/08 *Kozlowski* [2008] ECR I-6041 [115] and ff. The Court did not address the issue.

[117] Which falls within the jurisdiction of the Court by means of Art 46 TEU.

[118] See Sections 2.3.2.5 (third pillar) and 3.3.1 (second pillar).

where the Community method applies fully, rather than between the intergovernmental pillars and the EC pillar. In both cases, the application of the Community method seems to be the underlying distinction.[119]

Finally, whereas Article 47 TEU established the primacy of EC competences over EU ones, Article 40 TEU (after LT) seems to accord them equal weight. Its aim would be not to safeguard the *acquis communautaire* as much as to prevent mutual interference between the CFSP and any other policy. It should nevertheless be borne in mind that the Court already ensures under Article 230 EC that no measure is inappropriately adopted under the EC pillar when it should have had an intergovernmental legal basis.[120] The 'two-way street' of Article 40 TEU (after LT) can thus be seen as the fusion of two functions the Court has already been exercising under two different Treaty headings: it has protected EC competences from EU encroachment under Article 47 TEU, but it has also performed the converse task by enforcing the principle of conferral of powers and without the need to invoke Article 47 TEU. In practice, the difference would be that, in a situation such as the one at stake in *ECOWAS*, where the Court recognizes that the measure has two equally central aims or components, one falling within the scope of the CFSP and another one falling within another area of EU competence, a literal reading of Article 40 TEU would not necessarily supply us with the necessary conflict rule to choose one legal basis over the other.[121]

---

[119] An identical clause to Art 40 TFEU (after LT) had already been included in the Constitutional Treaty (Art III-308 Constitutional Treaty). Several members of the Convention expressed their concern that, if a safeguard equivalent to that of Art 47 TEU was not included in the Constitution, there would be 'a risk that acts relating to the former Community pillar would now be taken on the basis of procedures applicable to CFSP. Others expressed concern about "communitarising" CFSP, i.e. that decisions on issues covered by CFSP would be taken by applying rules of former first pillar areas.' 'Draft sections of Part Three with comments' (CONV 727/03. The European Convention. Praesidium, 2003) 52. This view was shared by the Discussion Circle on the Court of Justice in its Supplementary Report: 'Supplementary report on the question of judicial control relating to the common foreign and security policy' (CONV 689/1/03 REV 1. The European Convention. Discussion Circle on the Court of Justice, 2003).

[120] As in eg Joined Cases C-317/04 and C-318/04 *Parliament v Council and Commission* [2006] ECR I-4721 (PNR Agreement).

[121] Cremona has argued that an EC legal basis should still be chosen over a CFSP one: M Cremona, 'A Constitutional Basis for Effective External Action? An Assessment of the Provisions on EU External Action in the Constitutional Treaty' (2006) 30 EUI Working Paper http://cadmus.eui.eu/dspace/handle/1814/6293 (accessed March 2009), 20–1. See also J Heliskoski, 'Small Arms and Light Weapons within the Union's Pillar Structure: An Analysis of Article 47 of the EU Treaty' (2008) 33 ELR 898, 911–12.

3.4.3 The Protection of Individuals against Restrictive Measures

Within the framework of the Lisbon Treaty, the Court is given jurisdiction to control the validity of restrictive measures against individuals adopted under the CFSP. We will first consider the legal basis for these restrictive measures and their evolution, before examining the scope of the jurisdiction of the Court and the way in which it should be exercised.

3.4.3.1 The Legal Basis for Restrictive Measures; Evolution

Until now, restrictive economic measures against individuals have been adopted following a two-tier process: first, the Union adopts a CFSP common position; second, EC instruments are used to implement it. Articles 60 and 301 EC have been interpreted widely in order to allow for the adoption of restrictive measures against persons or associations that exercise control over a third country, following a CFSP common position. Article 308 EC has been added as a third joint basis in order to adopt economic sanctions against individuals who do not exercise control over a country.[122] On the other hand, restrictive non-economic measures (visa bans) have always addressed individuals in control of a third country, and they have been included in a common position and directly imposed by Member States.[123]

Within the framework of the Lisbon Treaty, Article 215 TFEU[124] (the successor of Article 301 EC) offers an explicit legal basis within the CFSP

---

[122] 'Judicial control relating to the common foreign and security policy' (Working Document 10. The European Convention. Secretariat, 2003) 2. On the adoption of restrictive measures against individuals who do not exercise control of a country using Arts 60, 301, and 308 EC, see Cases T-315/01 *Yassin Abdullah Kadi v Council and Commission* [2005] ECR II-3649; T-306/01 *Yusuf and Al Barakaat International Foundation v Council and Commission* [2005] ECR II-3533; Joined Cases C-402/05 P and 415/05 P *Yassin Abdullah Kadi, Al Barakaat International Foundation v Council and Commission* [2008] ECR I-6351; D Halberstam and E Stein, 'The United Nations, the European Union, and the King of Sweden: Economic Sanctions and Individual Rights in a Plural World Order' (2009) 46 CML Rev 13, 35–42; A Gattini, 'Annotation: Joined Cases C-402/05 P & 415/05 P, Yassin Abdullah Kadi, Al Barakaat International Foundation v Council and Commission, judgment of the Grand Chamber 2008, nyr' (2009) 46 CML Rev 213, 218–21, 223–4.

[123] See eg Council Common Position 2002/145/CFSP of 18 February 2002 concerning restrictive measures against Zimbabwe [2002] OJ L50/01, Annex and Arts 3–4. Art 62 EC could possibly be used to impose a visa ban as well, but in practice it has never happened; arguably this provision covers general decisions on visas and third countries, but not specific visa bans on individuals: M Cremona, F Francioni, and S Poli, 'Challenging EU Counter-Terrorism Measures through the Courts' EUI Working Paper (forthcoming).

[124] Art 215(2) TFEU: 'Where a decision adopted in accordance with Chapter 2 of Title V of the Treaty on European Union so provides, the Council may adopt restrictive measures under the procedure referred to in paragraph 1 against natural or legal persons and groups or non-State entities. [...] The acts referred to in this Article shall include necessary provisions on legal safeguards.'

for the adoption of restrictive measures (economic or not) against individuals with no control over a third country. This means that the Treaty acknowledges and supersedes the debate on competences that was at stake in *Kadi*, where it was unclear whether the EC Treaty allowed the Community to implement restrictive economic measures against individuals that do not have control of a state—a question that both the CFI and the ECJ answered in the affirmative, if for different reasons. Arguably the Treaty goes further than *Kadi* by foreseeing also the adoption of restrictive non-economic measures in the same circumstances.[125] The scope of the competence for the adoption of sanctions against individuals at European level thus continues to grow, even after *Kadi*.

Additionally, the Lisbon Treaty foresees the adoption of economic sanctions against individuals, this time within the AFSJ Title, under Article 75 TFEU,[126] the successor of Article 60 EC. Although the distinction between both provisions will have to be further clarified in the future, it is foreseeable that the CFSP legal basis (Article 215(2) TFEU) will be used to deal with 'external terrorism' (although EU citizens or organizations may be included, if the source of the listing is external—that is, stemming from the UN), and the AFSJ legal basis (Article 75 TFEU) will be used to deal with 'internal terrorism'.[127] This interpretation would also sit well with the

---

[125] These provisions have been kept on from the Constitutional Treaty. For an in-depth study of the evolution of these provisions from the works of the Convention to the Constitutional Treaty, see A Hinarejos, 'Judicial Control of CFSP in the Constitution: A Cherry Worth Picking?' (2006) 25 YEL 363, 378–83.

[126] Art 75 TFEU: Where necessary to achieve the objectives set out in Article 67, as regards preventing and combating terrorism and related activities, the European Parliament and the Council, acting by means of regulations in accordance with the ordinary legislative procedure, shall define a framework for administrative measures with regard to capital movements and payments, such as the freezing of funds, financial assets or economic gains belonging to, or owned or held by, natural or legal persons, groups or non-State entities. The Council, on a proposal from the Commission, shall adopt measures to implement the framework referred to in the first paragraph. The acts referred to in this Article shall include necessary provisions on legal safeguards.

[127] M Cremona, F Francioni, and S Poli, 'Challenging EU Counter-Terrorism Measures through the Courts' EUI Working Paper (forthcoming). Art 75 TFEU would then enable the Union to adopt restrictive economic measures against 'wholly internal' terrorism (the targets are domestic and the Union listing is autonomous rather than following UN listing), something that has not been done until now because of the 'foreign policy slant' of the current Arts 301 and 60 EC: rather, the Union has merely listed 'domestic' organizations, but no asset-freezing has been imposed by the Community (the situation at stake in *Segi*). See further C Eckes, 'Sanctions against Individuals: Fighting Terrorism within the European Legal Order' (2008) 4 EuConst 205, 201–11; E Spaventa, 'Fundamental What? The Difficult Relationship between Foreign Policy and Fundamental Rights' in M Cremona and B de Witte (eds), *EU Foreign Relations Law: Constitutional Fundamentals* (Hart: Oxford, 2008) 234–5, 238.

fact that a visa ban is possible under Article 215(2) TFEU (external) but not under Article 75 TFEU (internal). Needless to say, the decision between these two legal bases may often not be clear-cut. At any rate, Article 75 TFEU is not a CFSP provision and is thus fully subject to the standard jurisdiction of the Court; this section will only focus on the adoption of restrictive measures under the CFSP.

Under the Lisbon Treaty, then, the Council will be able to adopt CFSP decisions that foresee restrictive measures against individuals, be they economic or non-economic, under Chapter 2 of Title V TEU (after LT), on 'Specific Provisions on the Common Foreign and Security Policy' (hereafter 'CFSP Chapter'). These measures may then be implemented by more specific Council decisions imposing economic sanctions on individuals under Article 215 TFEU. To some extent, this system seems to mirror the current one, where a general CFSP common position is then implemented by an EC measure. Additionally, it is still possible that some CFSP decisions adopted under the above-mentioned CFSP Chapter and which provide for restrictive measures against individuals may be implemented directly by the Member States, as it is presently the case within the TEU with CFSP common positions that foresee visa bans.

3.4.3.2 *The Jurisdiction of the Court*

As a general observation, a first reading of Article 275 TFEU highlights the positive evolution that this provision has undergone from the draft Constitutional Treaty to the Constitutional Treaty and, finally, the Lisbon Treaty. After all, the draft CT allowed only the review of implementing measures imposing economic sanctions on individuals (Article III-282 draft CT).[128] At the other end of the spectrum, the Lisbon Treaty foresees the

---

[128] The Discussion Circle on the European Court of Justice could not reach an agreement on whether the Court should have jurisdiction to review restrictive measures which affect individuals other than from an economic point of view: 'Supplementary Report on the Question of Judicial Control Relating to the Common Foreign and Security Policy' (CONV 689/1/03 REV 1. The European Convention. Discussion Circle on the Court of Justice, 2003) 3. Accordingly, this was not included in the draft Constitutional Treaty submitted to the President of the European Council in Rome on 18 July 2003. It is in the Basic Document containing editorial and legal comments on the draft Treaty which the IGC Secretariat sent to the Working Party of IGC Legal Experts that the main changes were introduced: 'Editorial and Legal Comments on the Draft Treaty Establishing a Constitution for Europe: Basic Document' (CIG 4/03. Conference of the Representatives of the Governments of the Member States. IGC Secretariat, 2003) 436. For an overview of this evolution, see A Hinarejos 'Judicial Control of CFSP in the Constitution: A Cherry Worth Picking?' (2006) 25 YEL 363.

review of implementing and non-implementing decisions, be they economic or non-economic. These are of course welcome and necessary improvements in the future regulation of an area where measures are increasingly targeting or affecting the rights of individuals. It would have been unacceptable for the Union to be able to adopt restrictive non-economic measures against individuals that cannot be challenged before the Court; it would have been equally objectionable to restrict the Court's powers of review to implementing Union measures, in light of the fact that the Council may adopt CFSP (non-implementing) decisions that may be directly implemented by Member States—something that is routinely done at the moment in the case of visa bans.[129]

Yet this is not to say that Article 275 TFEU is necessarily straightforward or unproblematic. The first paragraph of Article 275 TFEU states that the Court shall not have jurisdiction with respect to 'the provisions relating to the common foreign and security policy nor with respect to acts adopted on the basis of those provisions'. On the face of it, this provision seems to exclude from the Court's jurisdiction both CFSP decisions adopted directly under the CFSP Chapter of the TEU and the decisions adopted to implement them under Article 215 TFEU. Although this is the most logical reading, it is not without its problems, and a different one may be possible or even desirable.

It should be remembered that adopting implementing measures under Article 215 TFEU has been equated with adopting EC measures to implement a CFSP common position under Articles 301/60/308 EC at present. Under this current mechanism, the general measure is a CFSP one, which is afterwards implemented by a more specific first pillar regulation; to some extent, this mechanism has been kept on in the Lisbon Treaty. In terms of judicial control, the current cross-pillar mechanism translates into the following: whereas the general CFSP measure cannot normally be challenged,[130] the implementing EC measure can be challenged through the normal avenues offered by the EC Treaty (that is, both direct and indirect review). Within the Lisbon Treaty, however, this

---

[129] See eg Council Common Position 2002/145/CFSP of 18 February 2002 concerning restrictive measures against Zimbabwe [2002] OJ L50/01, Annex and Arts 3–4.

[130] Although *Segi* allows for the review of common positions that have legal effects for third parties, it is doubtful that this may apply to a CFSP common position: the common position at stake in *Segi* was treated by the Court as a third pillar measure insofar as it affected the applicants, and Art 35 TEU (the channel through which such common positions may be challenged, according to the Court) only applies, in principle, to the third pillar.

pattern seems to have been changed: both general and implementing decisions are, to start with, outside the jurisdiction of the Court.

The second paragraph of Article 275 TFEU goes on to say that the Court may review directly (that is, under Article 263 TFEU) 'the legality of decisions providing for restrictive measures against natural or legal persons adopted by the Council on the basis of Chapter 2 of Title V of the Treaty on European Union'. Presumably, this could cover both CFSP decisions adopted directly under this Chapter as well as the Council decisions implementing them, adopted under Article 215 TFEU,[131] if necessary. Consequently, it could be argued that interpreting the first paragraph of Article 275 TFEU as putting both implementing and non-implementing decisions outside the jurisdiction of the Court is not a departure, in practice, from the current cross-pillar mechanism, because both types of measures are afterwards brought back in via the second paragraph, or the 'exception to the exception'. Yet this 'exception to the exception' has a limited scope, and it only allows the Court to deal with direct actions brought by individuals with the necessary standing. Accordingly, this reading would have the somewhat surprising effect of reducing the current jurisdiction of the Court in two ways.

First, the second paragraph of Article 275 TFEU is only open to individuals, but not to any privileged applicants. On the contrary, the current implementing measures adopted under Articles 60, 301, and 308 EC can be challenged not only by individuals, but also by a Member State, the European Parliament, the Council and the Commission, according to Article 230 EC.

Second, a literal reading of the same paragraph would indicate that the only action available to individuals is a direct one (under Article 263 TFEU), whereas current implementing measures adopted under Articles 60, 301, and 308 EC may be reviewed indirectly through the preliminary reference procedure.

Such a reduction of the scope of the Court's jurisdiction would be unfortunate. One of its consequences would be to leave implementing measures against third countries outside the jurisdiction of the Court: Article 215 TFEU may be used, just like Articles 60 and 301 EC at present, to adopt implementing measures interrupting or reducing economic

---

[131] This provision evolved substantially from the draft Constitutional Treaty to the Constitutional Treaty and, finally, the Lisbon Treaty. The main difference is that the draft Constitutional Treaty allowed only the review of implementing measures imposing economic sanctions on individuals (Art III-282 draft Constitutional Treaty).

relations with a third country generally, rather than against named individuals. These measures may at present be challenged by a Member State, the European Parliament, the Council, or the Commission (since individuals are not likely to have standing, even if collaterally affected).[132] They may also be reviewed indirectly through the preliminary reference procedure. If, within the framework of the Lisbon Treaty, these measures are outside the jurisdiction of the Court to start with, they may only be brought back in through Article 275 TFEU, which seems to offer only a direct action to individuals. Contrary to the current situation, individuals may be able to prove standing to bring a direct action against a general measure of this kind, if they can prove that it affects them directly; disappointingly, privileged applicants would be excluded.

Even when considering measures that do provide for sanctions against individuals rather than against third countries, it would seem unfortunate to adopt a reading of the TFEU that would reduce the jurisdiction that the Court has at present by allowing for direct review only of implementing measures adopted under Article 215 TFEU, while within the current cross-pillar pattern implementing measures adopted under Articles 60, 301, and 308 EC can be reviewed both directly (through Article 230 EC) and indirectly (through the preliminary ruling procedure).

Thus the most logical or literal reading of Article 275 TFEU is one that, in fact, reduces the current jurisdiction of the Court in certain aspects. To avoid this, it would be possible for the Court to interpret the first paragraph of this provision as only affecting CFSP decisions adopted directly under the CFSP Chapter of the TEU, but not the decisions adopted to implement them under Article 215 TFEU. This would mean that the latter are covered by the normal powers of the Court, because they were never part of the 'CFSP exception' to start with: as a result, decisions adopted directly under the CFSP could be reviewed only directly, whereas implementing decisions adopted under Article 215 TFEU could be challenged both directly by privileged applicants or individuals with standing, and indirectly. Such an interpretation would be in keeping with the historical evolution of Article 275 TFEU: its forebear in the Constitutional Treaty had a more specific wording and put only 'the provisions of Chapter II of Title V concerning the common foreign and security policy'[133] outside the

---

[132] eg Cases C-84/95 *Bosphorus Hava Yollari ve Ticaret AS v Minister for Transport, Energy and Communications, Ireland and the Attorney General* [1996] ECR I-3953; C-162/96 *A. Racke GmbH & Co. v Hauptzollamt Mainz* [1998] ECR I-03655.   [133] Art III-376 Constitutional Treaty.

jurisdiction of the Court: this earlier wording would seem to include CFSP acts adopted under the CFSP Chapter, but not their implementation (adopted under a provision outside said chapter).

Alternatively, the Court could interpret the second paragraph of Article 275 TFEU extensively, and thus granting it not only powers of direct review (which would be the most literal interpretation) but also of indirect review, through the preliminary ruling procedure.[134] This reading would allow individuals to review both decisions adopted directly under the CFSP and implementing decisions adopted under Article 215 TFEU directly and indirectly, but it would not be completely satisfactory to the extent that privileged applicants would remain excluded.

Finally, the Court could do both: interpret the second paragraph of Article 275 TFEU as only 'bringing back in' CFSP decisions (presupposing that their implementing acts would not be excluded from the Court's jurisdiction in the first place), but also as allowing for both direct and indirect review of such CFSP decisions. This would be the widest reading possible of the Court's jurisdiction.[135]

Ultimately, it seems unlikely that the Court would adopt a reading of the Lisbon Treaty that diminishes its current jurisdiction. It is far more probable that the Court would (rightly) hang on to its powers to review measures implementing a CFSP act in an indirect manner, as well as to deal with direct actions brought by privileged applicants against such implementing measures, and that the only change that Article 275 TFEU would bring would be to expand the Court's jurisdiction by allowing individuals to challenge not only the implementing measure that imposes a sanction on them following a CFSP measure, but also the CFSP measure itself. The next section will briefly revisit the reform of the standing rules for individuals put forward in the Lisbon Treaty.

3.4.3.3 Standing

Article 263(4) TFEU establishes that an individual may 'institute proceedings against an act addressed to that person or which is of direct and

---

[134] This was already Tridimas' interpretation of the predecessor of Art 275(2) TFEU in the draft Constitution (Art III-282(2)): T Tridimas, 'The European Court of Justice and the Draft Constitution: A Supreme Court for the Union?' in T Tridimas and P Nebbia (eds), *European Union Law for the Twenty-First Century: Rethinking the New Legal Order* (Hart: Oxford, 2004) 128.

[135] At least initially; it may be also be discussed whether the action for failure to act and the action for damages could be made available in the future within the scope of Art 275(2) TFEU.

individual concern to them, and against a regulatory act which is of direct concern to them and does not entail implementing measures'.

It has already been pointed out that 'regulatory acts' could be taken to mean 'all Union acts of general application', an interpretation that would drastically widen the access of individuals to the Court. It seems, however, that the Convention had something different in mind when originally drafting this provision for its inclusion in the Constitutional Treaty. Both this document and its successor, the Lisbon Treaty, distinguish elsewhere between legislative and non-legislative acts,[136] and its seems clear from the preparatory works that the Convention seemed to use 'regulatory acts' in the sense of 'non-legislative acts of general application'. [137]

Article 31 TEU (after LT) excludes the adoption of legislative decisions within the CFSP.[138] As a result, all CFSP measures (or at least those adopted under Title V TEU) are bound to be non-legislative decisions taken generally by the European Council and the Council unanimously. For the purposes of standing of individuals, this leaves us with two scenarios: in the first one, an individual wishes to challenge a CFSP decision with national implementing measures.[139] In that case, the individual must still prove direct and individual concern. In the second scenario, however, the individual wishes to challenge a CFSP measure without national

---

[136] Arts 290 and 297 TFEU refer to 'non-legislative acts', whereas Arts 263(4) and 207 TFEU refer to 'regulatory acts'.

[137] It seems that the distinction between legislative and regulatory acts was used for the first time in CONV 572/03, 10 March 2003, and CONV 575/03, 10 March 2003. Throughout the ensuing discussion, the term 'regulatory act' seems to be used as a synonym for 'non-legislative act of general application'. For an overview of the terminology in the preparatory works, see J Bering Liisberg, 'The EU Constitutional Treaty and its Distinction between Legislative and Non-legislative Acts: Oranges into Apples?' Jean Monnet Working Paper 01/06 http://www. jeanmonnetprogram.org/papers/06/060101.html (accessed January 2009), 37–9.

[138] Except in cases foreseen in the second paragraph of the same provision.

[139] 'Implementing measures', as referred to by Art 263(4) TFEU, must be taken to refer to the existence of national implementing measures and not those adopted at Union level, given that the background of this provision points towards the will to liberalize access to the Court and to avoid situations like those encountered in *UPA* and *Jégo-Quéré*, where individuals could not resort to an indirect challenge because there was no national implementing measure they could challenge before national courts. The existence of implementing measures at Union level (ie under Art 215 TFEU in this case) does not have any relevance in this regard. The 'implementing measures' referred to in Art 230(4) TFEU are thus different from those adopted by the Council under Art 188k(2): the reason to apply (b) or (c) is whether national implementing measures have been adopted, and it would be indifferent whether the Council has been called upon to implement this European decision at Union level: Cases C-50/00 *Unión de Pequeños Agricultores v Council* [2002] ECR I-6677; C-263/02 *Commission v Jégo-Quéré* [2004] ECR I-03425.

implementing measures; according to the new test laid down in Article 263 (4) TFEU, he or she would only have to prove direct concern.

The same rules would apply in order to challenge an implementing decision adopted under Article 215 TFEU, since these measures are also regulatory (they are not adopted following the legislative procedure, neither ordinary nor extraordinary).[140]

3.4.3.3.1 The Relationship between Jurisdiction and Standing.

Article 275 TFEU grants jurisdiction to the Court in a very limited field ('decisions providing for restrictive measures against natural or legal persons adopted by the Council on the basis of Chapter 2 of Title V of the Treaty on European Union'). These words determine the scope of the Court's jurisdiction and, as such, they will have to be interpreted by the Court in a step prior to examining the question of standing. Two plausible interpretations deserve mention: on the one hand, 'restrictive measures against natural or legal persons' could be taken to refer to measures which name individuals,[141] in which case the standing question would have been preempted, since it would be logical to allow only the named individuals (or 'real addressees', as opposed to formal ones)[142] to challenge the measure. On the other hand, the Court could consider itself competent to review the legality of any CFSP measure that happens to have a restrictive effect on an unnamed individual's rights, if he or she can satisfy the standing rules. The upshot is that, by adopting a very strict interpretation of the limits of its jurisdiction under Article 275 TFEU, the Court could prejudge the question of standing. On the other hand, it could also adopt a more relaxed interpretation of Article 275 TFEU that ultimately depends on whether an individual can satisfy the rules of standing. It will be necessary to wait and see whether the Court places the *crux* of the question on the scope of its jurisdiction or on the standing test.

---

[140] According to Art 215 TFEU, the Council acts by a qualified majority on a joint proposal from the High Representative of the Union for Foreign Affairs and Security Policy and the Commission. The European Parliament shall be informed.

[141] The most obvious example would be the 'terror lists' that have been studied at length in the previous section (regardless of whether the list has been autonomously drafted or is the implementation of a UN list).

[142] In all cases named above, the people whose names are on a list cannot be considered formal addressees, as clarified by the CFI and ECJ in *Kadi*: the prohibition contained in the regulation at stake was 'addressed to whoever might actually hold the funds or economic resources in question' ECJ *Kadi* [244].

As a general observation, it is unlikely that the Court will take to itself the competence to review directly measures of a general (regulatory) nature adopted under the CFSP Chapter on the basis that the decision affects individuals' rights in a very vague fashion. On the contrary, the ECJ has a long record of being extremely cautious when it comes to allowing the challenge of a Community measure by non-privileged applicants, and one can also expect great awareness of the political delicacy of the field in question, even in the face of laxer standing rules. Yet a very strict approach to the letter of Article 275 TFEU—allowing only for measures that name their 'real addressees' to be challenged—may be problematic. It is well known that the Court has taken a strict stance on allowing individuals to challenge measures of EC law directly, but this has only been justifiable to the extent that an indirect path remained open to individuals in the guise of Article 234 EC.[143] When it comes to CFSP measures that affect individuals within the framework of the Lisbon Treaty, however, direct review through the channel of Article 275 TFEU may be the only remedy available, and it would therefore be desirable for the Court to adopt an approach that is as conducive to judicial protection as possible. This would change if the Court adopted an extensive reading of Article 275 TFEU that allowed it to exercise powers of indirect review as well.

It will also be recalled that it is not yet clear whether implementing decisions adopted under Article 215 TFEU will be considered as placed outside the jurisdiction of the Court via Article 275(1) TFEU but brought back in via the second paragraph of the same provision, or within the jurisdiction of the Court from the beginning (that is, unaffected by the first paragraph of Article 275 TFEU). This may be significant if the Court adopts a very restrictive interpretation—both as regards the kind of measure that may be reviewed, and as to whether indirect review is possible—of the second paragraph of Article 275 TFEU. In that case, only if Article 215 TFEU is deemed to be within the jurisdiction of the Court per se—rather than because of Article 275 TFEU—would it be possible for an individual to challenge an implementing measure that does not name him explicitly: because laxer rules would apply to a direct action, but also because an indirect challenge would remain possible.

There are further factors—arising out of the unique context in which the Court has shaped and continues to shape the legal order over which it

---

[143] See eg 294/83 *Parti Écologiste 'Les Verts' v European Parliament* [1986] ECR 1339 [23]; C-50/00 *Unión de Pequeños Agricultores v Council* [2002] ECR I-6677.

presides—which could, in the future, push the Court towards an extensive interpretation of its powers. On the one hand, because the Court may wish to avoid external scrutiny by the European Court of Human Rights. On the other, because thorough protection on a case-by-case basis could make national constitutional courts refrain from controlling CFSP measures in certain cases. Both of these possibilities will be considered in detail in Section 3.5.

3.4.4 Judicial Control of International Agreements

According to Article 37 TEU (after LT), '[t]he Union may conclude agreements with one or more States or international organisations in areas covered by this Chapter' (Chapter 2, 'Specific Provisions on the CFSP', of Title V TEU, 'General Provisions on the Union's External Action and Specific Provisions on the CFSP'). Contrary to the current provision authorizing the Union to conclude CFSP agreements,[144] Article 37 TEU (after LT) does not lay down itself a specific procedure applicable to this kind of agreement. As a result, the rules for the conclusion of all international agreements found in Article 218 TFEU apply.[145] This provision foresees, in paragraph 11, that:

> A Member State, the European Parliament, the Council or the Commission may obtain the opinion of the Court of Justice as to whether an agreement envisaged is compatible with the Constitution. Where the opinion of the Court of Justice is adverse, the agreement envisaged may not enter into force unless it is amended or the Constitution is revised.[146]

This paragraph would bring CFSP international agreements within the scope of the Court's jurisdiction. Article 218 TFEU itself does not consider CFSP agreements an exception in this respect, whereas it does so explicitly in others: it sets out special rules on the opening of negotiations

---

[144] Art 24 TEU. This provision lays down the powers of the Union, the decision-making procedure and the effects of CFSP agreements. It grants no powers to the Court of Justice, with the result that the question of whether the Court can give a prior opinion on the validity of a CFSP agreement does not arise at present.

[145] Art 218(3) TFEU does lay down some specific rules on the negotiation of a CFSP agreement: 'The Commission, or the High Representative of the Union for Foreign Affairs and Security Policy where the agreement envisaged relates exclusively or principally to the common foreign and security policy, shall submit recommendations to the Council, which shall adopt a decision authorising the opening of negotiations and, depending on the subject of the agreement envisaged, nominating the Union negotiator or the head of the Union's negotiating team.'

[146] This mechanism is currently found (for EC agreements only) in Art 300(6) EC.

(paragraph 3) and it establishes that the Parliament's consent is not necessary (paragraph 6).

We have already seen, however, that Article 275 TFEU excludes from the Court's jurisdiction all provisions relating to the CFSP, as well as 'acts adopted on the basis of these provisions'. The wording of this exception seems to include CFSP agreements, since they would be adopted under the basis of Article 37 TEU (a 'CFSP provision') rather than under Article 218 TFEU, a non-CFSP specific provision that does not provide for a legal basis but establishes only a procedure for adoption. On the other hand, this is a conclusion that seems at odds with the working documents of the Convention that dealt with the matter:[147] according to these documents, it is possible to argue that it was the drafters' intention to make CFSP agreements amenable to judicial review. It is at any rate unfortunate that the wording of such a crucial provision as Article 275 TFEU should be ambiguous. The catalogue of exceptions to judicial review should be unequivocal, closed, and conducive to legal certainty—something that the language of Article 275 TFEU has arguably failed to attain.

3.5 What the CFSP is Missing and its Consequences

3.5.1 The Role of the ECJ

The jurisdiction of the Court of Justice under the CFSP Chapter within the framework of the Lisbon Treaty has been the focus of the previous section: although the specific scope of its powers will have to be clarified in future case-law, Article 275 TFEU allows the Court to review the substance of CFSP acts only in those cases where an individual that is affected by a restrictive measure decides to challenge it.[148]

Additionally, it has been argued that the original drafters' intention was to allow for the a priori judicial control of international agreements adopted in the realm of the CFSP. Yet this is in contradiction with a literal reading of the Lisbon Treaty, which seems to exclude such agreements from the jurisdiction of the Court. This exclusion seems unfortunate; allowing privileged applicants to ask the Court to control the legality of

---

[147] For an in-depth study of the Convention documents, see A Hinarejos, 'Judicial Control of CFSP in the Constitution: A Cherry Worth Picking?' (2006) 25 YEL 363, 376–8 with further references.

[148] Assuming that Art 275 TFEU is taken to exclude the prior review of CFSP agreements.

these agreements before they become law would appear reasonable. In general, allowing for some sort of judicial control of the legality of international agreements would seem to be more in keeping with the traditions of the Member States: in France, for example, the Constitution foresees that the Conseil Constitutionnel will exercise a preventive control in reviewing the constitutionality of international agreements before they are ratified by Parliament and occupy their place in the legal hierarchy.[149] In Germany, although the legality of international agreements cannot be challenged directly, the Bundesverfassungsgericht ensures the constitutionality of the implementing laws.[150] It should however be borne in mind that, to the extent that it is foreseeable that primacy in CFSP matters may be reduced to a theoretical claim, CFSP measures may in fact be reviewed by national courts for compliance with national standards. The lack of constitutional review at Union level of CFSP measures for compliance with Union standards goes, however, to the question of internal coherence of a legal system. At any rate, although an extensive reading of the jurisdiction of the Court seems desirable in this respect, it would remain to be seen how the Court chooses to deal with this issue in the future.

For now, then, the powers of the Court under the CFSP Chapter would be restricted, under a literal reading of Article 275(2) TFEU, to those specific cases where an aggrieved individual brings a complaint or direct action. In broad terms, the main aim of this sort of procedure is to repair or avoid the breach of an individual's rights, and it is directly linked to the role of courts as guarantors of fundamental rights. To the extent that the Court considers itself competent in the future to review the sort of CFSP measure that is likely to affect an individual's rights directly, it may successfully function as a guarantor of rights in specific cases within the CFSP.

Yet this is not the only aim that a system of judicial review normally seeks to fulfil. Some European constitutional courts may function as guarantors of fundamental rights in specific cases, but what they all have in

---

[149] Art 54 of the French Constitution foresees the review of international agreements by the Conseil Constitutionnel. Art 55 places international agreements above all other norms of legal rank, but below the Constitution itself. See further 'Draft Report on the Legal Foundation for Foreign Policy and Appendix' (CDL-DI(1997)001e-rev-restr. Council of Europe. Venice Commission, 1997).

[150] Either through the *Abstrakt Normenkontrolle* (Art 93(2) *Grundgesetz*, available to privileged applicants only) or through the *Konkrete Normenkontrolle* (Art 100 *Grundgesetz*, whereby ordinary courts refer a question on the validity of a law that is central to a case pending before them). cf generally M Schweitzer, *Staatsrecht III* (8th edn, CF Müller Verlag: Heidelberg, 2004) 267–72.

common in any case is that they strive to build a coherent legal system, ensure uniformity of interpretation, and act as an arbiter in case of conflict (in federal systems not only horizontal but also vertical conflict, that is, between the centre and the states). These will be referred to as 'general aims', because they concern the legal system as a whole and go further than protecting the rights of a specific individual. These general aims can also be realized, to a certain extent, if the constitutional court is faced with an individual's complaint: insofar as the court is necessarily interpreting the rules it applies to a specific complaint in a certain way, it is also shaping the legal system and ensuring uniformity. If, for example, the individual argues that there was no competence to adopt the measure at stake, a competent court would have to address the balance of powers to be struck between the different levels of the system. Yet, within the framework of an individual complaint, all these general aims will only be realized to the extent that they are relevant to the individual's situation. Other avenues, not open to aggrieved individuals but to privileged applicants or ordinary courts, are better suited to achieve such general aims.

To return to the examples used above, both the German and the French legal system foresee the abstract review of foreign policy measures, allowing their courts to address the more abstract aims of, among others, ensuring the coherence of the legal system or safeguarding the competence division. Thus the Conseil Constitutionnel reviews measures of legal rank a priori and in the abstract for their compliance with the Constitution.[151] Equally, the Bundesverfassungsgericht may conduct an abstract review of constitutionality of legislation, prompted either by privileged applicants or by an ordinary court; such review typically concerns compliance with the constitutional provisions on fundamental rights, competence, and the aims of the state or *Staatszielbestimmungen*.[152]

In the case of the ECJ, general aims may be better fulfilled through preliminary rulings, infringement proceedings, etc.—yet the Court, at least under a literal reading of the Lisbon Treaty, is bereft of these powers within the CFSP. Of course, general aims may be fulfilled, to some extent,

---

[151] This control includes, but is not restricted to, ensuring conformity in the abstract with the Declaration of the Rights of Man and of the Citizen (*Déclaration des droits de l'homme et du citoyen*, 1789), and with the Preamble to the Constitution of 1946. Both documents are cross-referenced in the Preamble to the Constitution of 1958; this Preamble grants them the same legal status that it itself enjoys. B Dickson, *Introduction to French Law* (Pitman Publishing: London, 1994) 82.

[152] cf generally M Schweitzer, *Staatsrecht III* (8th edn, CF Müller Verlag: Heidelberg, 2004) 267–72.

through the direct action contained in Article 275 TFEU, but this is bound to be contingent upon the directly affected individual bringing an action, and these aims are likely to be dealt with only to the extent that they are relevant to the individual's situation. Finally, the scope of Article 275 TFEU is not only reduced to individual actions; let us not forget that this provision allows only a particular kind of individual action that, although ultimately depending on the interpretation of the Court, is likely to be very narrowly defined.

The fact that the Court can only fulfil any of the functions of constitutional review on a case-by-case basis does not have to be problematic in itself; after all, concrete review is one of the main features of the US system of judicial review, and many consider it less problematic from the point of view of separation of powers.[153] Yet the ECJ's situation seems different because of two factors: first, because it sits at the apex of a centralized system of review of Union law, as opposed to the US system where all courts may exercise constitutional review on a case-by-case basis. And second, because the ECJ's powers are not just limited to concrete review, but to concrete review of direct actions brought by individuals in a narrowly defined range of cases. Both factors decrease the number of occasions on which constitutional adjudication will take place.

Accordingly, although it remains to be seen how actively the Court strives to fulfil more general aims (such as building and shaping a coherent legal system) within the CFSP, it is bound to be very limited in this endeavour by the narrow channel through which it will have to operate. As a result, the Court of Justice may act as a guarantor of rights in specific situations in this area, but it will not be able to act as a fully fledged constitutional court. Finally, it has already been argued that, in practice, CFSP measures may end up being reviewed by national courts for compliance with national standards. Nevertheless, the lack of a wider power of review at the EU level impairs the internal coherence of the legal system of the EU, something that national courts are not in a position to address.

---

[153] For a general discussion of why concrete review is less problematic, W Sadurski, *Rights before Courts: A Study of Constitutional Courts in Postcommunist Countries in Central and Eastern Europe* (Springer: Dordrecht, 2005) 65–74. On judicial minimalism and its critique, see respectively C Sunstein, *One Case at a Time: Judicial Minimalism on the Supreme Court* (Harvard University Press: Cambridge, 1999); O Fiss, 'The Perils of Minimalism' (2008) 9 Theoretical Inquiries 643.

3.5.2 *The National Comparison*

When considering the restricted competence of the European Court of Justice to review acts adopted pursuant to the CFSP, it is often pointed out that national courts also enjoy a very limited jurisdiction over foreign policy and defence matters at the national level. Yet the jurisdiction of national courts to review foreign policy issues varies indeed widely from one system to the other. At one end of the spectrum, the so-called 'political questions doctrine' submits that issues of foreign policy must remain outside the scope of judicial control exercised by any national court. This doctrine finds its most clear expression in judicial abdication in the USA.[154] European states, on their part, have set out different approaches to judicial control in this field. Once again, the German and French cases may provide a useful term of comparison: a cursory glance at these two national legal systems yields the conclusion that, first, different approaches to this issue are possible at the national level, and second, it is not the case that the realm of foreign policy is necessarily subject to a sweeping exception to judicial control, for the mere reason of being foreign policy. In France as well as in Germany, judicial reasoning has tried to find more meaningful criteria to distinguish between areas where the courts' intervention is legitimate and necessary, and otherwise.

In the French case, we have already seen how the constitutionality of international agreements is ensured by the Conseil Constitutionnel. On the other hand, the control of non-legislative acts by the administrative courts in this area has undergone an interesting evolution:[155] originally, judges acted in accordance with the *théorie du mobile politique*, thus considering themselves not competent to control whether an act was lawful if there were political reasons behind its adoption.[156] This changed however when the Conseil d'État handed down its judgment on *Prince Napoléon* in 1875.[157] Although the Conseil abandoned at this point such doctrine, the notion of *acte de gouvernement* was to be kept. Albeit narrowing down the

---

[154] T Franck, *Political Questions/Judicial Answers: Should the Rule of Law Apply to Foreign Affairs?* (Princeton University Press: Princeton, 1992); L Henkin, *Foreign Affairs and the United States Constitution* (Clarendon: Oxford, 1996); L Henkin, 'Is there a "Political Question" Doctrine?' (1976) 85 Yale L J 597.

[155] Note that ordinary courts also exercise a so-called 'conventionality control': O Beaud, 'Reframing a Debate among Americans: Contextualizing a Moral Philosophy of Law' (2009) 7 I-CON 53, 60.

[156] CE, 1 May 1822, *Laffitte*; CE, 9 May 1867, *Duc d'Aumale* D. 1867.3.49.

[157] CE, 19 February 1875, *Prince Napoléon* D. 1875.3.18.

field that would escape judicial scrutiny, the Conseil recognized the existence of a series of measures that should remain out of its reach because of their political significance and delicacy. Unlike before, this range of measures did not include any act adopted on political grounds, but only those decisions of high governmental responsibility which require a high degree of sensitivity and knowledge in matters in which the courts are not competent to form a judgment.[158] Nowadays, this means acts concerning the relation of the executive with the legislative power and the conduct of international relations.[159] Nevertheless, control will be exercised when some aspect of an issue in the field of international relations has domestic effects that are severable from the conduct of foreign policy (*actes détachables*).[160] It seems that French courts are very cautious when dealing with foreign policy measures, and do not wish to interfere with the discretion of the executive in an unwarranted manner; yet they have also tried to find the necessary criteria to delineate the scope of non-justiciable activity.

The Bundesverfassungsgericht, on its part, has explicitly rejected the political questions doctrine and has considered it its duty, in principle, to control government activity in this area, if allowing for a very wide scope of discretion. In the *Saarstatut* case,[161] the German Court made it plain that it would not accept the Government's claim that the issue raised was essentially of a political nature and therefore nonjusticiable. The act in question was a treaty between the Federal Republic of Germany and France creating an especial status for the Saar. The Court asserted that the Treaty would be

---

[158] J Bell, S Boyron, and S Whittaker, *Principles of French Law* (OUP: Oxford, 1998) 179.

[159] TC 2 February 1950, *Radiodiffusion Française*. Thus the Conseil d'État refused to entertain an action brought by Greenpeace against the President's decision to resume a series of nuclear tests; in this case, it was impossible to separate this decision from the conduct of international relations: CE Ass. Plén. 29 September 1995, *Greenpeace*, AJDA 1995. 749. The same occurred when an action was brought to challenge the suspension of financial aid to Iraq: CE 23 September 1992, *GISTI-MRAP*, AJDA 1992 752.

[160] An *acte détachable* is, for example, the legality of a building permit granted to a foreign embassy: CE 22 December 1978, *Vo Thanh Nghia*, AJDA 1978. 4. 36. This category has been constantly enlarged: for instance, military activities unconnected with warlike operations are considered reviewable. TC 9 June 1986, *Eucat*, AJDA 1986. 456. The Conseil d'État followed this approach when deciding that it was competent to review a refusal of extradition from France of a Malaysian businessman, following a request placed by the British Government and the Governor of Hong Kong. The court considered that this refusal was severable from the conduct of foreign relations between France and the United Kingdom: CE 13 October 1993, *Royaume-Uni de Grande Bretagne et d'Irlande du Nord et Gouverneur de Hong Kong*, AJDA 1993. 886. It has been pointed out that the Conseil d'État has shown itself increasingly willing to apply this doctrine: J Bell and L Brown, *French Administrative Law* (Clarendon Press: Oxford, 1998) 139. See also CE 19 February 1988, *Societé Robatel*, AJDA 1988. 354.   [161] BVerfGE 4, 157.

amenable to judicial review just like any other piece of legislation, as long as the procedural requisites were complied with, and that the fact that the subject-matter concerned foreign policy did not place the issue outside the realm of judicial control altogether. The field of foreign policy must also comply with the requirements laid down by the *Grundgesetz* and, as ultimate guardian of the latter, the German Court considers its jurisdiction undisputable. The political questions doctrine was again rejected in the *Grundlagenvertrag* case,[162] where the Court declared that the meaning of the concept of *Rechtsstaat* made it impossible for the realm of international relations to be free of the constitutional limits imposed on political power at the domestic level. The fact that this affected all foreign-policy acts, and not only treaties, was pointed out in the *Rudolph Hess* case.[163] Finally, once the amenability for judicial review is established, the Court readily admits a far greater space for discretion left to the executive branch in the specific field of foreign policy. This responds to the peculiar essence of this sphere of action; the Constitution does not allow the Court to substitute the political choices of the Government for those of its own. It is in this restricted sense that the German Court interprets the meaning of 'judicial restraint',[164] and not as meaning that a court should not adjudicate when the executive branch determines that the issue at stake belongs to the field of foreign policy, the central tenet of the political questions doctrine.[165]

Although the German and French legal systems have adopted very different approaches in this field, it seems that, in both cases, judges are entrusted with the task of delineating the area where legal criteria are at hand. The argument can be made that there is no legal impediment—albeit

---

[162] BVerfGE 36, 1.

[163] BVerfGE 55, 349.

[164] 'Der Grundsatz des judicial self-restraint zielt darauf ab, den von der Verfassung für die anderen Verfassungsorgane garantierten Raum freier politischer Gestaltung offenzuhalten' BVerfGE 36, 1 (1). See generally E Petersmann, 'Act of State Doctrine, Political Question Doctrine und gerichtliche Kontrolle der auswärtigen Gewalt' (1976) 25 Jahrbuch des öffentlichen Rechts der Gegenwart NF 587; FC Zeitler, 'Judicial Review und Judicial Restraint gegenüber der auswärtigen Gewalt' (1976) 25 Jahrbuch des öffentlichen Rechts der Gegenwart NF 621. While allowing this exceptional discretion to the executive branch, the Court will check 'whether they went beyond the limits of their allotted discretion, or whether in their action they were guided by an erroneous belief about the legal constraints on their discretion': BVerfGE 55, 349, 354. The Court has added that it shall also control the means chosen to pursue a foreign-policy aim, and disallow them only if arbitrariness or bad faith can be proven: BVerfGE 55, 349, 366; double test used in BVerfGE 46, 160.

[165] For a general account, T Franck, *Political Questions/Judicial Answers: Should the Rule of Law Apply to Foreign Affairs?* (Princeton University Press: Princeton, 1992) 107–25.

strong political ones—why the same should not happen at the EU level. In fact, the approach has already been mirrored by the ECJ to the limited extent that it has had to deal with national measures that touched upon foreign policy. The Court has not shied away from such control, in spite of the nature of the measures.[166] AG Jacobs considered the question of justiciability at length in his Opinion in *Commission v Greece*,[167] freely acknowledging that the Court should not enter an area such that legal standards are not anymore at hand.[168] More recently, the Court of Justice implicitly resisted the urgings of the Commission, the Council, and the UK to consider the sort of anti-terrorism legislation at stake in *Kadi* as a political question that should remain outside the scope of judicial control. In so doing, the Court followed AG Maduro's explicit rejection of this approach.[169]

Furthermore, in comparing judicial control of foreign policy at the EU and at the national level, we should be aware of the fact that patterns of political (as opposed to judicial) oversight of executive action in the field of foreign policy differ widely between national legal systems, on the one hand, and the Union, on the other. In the first instance, judicial control is part of a system of checks and balances that includes political control, generally exercised by national parliaments.[170] This is, however, not

---

[166] C-124/95 *The Queen, ex parte Centro-Com Srl v HM Treasury and Bank of England* ECR [1997] I-81; C-120/94 *Commission v Greece* [1996] ECR I-3037.

[167] Opinion of AG Jacobs in *Commission v Greece*, ibid.

[168] On whether international law criteria are available, P Eeckhout, *External Relations of the European Union: Legal and Constitutional Foundations* (OUP: Oxford, 2004) 133; M Koskenniemi, 'International Law Aspects of the Common Foreign and Security Policy' in M Koskenniemi (ed), *International Law Aspects of the European Union* (Kluber Law International: The Hague, 1998).

[169] Opinion of AG Maduro in Joined Cases C-402/05 P and 415/05 P *Yassin Abdullah Kadi, Al Barakaat International Foundation v Council and Commission* [2008] ECR I-6351 [33]-[35].

[170] Albeit that the dominance of the executive is a common feature of contemporary political practice. In the case of France, it is for the Parliament to ratify all types of international agreements listed under Art 53 of the Constitution; the debate on the annual budget includes a vote on the appropriations to the Minister for Foreign Affairs which usually includes a debate on the broad directions that foreign policy should take; and, lastly, when the Prime Minister presents his or her action programme and seeks confirmation by Parliament, a large and crucial part of such programme is concerned with foreign policy: 'Draft Report on the Legal Foundation for Foreign Policy and Appendix' (CDL-DI(1997)001e-rev-restr. Council of Europe. Venice Commission, 1997). As regards Germany, apart from the general function of control and debate exercised by Parliament, both the Bundestag and Bundesrat are involved in the ratification of international treaties, and in some circumstances in the enactment of unilateral legal acts: For more information on the political oversight of foreign policy in Germany, see R Wolfrum, 'Kontrolle der auswärtigen Gewalt' (1997) 56 Veröffentlichungen der Vereinigung der Deutschen Staatsrechtslehrer 38.

applicable to the Union, given that, even in theory, there is no effective parliamentary control in matters of CFSP under the Lisbon Treaty, and political checks are only present in the form of the decision-making rules within the Council. What is a common thread in all systems is that the judicial role must be respectful of the political patterns of representation and accountability. If anything, the relative lack of these values in matters of CFSP means that a case could be made in favour of a more embracing role for the ECJ.

In reality, however, this is unlikely to happen. The CFSP has not attained the level of integration that other policies of the Union have. This is neither surprising nor likely to change in the near future, given that autonomy in foreign policy and defence matters is a crucial part of the core of the traditional conception of sovereignty. The lack of a more integrated policy explains the lack of a fully fledged constitutional court, a role that the Court of Justice is set to attain in the AFSJ and that it has already been playing in the first pillar for some time. At the same time, the fact that the Court cannot play this role within the CFSP means that it cannot push the integration process as it has done in other areas in the past.

It is not my intention to argue that further integration in this field is desirable; that is a matter for political discussion. It has been mentioned that the Member States are willing to cooperate in the future on what can be considered a quasi-intergovernmental basis: albeit including the CFSP within the single structure of the Union, the Lisbon Treaty does not impose on it the most important elements of what is currently termed the Community method. The contemporary challenges of a globalized world make it necessary and much more efficient for national governments to cooperate; in doing so, however, they are not subject to the controls of domestic politics. Insofar as the CFSP is a forum for such cooperation, the general argument can be made that it would be beneficial for the Union to impose certain controls on it, be they of a political or judicial nature. Although crucial, these are general problems of institutional design that go beyond the scope of this monograph. Instead, the next section will focus on two likely consequences of the very limited scope of judicial review at EU level in this area: on the one hand, national constitutional courts are likely to reject a hypothetical extension of the *Foto-Frost* principle, as well as the unconditional primacy of CFSP measures over national law (that is, not even to the extent that the primacy of EC law is de facto respected). On the other hand, Union actions under the CFSP may come under the unfavourable scrutiny of the European Court of Human Rights.

3.5.3 A Likely Response from National Constitutional Courts

As a result of the very limited system of remedies available at EU level within the CFSP, it has already been suggested that the *Foto-Frost* principle should not be deemed to apply in this area.[171] This section will further show that, if the *Foto-Frost* principle were deemed to apply, national constitutional courts would be bound to disobey it, causing an open conflict within the judicial system of the EU. Finally, if these courts do review CFSP measures, they are likely to deprive CFSP measures of primacy by applying national rather than EU standards.[172]

At the moment, some national constitutional courts could (at least as a matter of EU law) exercise an abstract control of CFSP measures for compliance with the national constitution, and ultimately leave these intergovernmental measures without effect within the territory of their Member State. The Lisbon Treaty and the 'default' extension of primacy would, in theory, put an end to this possibility, since CFSP measures could not be reviewed against national standards. The *Foto-Frost* principle would even go one step further, not allowing national courts to exercise any review—not even for compliance with EU standards.

To the extent that there is a channel for the judicial protection of individuals (and always, of course, depending on how the Court discharges this task), the Lisbon Treaty addresses the most pressing legal problem in this area. The lack of abstract control of CFSP measures at EU level,[173] however, is likely to drive some national constitutional courts to exercise their jurisdiction in the future, regardless of any duties imposed on them as a matter of EU law.

Two functions that are exercised by national constitutional courts within the framework of an abstract control of measures are of interest here: on the one hand, national courts may verify the compatibility of the measure with a hard core of general principles and fundamental rights embedded in the national constitution; on the other, they may verify whether a measure

---

[171] Arnull, for example, believes that *Foto-Frost* should not be deemed to apply in the absence of a preliminary ruling mechanism: A Arnull, *The European Union and its Court of Justice* (2nd edn, OUP: Oxford, 2006) 134–5.

[172] The main consequence of the primacy of EC law is that national standards (including the national constitution) cannot be applied as a standard of review of its legality. AG Mengozzi already argued in favour of allowing national courts to review Union measures according to Union standards in his Opinion in C-355/04 P *Segi* [2007] ECR I-1657.

[173] By 'abstract control' I am referring here to any constitutional review of a measure that does not come within the scope of an individual's direct action under Art 275 TFEU.

was properly adopted, in an area where there is the necessary competence to do so. Let us examine both functions in turn.

As regards ensuring the compatibility of legislation with a hard core of general principles and fundamental rights, a conflict between national constitutional courts and the ECJ would be nothing new: indeed, a similar feud contributed significantly to one of the most significant changes in EC constitutional law, where the resistance of several national courts to the primacy of EC law in the terms mapped out by the ECJ led to a change in the place of fundamental rights in the EC legal order.

It will be recalled that national constitutional courts have not recognized the unconditional supremacy of EC Law in the terms mapped out by the ECJ.[174] In some cases, the main worry of these courts was whether EC Law could breach fundamental rights guaranteed in the national constitution. The most famous example is that of the German Bundesverfassungsgericht, which decided that the transfer of powers to the EC could not amend an essential feature of the *Grundgesetz*, such as the protection of fundamental rights. In the *Solange* case,[175] the court claimed that:

[I]n the hypothetical case of a conflict between law and [...] the guarantees of fundamental rights in the Constitution, there arises the question of which system of law takes precedence, that is, ousts the other. In this conflict of norms, the guarantee of fundamental rights in the Constitution prevails as long as the competent organs of the Community have not removed the conflict of norms in accordance with the Treaty mechanism.[176]

In its later judgment *Solange II*,[177] however, the Court reconsidered the level of protection of fundamental rights within the legal system of the Community and decided that it was substantially similar to the one envisaged by the German constitution. It therefore claimed that it would 'no longer exercise its jurisdiction to decide on the applicability of secondary community legislation [...] and it [would] no longer review such legislation by the standard of the fundamental rights contained in the Constitution'.[178]

As has been rightly pointed out,[179] the Bundesverfassungsgericht did not find in this judgment that it lacked jurisdiction to review EC law according

---

[174] For a general account, cf S Weatherill, *Cases and Materials on EU Law* (8th edn, OUP: Oxford, 2007) 661–74; P Craig and G De Búrca, *EU Law: Text, Cases and Materials* (4th edn, OUP: Oxford, 2007), 353–74.

[175] *Internationale Handelsgesellschaft mbH v Einfuhr- und Vorratsstelle für Getreide und Futtermittel (2 BvL 52/71)* [1974] 2 CMLR 540. [176] Ibid, 551.

[177] *Re Wünsche Handelsgesellschaft (Case 2 BvR 197/83)* [1987] 3 CMLR 225.

[178] Ibid, 265. [179] J Fröwein, 'Solange II' (1988) 25 CML Rev 201, 203–4.

to the national standard of protection of fundamental rights. It rather claimed that, although such jurisdiction existed, it would not be exercised as long as the Court remained satisfied that there was an equivalent protection of fundamental rights ensured by the Community institutions. This view was further stressed in the *Maastricht* judgment[180], as later explained in the *Bananas* decision.[181] The latter decision indeed also stresses the improbability that the Court will exercise its jurisdiction to rule in favour of the disapplication of a Community measure in German territory, because the burden placed on the plaintiff is extremely heavy.

The Bundesverfassungsgericht was not the only national constitutional court to voice such reservations with regard to the primacy of EC law and the protection of fundamental rights.[182]

Let us now consider the situation envisaged in the Lisbon Treaty in CFSP matters: given that the ECJ is not competent as a matter of course to ensure the compliance of CFSP legislation with general principles (including fundamental rights), national constitutional courts are likely to feel justified in reasserting their role as ultimate adjudicators within their national legal orders, regardless of whether the *Foto-Frost* principle is deemed to apply in this area as a matter of EU law. Further, if national constitutional courts do review CFSP measures, they are most likely to do so by applying national standards, which would turn the primacy of CFSP measures into a merely theoretical claim.

This, of course, has to be differentiated from—although taken into account with—the competence of the ECJ to review CFSP restrictive measures which directly affect the rights of an individual under Article 275(2) TFEU, the 'constitutional complaint' studied in the previous section. It could be that constitutional courts do not find it necessary to exercise abstract

---

[180] *Manfred Brunner and Others v The European Union Treaty (Cases 2 BvR 2134/92 & 2159/92)* [1994] 1 CMLR 57.   [181] BVerfGE 102, 147.

[182] Similar reservations had already been voiced by the Italian Constitutional Court, reaching the conclusion that: '[I]t should therefore be excluded that such limitations of sovereignty, concretely set out in the Rome Treaty [...] can nevertheless give the organs of the EEC an unacceptable power to violate the fundamental principles of our constitutional order or the inalienable rights of man. And it is obvious that if ever Article 189 had to be given such an aberrant interpretation, in such a case the guarantee would always be assured that this Court would control the continuing compatibility of the Treaty with the above-mentioned fundamental principles.' *Frontini v Ministero delle Finanze (Case 183)* [1974] 2 CMLR 372, 389. This position was later on reinforced in *Fragd. Corte Constituzionale, 21 Aprile 1989 n. 232 - Pres. Conso; red. Ferri - S.p.a. Fragd c. Amministrazione delle finanze dello Stato* [1989] 72 Rivista di Diritto Internazionale 104.

review of CFSP measures for compliance with constitutionally protected fundamental rights if they are satisfied that the Court protects individuals consistently through this channel on a case-by-case basis, although it has no jurisdiction to monitor compatibility of legislation with the general principles of Union law (including fundamental rights) and with the Charter of Fundamental Rights in the abstract. This could be another incentive for the Court to interpret the wording of Article 275(2) TFEU in an expansive manner, both when determining whether it has competence and whether the plaintiff has standing. Otherwise, the possibility remains for national constitutional courts to review the validity of these Union acts against national standards and, ultimately, to render them without effect within their national territory. The nature of legal reasoning is such that it is impossible to prove a firm connection between the course selected by the European Court in interpreting EC law and the anxieties and preferences expressed by national courts, but, in particular in matters associated with the protection of fundamental rights, it is very tempting to conclude from available rich evidence in the case-law that practice in Luxembourg has been influenced by the vital need to maintain the loyal support of national judiciaries, especially those in the superior constitutional courts of Europe, whose voice cannot be lightly ignored in the shaping of EC law;[183] there is no reason to believe that the Lisbon Treaty would alter the dynamics of this relationship.

Let us now consider the second aspect of an abstract control of legislation, that is, ensuring the correct use of competences and procedures. National constitutional courts have also expressed concern in this respect in the past: the Bundesverfassungsgericht exposed clearly in the *Maastricht* judgment its intention to monitor the exercise of the competences of the Community,[184] making sure its institutions remained within their powers. Although the tone of the *Bananas* decision is far more conciliatory,[185] this 'subsidiary emergency jurisdiction' remains.[186] The Italian Constitutional

---

[183] A-M Slaughter, AS Sweet, and JHH Weiler (eds), *The European Courts and National Courts: Doctrine and Jurisprudence* (Hart: Oxford, 1998); J Schwarze (ed), *The Birth of a European Constitutional Order: The Interaction of National and European Constitutional Law* (Nomos: Baden-Baden, 2000); S Weatherill, 'Activism and Restraint in the European Court of Justice' in P Capps, M Evans, and S Konstadinidis (eds), *Asserting Jurisdiction: International and European Legal Perspectives* (Hart: Oxford, 2003).

[184] *Manfred Brunner and Others v The European Union Treaty (Cases 2 BvR 2134/92 & 2159/92)* [1994] 1 CMLR 57. [185] BVerfGE 102, 147.

[186] A Peters 'The Bananas Decision 2000 of the German Federal Constitutional Court: Towards Reconciliation with the ECJ as regards Fundamental Rights Protection in Europe' (2000) 43 German Yearbook of International Law 276, 281.

Court, on its part, also signalled readiness to monitor correct use of competence in *Granital*[187] and *Fragd.*[188] The Danish Supreme Court came to a similar result in *Carlsen.*[189]

The national constitutional courts' 'pending threat' as regards the competence creep of the Community may, in theory, materialize in any field of Union activity in the future. But this danger is, again, more acute in the CFSP, where the Court is less able than in other areas to monitor the use of Union competence. We have already seen how the Court may, according to Article 40 TEU (after LT), police the borders between the CFSP and other policies of the Union. Yet national constitutional courts' worries concern 'alleged trespass beyond the outer limits of Treaty-conferred competence',[190] rather than the internal boundaries within the different competences granted by the Treaty. To put it more clearly, the national courts do not worry about whether a certain Union measure should have been adopted within the AFSJ or the CFSP, but about whether the Union had the power to act at all. The Court has the power to generally monitor the outer limits of Union competence under Article 263 TFEU,[191] but this power does not extend to the CFSP. As a result, again, national constitutional courts may feel the need to step in and monitor the use of CFSP competences in specific cases.

This section has focused on two functions of the abstract control of CFSP measures that may not be exercised by the ECJ and may therefore be claimed by national constitutional courts, if national law so allows.[192] This, in itself, would only amount to an act of defiance if the *Foto-Frost* principle were deemed to apply in this area. Apart from the fact that the extension of this principle does not seem justified in an area where the EU legal system

---

[187] Unofficial translation in G Gaja, 'Constitutional Court (Italy) Decision No. 170 of 8 June 1984, S.p.a. granital v Amministrazione delle Finanze dello Stato.' (1984) 21 CML Rev 756.

[188] *Corte Costituzionale, 21 Aprile 1989 n. 232 - Pres. Conso; red. Ferri - S.p.a. Fragd c. Amministrazione delle finanze dello Stato* [1989] 72 Rivista di Diritto Internazionale 104.

[189] *Hanne Norup Carlsen and others v Prime Minister Poul Nyrup Rasmussen. Danish Supreme Court, 6 April 1998* [1999] 3 CMLR 854.

[190] S Weatherill, *Cases and Materials on EU Law* (8th edn, OUP: Oxford, 2007) 668. This comment specifically refers to the Maastricht judgment of the Bundesverfassungsgericht, but it can be generalized to other similar cases.   [191] The current Art 230 EC.

[192] Within the debate on the UK Supreme Court, for example, Arden has argued that the creation of such a court would be of particular importance within the CFSP, given the lack of pervasive ECJ jurisdiction. In her opinion, it is possible that national courts (and among them the new Supreme Court of the United Kingdom) have jurisdiction to review such measures, if national legislation so provides: LJ Arden, 'Jurisdiction of the new United Kingdom Supreme Court' [2004] Winter PL 699.

does not offer a complete system of remedies, it is a further argument against its extension that national constitutional courts are very likely to disobey it. Yet to the extent that national constitutional courts are also likely to apply national standards rather than EU ones when reviewing CFSP measures, they would not only be acting against a hypothetical application of the *Foto-Frost* principle to this area, but also against the principle of primacy of Union law. The claim to primacy of CFSP measures is likely to be accordingly reduced to a theoretical claim that cannot have the practical effects that primacy has at the moment in the EC pillar, or that it will have in all other areas of Union activity if the Lisbon Treaty is ratified. Ultimately, these practical effects seem unavoidable; they are the consequence of a certain set of features that are generally present in the Union judicial system but that are nevertheless absent in the CFSP.

3.5.4 The Control of the ECtHR

Depending on the Court's approach when determining the scope of its competence and the conditions for standing under Article 275(2) TFEU, it may be that certain individuals are denied access to a court at the EU level and have to resort to the European Court of Human Rights (hereafter ECtHR). This section will briefly deal with this possibility and its consequences.

Article 6(2) TEU (after LT) establishes that '[t]he Union shall accede to the European Convention for the Protection of Human Rights and Fundamental Freedoms' (hereinafter 'the Convention'). To the extent that the terms of such accession would have to be determined in the future, we can only venture some hypothesis as to its likely consequences in terms of judicial protection in CFSP matters. It will be in any case assumed that the Union would accept the jurisdiction of the ECtHR and that the latter would be, in principle, open to individuals' actions against the Union. The ECtHR could then deal with such an action in two different ways: on the one hand, it could treat the Union just like any other signatory to the Convention, meaning that it would simply examine the substance of each complaint, if admissible. On the other hand, the Court could establish a presumption in favour of the Union, applying the 'equivalent protection' doctrine that it has developed in relation to the EC.

In the first scenario, the ECtHR chooses to exercise a full review in each admissible case brought against the Union. If an individual's rights have been breached by a CFSP measure and he or she has not been allowed access to the ECJ, the ECtHR is likely to find against the Union, at least in the absence of a convention whereby national courts do review these measures.

In the second scenario, the ECtHR decides to treat the Union more favourably than other signatories to the Convention on account of its singular nature. In this case, the Court would establish the assumption that the Union offers a level of protection of fundamental rights that is generally equivalent to that of the Convention. In other words, the ECtHR could decide to apply its 'equivalent protection' doctrine, elaborated in relation to the EC, to the post-Lisbon Union. The ECtHR has developed this doctrine in cases concerning the responsibility of Member States for EC action because the EC is not a signatory to the Convention. As a result, the EC cannot be accused or held responsible before the ECtHR for its actions; instead, Member States may be.[193]

3.5.4.1 The 'Equivalent Protection' Doctrine

In *M & Co v the Federal Republic of Germany*,[194] the ECtHR laid down the foundations of the 'equivalent protection' doctrine: state action taken in compliance with international obligations is justified as long as the relevant organization protects human rights in a manner equivalent to that provided by the Convention. In *Matthews v UK*,[195] this test was applied and the Community failed because there was no remedy left to the individual: the ECJ had no jurisdiction to review the measure in question (a measure of primary law). Finally, in *Bosphorus*,[196] the ECtHR further clarified the conditions under which an individual Member State would be held

---

[193] For a fuller account of the arguments contained in this section, see A Hinarejos, 'Bosphorus v Ireland and the Protection of Fundamental Rights in Europe' (2006) 31 ELR 251. For comments on the *Bosphorus* Case, see C Costello, 'The Bosphorus Ruling of the ECHR: Fundamental Rights and Blurry Boundaries in Europe' (2006) 6 EHRLRev 87; S Douglas-Scott, 'Bosphorus Hava Youllari Turizm Ve Ticaret Anonim Sirketi v Ireland' (2006) 43 CML Rev 243. On the relationship between the ECJ and the ECtHR: G Harpaz, 'The European Court of Justice and its Relations with the European Court of Human Rights: The Quest for Enhanced Reliance, Coherence and Legitimacy' (2009) 46 CML Rev 105; L Garlicki, 'Cooperation of Courts: The Role of Supranational Jurisdictions in Europe' (2008) 6 I-CON 509; S Douglas-Scott, 'A Tale of Two Courts: Luxembourg, Strasbourg and the Growing European Human Rights Acquis' (2006) 43 CML Rev 619; I Canor, 'Primus Inter Pares: Who is the Ultimate Guardian of Fundamental Rights in Europe' (2000) 25 ELR 3.

[194] *M & Co v The Federal Republic of Germany* (App 13258/87) (1990) 64 DR 138.

[195] *Matthews v The United Kingdom* (App 24833/94) Series A 1999-I 251 (1999) 28 EHRR 361.

[196] *Bosphorus Hava Yollari Turizm ve Ticaret Anonim Sirketi v Ireland* (App no 45036/98) (2006) 42 EHRR 1.

responsible for the actions of the Community.[197] It seems that the test of 'equivalent protection', a tool which enables the ECtHR to determine whether its intervention is required, may be used, first, when only EC law measures are at stake (as in *Matthews*) and, second, when national implementation of EC law measures is at stake, if national authorities enjoyed no discretion in the matter (*Bosphorus*). The Community will fail this test if there is a manifest deficiency in its standard of protection of fundamental rights:

[A]ny such presumption can be rebutted if, in the circumstances of the particular case, it is considered that the protection of Convention rights was manifestly deficient. In such cases, the interest of international co-operation would be outweighted by the Convention's role as a 'constitutional instrument of European public order' in the field of human rights.[198]

Judge Ress clarified in his concurrent opinion in *Bosphorus* that protection of fundamental rights within the Union would be considered 'manifestly deficient' when 'there has, in procedural terms, been no adequate review in the particular case'. Examples given of this dysfunction included cases where the ECJ lacks competence, when it has been too strict in its interpretation of *locus standi*.[199]

Coming back to our earlier discussion, it would thus be possible for the ECtHR to operate under the assumption that the Union (post-Lisbon) offers a level of protection that is equivalent to that of the Convention. It would then be up to the individual to rebut this assumption by showing that there has been a manifest deficiency in the specific case before the Court. It would seem, however, that a very strict interpretation of the ECJ's jurisdiction under Article 275 TFEU that systematically deprives individuals of an effective remedy would qualify as a manifest deficiency.

On a different note, it may be possible to think of a scenario where the Lisbon Treaty has been ratified but accession has not yet taken place, or it has taken place in a way so as not to allow individuals to bring an action against the Union (unlikely as this possibility may be). In that case, it can be reasonably expected that the ECtHR would extend to the whole of the Union its case-law on the responsibility of Member States for EC action. As a result, Member States would be held responsible for breaches caused

---

[197] The test in *Bosphorus* seems applicable to both the EC and the EU. The difference would be that lack of discretion on the Member State's part may be more difficult to prove when an EU measure is at stake.   [198] Ibid, [156].

[199] Concurring opinion of Judge Ress in *Bosphorus*, [3].

by CFSP measures. How often this would happen in practice would depend on whether national courts have taken it to themselves to review CFSP measures for compliance with either EU or national standards.[200]

Regardless of whether the Union or the Member States are ultimately held accountable, the need for external control of CFSP measures by the ECtHR remains a possibility that the Union should be keen to avoid. To this effect, the Court of Justice may—and arguably should—adopt a broad reading of its jurisdiction under Article 275 TFEU.

---

[200] There is another way in which it could be possible to hold the Union responsible indirectly for a breach of human rights; in this case it would not be necessary for a Member State to be implementing a Union measure. The potential context in which such situations may take place is illustrated by the *Senator Lines* case: *Senator Lines v Austria, Belgium, Denmark, Finland, France, Germany, Greece, Ireland, Italy, Luxembourg, the Netherlands, Portugal, Spain, Sweden and the United Kingdom* (App 56672/00) 39 EHRR 13. The same mechanism was used in *Segi and Gestoras pro-Amnistía*, where the applicants brought an action before the European Court of Human Rights against all Member States of the European Council: *Segi and others and Gestoras pro-Amnistía and others v Germany, Austria, Belgium, Denmark, Spain, Finland, France, Greece, Ireland, Italy, Luxembourg, the Netherlands, Portugal, the United Kingdom and Sweden* (App 6422/02, 9916/02) Series A 2002–V 371. Both cases were declared inadmissable.

4

Concluding Remarks: A Constitutional Court for the EU?

We have already seen how the Court understood its Treaty mandate under Article 220 EC to mean that it had to develop a 'firm legal base' for the Community to stand on. The European Court of Justice took to itself the task of developing the Community legal order, a task that has been inextricably linked to its position as a guarantor of rights, and that involved 'discovering' the foundations of the EC legal system in the Treaty, a vague and heterogeneous text.

The technique used by the ECJ in this quest entailed finding the general principles of EC law, enshrined primarily in the Treaty and in the shared heritage of the EC national legal systems. The 'discovery' of general principles of law entails the establishment of a hierarchy; thus the Court established the 'supra-constitutionality' of some fundamental norms (such as judicial protection) above other norms of a lesser importance. Hence it was possible for the Court, for instance, to resolve the conflict in *les Verts* between a fundamental norm (the principle of judicial protection) and a Treaty provision which established very strict conditions for the admission of an annulment action against Parliament acts.[1] This is seen by some as one of the duties of the Court—not merely 'to respect the will of the constitutional powers, but also to bring coherence to the articulations between principles and rules, establishing an order of preference and therefore contributing to the reconstruction of the normative system

[1] V Constantinesco, 'The ECJ as a Law-Maker: Praeter aut Contra Legem?' in D O'Keeffe (ed), *Judicial Review in European Union Law* (Kluwer: The Hague, 2000). Case 294/83 *Parti Écologiste 'Les Verts' v European Parliament* [1986] ECR 1339.

instead of deconstructing it'.[2] There is therefore an arguable logic to how the European Court of Justice can sometimes seem to be pushing the boundaries of some Treaty provisions—sometimes just falling short of even ignoring them altogether—in favour of a hierarchically superior general principle or 'supra-constitutional' rule.[3] A different question is, of course, whether one agrees with the labelling of a particular principle as hierarchically superior in a specific case. At any rate, one of the principles recognized by the Court as supra-constitutional rules is the principle of effective judicial protection and the generality of judicial review.[4] As the Court put it, the Community 'is a Community based on the rule of law, inasmuch as neither its Member States nor its institutions can avoid a review of the question whether the measures adopted by them are in conformity with the basic constitutional charter, the Treaty'.[5]

Does the Court have the same mandate to ensure that 'the law is observed' and, by extension, to provide a firm legal base for the Union as it does for the EC under its interpretation of Article 220 EC? Although there is no textual equivalent of Article 220 EC in the TEU, Article 46 TEU, at least, entails that the provisions of the EC Treaty concerning the powers of the ECJ apply to the provisions in the TEU on police and judicial cooperation in criminal matters:[6] this would include the Court's mandate under Article 220 EC. More importantly, it seems clear from its case-law that the Court of Justice considers it its duty to build a logically coherent legal system for the Union, a visible endeavour behind ambitious decisions such as *Pupino*, extending the duty of loyal cooperation and the duty of conform interpretation, *Segi*, extending judicial review, or all cases where the Court asserts its powers to police the allocation of competences under Article 47 TEU. The Court strives to shape the legal system of the Union, albeit with a watchful eye on restrictions set by the Treaty

---

[2] Constantinesco, ibid, 79.

[3] Constantinesco's term: ibid.

[4] Ibid. The Court has declared that the right to judicial protection is one of the general principles of law stemming from the constitutional traditions of the Member States: see for instance Case 222/84 *Johnston v Chief Constable of the Royal Ulster Constabulary* [1986] ECR 1651 [18]; Case C-50/00 *Unión de Pequeños Agricultores v Council* [2002] ECR I-6677 [39]; Case C-263/02 *Commission v Jégo-Quéré* [2004] ECR I-03425 [29]. For a general overview of the general principle of effective judicial protection, T Tridimas, *The General Principles of EU Law* (2nd edn, OUP: Oxford, 2006) 443-56.

[5] Case 294/83 *Parti Écologiste 'Les Verts' v European Parliament* [1986] ECR 1339 [23].

[6] Case C-170/96 *Commission v Council (airport transit)* [1998] ECR I-02763 [15]; Opinion of AG Maduro in Case C-160/03 *Spain v Eurojust* [2005] ECR I-2077 [17].

structure. It is the logical result of these restrictions that the Courts' advances have mostly taken place within the third pillar, rather than the second one.

The restrictions contained in the Treaty are indeed substantial, even within the third pillar: notwithstanding the Court's reading of Article 6(2) TEU,[7] the Court does not have its full array of powers at its disposal, and so it cannot shape the legal order, ensure its coherence, or safeguard individual rights to the same extent: the Court cannot review national action directly, it can review Union measures directly only in certain circumstances (never prompted by individuals), and it can only enter a dialogue with certain national courts but not with others. Nevertheless, the thesis can be put forward that, within the realm of its possibilities, the Court seeks to build and develop a coherent legal system for the Union. In some cases, this entails undertaking an exercise of hierarchization in the intergovernmental areas, similar to that undertaken in the first pillar, by singling out supra-constitutional rules that trump less important treaty provisions.[8] The restricted availability of procedural vehicles means, of course, that the Court has much less opportunity to do this than in the first pillar.

The fact that the principle of effective judicial protection has, again, been singled out as a supra-constitutional rule, this time outside the realm of the EC, should come as no surprise. Article 6(2) TEU states that 'the Union shall respect fundamental rights, as guaranteed by the European Convention for the Protection of Human Rights and Fundamental Freedoms signed in Rome on 4 November 1950 and as they result from the constitutional traditions common to the Member States, as general principles of Community law'. This means that the principle of effective judicial protection, a fundamental right laid down in Articles 6 and 13 ECHR and a general principle of Community law, must also underpin the Union's legal system. Further, regardless of whether one defends a merely formal or

---

[7] 'As is clear from Article 6 TEU, the Union is founded on the principle of the rule of law and it respects fundamental rights as general principles of Community law. It follows that the institutions are subject to review of the conformity of their acts with the treaties and the general principles of law, just like the Member States when they implement the law of the Union.' Case C-355/04 P *Segi* [2007] ECR I-1657 [51].

[8] Chalmers believes that the Court has made it clear that, if more judicial guarantees are not created within the third pillar, 'judicial creativity might have to be used instead'. D Chalmers, 'The Court of Justice and the Third Pillar' (2005) 30 ELR 773, 773.

a substantive definition of the rule of law,[9] the principle of judicial review is one of its essential elements: 'the existence of an independent and impartial judiciary with responsibility for resolving disputes over precisely what the law requires and providing effective remedies where the law is breached' is considered as a basic element of the most minimalist conception of the rule of law.[10] Since Amsterdam, the rule of law is one of the principles among which the Union is founded, according to Article 6(1) TEU, and has taken on increasing significance since it was first included in the preamble to the TEU at Maastricht.[11] Thus the principle of judicial review—be it considered a formal requirement of the legal system or a fundamental right of recourse to a court—applies fully to the legal system of the Union.

AG Maduro had already argued in *Eurojust* that the principle of judicial protection and the generality of judicial review should trump a limitation on the jurisdiction of the Court under the TEU as well. The European Union, he argued, is also a community of law—a term used by the ECJ in reference to the European Community in *les Verts*—making it necessary 'for measures of Union institutions and bodies to be amenable to review by a Union Court, so long as they are intended to produce legal effects vis-à-vis third parties'.[12] The principle of effective judicial protection and the generality of judicial review extend to the whole of the Union, AG Maduro argued, and can have the same 'trumping' effect that they have within the framework of the Community.[13] Although the Court did not follow the

---

[9] This refers to the cleavage between those academics who consider that the rule of law is merely formal or technical, in that it only deals with the mechanics of the legal system, and those who consider that the concept includes an element of substantive justice, such as the protection of fundamental rights or democratic values. For a comprehensive overview of the literature on this point, see P Craig, 'Formal and Substantive Conceptions of the Rule of Law: An Analytical Framework' [1997] PL 467. Some of the best-known proponents of these different conceptions are: J Raz, 'The Rule of Law and its Virtue' (1977) 93 LQR 195; A Dicey, *The Law of the Constitution* (10th edn, Macmillan: London, 1959); R Unger, *Law in Modern Society: Toward a Criticism of Social Theory* (Free Press: New York, 1976); R Dworkin, *A Matter of Principle* (Clarendon Press: Oxford, 1986); J Laws, 'Law and Democracy' [1995] PL 72; T Allan, *Law, Liberty and Justice, the Legal Foundations of British Constitutionalism* (Clarendon Press: Oxford, 1993).

[10] A Arnull, 'The Rule of Law in the European Union' in A Arnull and D Wincott (eds), *Accountability and Legitimacy in the European Union* (OUP: Oxford, 2003) 240.

[11] Arnull ibid, 239; 'Editorial Comments: The Rule of Law as the Backbone of the EU' (2007) 44 CML Rev 875.

[12] Opinion of AG Maduro in C-160/03 *Spain v Eurojust* [2005] ECR I-2077 [17].

[13] The Court, however, decided that the action was inadmissible because it had been brought under Art 230 EC and sustained that there was no breach of the right to judicial protection, since specific affected individuals could have access to the Court under Art 91 of the Staff Regulations: Case C-160/03 *Spain v Eurojust* [2005] ECR I-2077 [35]-[44].

AG's urgings in this case, his reasoning seems to have influenced later outcomes.

Thus the Court used the principle of effective judicial protection to trump a limitation on its jurisdiction to give a preliminary ruling on the validity or interpretation of a common position in *Segi* and *Gestoras pro Amnistía*. The principle of effective judicial protection was presented as a consequence of the fact that the Union is committed to the rule of law and the respect of fundamental rights.[14] The Court further grounded its conclusions on its consideration of the preliminary ruling procedure as a tool designed 'to guarantee observance of the law in the interpretation and application of the Treaty'[15] (paraphrasing Article 220 EC and thus referring to its duty to ensure the law is observed and to develop the basis of the legal system, this time outside of the first pillar): a literal reading of Article 35(1) TEU would make the fulfilment of this function impossible, and was therefore precluded. Later on, in *Advocaten*,[16] the Court reasserted the Union's commitment to the rule of law and the respect of fundamental rights in the same terms as in *Segi*. Albeit not concerning measures of EU law directly, the need for effective review has also been forcefully reasserted in CFSP-related cases such as *OMPI* and others, and the idea of a community based on the rule of law was instrumental in the affirmation of the autonomy of the legal order in *Kadi*, where the Court of Justice stated that there could be no derogations from 'the principles of liberty, democracy and respect for human rights and fundamental freedoms enshrined in Article 6(1) EU as a foundation of the Union'.[17]

The Court's vigorous approach to the need for judicial protection and the generality of judicial review is of special interest in the period leading up to the entry into force of the Lisbon Treaty. Should the ratification process fail, the pressure on the Court to assert a firm approach to review in the intergovernmental pillars will become stronger. This is not only the result of a slow approximation or *Reflexwirkung* between the pillars,[18] the dynamics of the system that work in favour of placing the European Court of Justice in an increasingly similar position within the two 'integrated but

---

[14] Ibid, [51].

[15] Ibid, [53].

[16] Case C-303/05 *Advocaten voor de Wereld* [2007] ECR I-3633 [45].

[17] Joined Cases C-402/05 P and 415/05 P *Yassin Abdullah Kadi, Al Barakaat International Foundation v Council and Commission* [2008] ECR I-6351 [303].

[18] C Timmermans, 'The Constitutionalisation of the European Union' (2002) 21 YEL 1, 10; M Claes, *The National Courts' Mandate in the European Constitution* (Hart: Oxford, 2006) 105.

separate legal orders' of the Union and the EC.[19] In addition, the Court is ever more likely to use the principle of judicial protection to trump treaty limitations in cases where it is necessary in order to protect the rights of third parties, due to the fact that an increasing number of measures with an adverse effect on individuals are being adopted in the intergovernmental areas and national constitutional courts expect the ECJ to be able to review these measures effectively,[20] as AG Ruiz Jarabo-Colomer and AG Mengozzi highlighted in their Opinions in *Advocaten* and *Segi*, respectively.[21] Furthermore, it has already been argued in this monograph that the way in which third pillar law is treated by courts is likely to suffer a gradual change in the absence of a Treaty reform, and that these measures may end up being accorded primacy over national law. This would greatly increase the pressure on the Court of Justice to exercise effective judicial control in this area, not only because of internal concerns as to the Union's commitment to the rule of law, but also because of the need to avoid a conflict with national constitutional courts.

The Court's likely role in this area is thus problematic because demand will mount on the Court to use the principle of judicial protection and the generality of judicial review as requirements of the rule of law to expand the boundaries of its jurisdiction. Yet this expansion can only take place within certain limits. Even if the Court can push some Treaty boundaries, it is not likely to ignore them altogether. Nor is it desirable for the Union to acquire better judicial control solely on the basis of judicial activism. This would necessarily be a piecemeal approach, which is liable to create legal uncertainty and understandable doubts as to its political legitimacy.

The legitimacy problem is an inevitable one, given that the Court is reinterpreting the letter of the Treaty in ways that can be difficult to discern from plain rewriting; the Court has to assume the role of a legislator of sorts, something that is, as discussed earlier, necessarily controversial.

---

[19] Joined Cases C-402/05 P and 415/05 P *Yassin Abdullah Kadi, Al Barakaat International Foundation v Council and Commission* [2008] ECR I-6351 [202].

[20] This threat is not as great as within the first pillar, given that in these areas constitutional courts are not necessarily relinquishing their power of review totally. These are still, in theory, measures of public international law and the *Foto-Frost* principle does not apply. The perception of Union law is, however, increasingly different from that of traditional public international law and it is not likely that constitutional courts will treat them alike. It is far more likely that, in practice, national constitutional courts will expect the ECJ to review these measures.

[21] Opinion of AG Ruiz Jarabo-Colomer in *Advocaten* [80]; Opinion of AG Mengozzi in *Segi* and *Gestoras pro Amnistía* [90].

Furthermore, it has already been pointed out that the legitimacy of the ECJ can be more easily contested than that of a national constitutional court because of the transnational context in which the former operates and the lack of consensus on the values it should defend. The problem of legal uncertainty is no less important, since legal certainty is also a basic element of the rule of law. We are thus faced with the dilemma that, in trying to enhance the rule of law by extending judicial control, the Court also damages the rule of law by creating legal uncertainty. It is accepted that the different elements of the rule of law may be difficult to reconcile on some occasions,[22] and this is one of them. It is submitted that, in those cases where the ECJ pushes the boundaries of its jurisdiction in order to extend judicial control, arguably at the expense of legal certainty, what the Union gains in terms of compliance with the rule of law offsets what it loses. Ideally, however, the Union should not be losing anything in terms of compliance with the rule of law—hence the recommendation for a more embracing reform as a means to tackle possible deficiencies: a Treaty reform would extend judicial control without endangering legal certainty, and both elements of the rule of law would thus be better reconciled than by leaving the job to the Court of Justice. Such a constitutional reform would also assuage any worries about political legitimacy. The extension of judicial control envisaged in the Lisbon Treaty would therefore be a welcome change, from this point of view; although the Court has proven that it is not afraid to act, an overarching, more ambitious Treaty reform is, without doubt, preferable.

Finally, a Treaty reform is also desirable as regards the nature of third pillar law. It has been argued that the current state of uncertainty may lead national courts and/or the ECJ to treat third pillar law as having primacy over national law, and the problems that this would cause have already been highlighted. Notably, this development would also be likely to drive the ECJ towards a more expansive interpretation of its jurisdiction. On the other hand, the reform envisaged in the Lisbon Treaty has the advantage of clarifying the change in the nature of third pillar law, coupling it with other necessary changes (especially in terms of judicial control) and thus removing, to some extent, the need for judicial activism.

---

[22] A Arnull, 'The Rule of Law in the European Union' in A Arnull and D Wincott (eds), *Accountability and Legitimacy in the European Union* (OUP: Oxford, 2003) 247.

4.1 The Lisbon Treaty

The Lisbon Treaty would extend the Court's mandate in an explicit manner: the duty of the Court to ensure that 'in the interpretation and application of the Treaties, the law is observed' (Article 19 TEU, after LT), currently contained in Article 220 EC, would apply to the whole of the Union legal system.

More specifically, the removal of the most significant restrictions that currently curtail the Court's powers within the AFSJ would place it on the same footing in this area as within the orthodox areas of the current EC pillar, where the Court has long functioned as an effective constitutional adjudicator. The same cannot be said, however, of the CFSP, where the Court's powers continue to be very restricted. The Court's competence to review the validity of measures providing for restrictive measures against individuals in this field has already been studied; granting this power to the Court is clearly a positive development that has the potential to assuage concerns as to the protection of fundamental rights in the CFSP. Yet protecting individual rights is only one of the functions that a constitutional adjudicator routinely performs. The Court will engage in achieving other aims, such as shaping a coherent legal order, only to the extent that it is necessary in the case at stake, and to the extent that any court shapes the legal order by interpreting any of its rules. The Court is therefore limited by the fact that the only procedural vehicle available within the CFSP is a sort of constitutional complaint that aims, first and foremost, at safeguarding the rights of specific individuals. Although this will bring the Court closer to what Bickel celebrated as 'passive virtues', since the Court's role will largely be restricted to adjudicating on specific controversies, rather than on abstract constitutional issues,[23] the type of controversy that may reach the Court is so narrowly defined that the Court will not be in a position to exercise the role of a fully fledged

---

[23] Bickel celebrated the 'passive virtues' in a court: avoiding constitutional issues if possible, deciding only on the case at stake, deciding constitutional issues only when the time is ripe. See generally A Bickel, *The Least Dangerous Branch* (Yale University Press: New Haven, 1962) 111-98. Ferreres Comella has argued that the European model of constitutional court (centralized) finds it difficult to cultivate these virtues, in part because there is no case-by-case minimalism whenever a question reaches the Court in the form of an abstract challenge: V Ferreres Comella, 'The Consequences of Centralizing Constitutional Review in a Special Court: Some Thoughts on Judicial Activism' (2004) 82 Texas L Rev 1705, 1712-22. The possibility of abstract challenge is precluded in the case of the ECJ when dealing with CFSP matters, making case-by-case minimalism more likely.

constitutional adjudicator in this area. As a result, first, problems of legal coherence will arise and, second, the Court will not be in a position to push the process of integration as it has done in other areas. The question of whether further integration is in fact desirable is, of course, a political one.

Until now, the Court's active approach in the intergovernmental pillars has not attracted general criticism in the literature, probably because it has involved the judicial control of Union measures rather than national ones. Thus the Court has, to some extent, upset the balance of power at EU level, but it has not yet 'trumped' regulatory choices made at the national level. This is, of course, bound to change if the Court, pursuant to the Lisbon Treaty, emerges as a fully fledged constitutional/supreme court, at least within the AFSJ. The Court's bold style within the first pillar attracts periodic bouts of disapproval,[24] something that is not surprising: the legitimacy problems of constitutional adjudication—most notably, the countermajoritarian difficulty—are well-known and have long been the focus of academic discussion in the US.[25] European constitutional courts, on the contrary, seem to enjoy a high degree of social and academic support when discharging their functions.[26] Yet the same degree of support is not extended to the Court of Justice, in part because of the mentioned lack of social consensus as to the specific values that the Court is seen to be promoting.

At any rate, the classic countermajoritarian argument against constitutional adjudication apply to the Court's role as a protector of individual

---

[24] For the most recent controversy, see R Herzog and L Gerken, 'Stop the European Court of Justice' http://www.cep.eu/678.html?&l=1 (accessed Jan 2009) and a reply in: Editorial, (2008) 45 CML Rev 1571.

[25] For two recent and compelling overviews from opposite standpoints and further references, see: J Waldron, 'The Core of the Case against Judicial Review' (2006) Yale L J 1346; R Fallon, 'The Core of an Uneasy Case for Judicial Review' (2008) 121 Harvard LR 1693. There is a long tradition of challenging constitutional review in the US, contrary to what happens in Europe— see, for example, M Tushnet, *Taking the Constitution away from the Courts* (Princeton University Press: Princeton, 1999); R Hirschl, *Towards Juristocracy: The Origins and Consequences of the New Constitutionalism* (Harvard University Press: Cambridge, 2004). Judicial review has often been defended on substantive or procedural conceptions of minority protection: R Dworkin, *Taking Rights Seriously* (Harvard University Press: Boston, 1977); JH Ely, *Democracy and Distrust: A Theory of Judicial Review* (Harvard University Press: Cambridge, 1981).

[26] For a useful overview of possible reasons for this support: W Sadurski, *Rights before Courts: A Study of Constitutional Courts in Postcommunist Countries in Central and Eastern Europe* (Springer: Dordrecht, 2005) XIV-XVIII; see also, for the specific cases of Germany and France: M Rosenfeld, 'Constitutional Adjudication in Europe and the United States: Paradoxes and Contrasts' (2004) 2 I-CON 633, 663-7.

rights, and as a federal court that has to enforce the vertical distribution of powers.[27] To the extent that the Union is, however, not a strictly democratic lawmaker, the countermajoritarian argument is not very powerful when it comes to situations where the Court of Justice strikes down Union measures.[28] On the contrary, the most problematic instances of constitutional adjudication (within the AFSJ or at all) are likely to be those where the Court, in practice, strikes down national legislation that is the product of the national democratic process, regardless of whether this is framed in terms of the protection of individual rights or in terms of a competence dispute. Although it may be possible to argue that the Court is, in such cases, defending the rights of out-of-state actors who do not have a stake in the national democratic process,[29] the fact remains that the Court, rather than a Union-wide demos, is deciding the scope and content of those prevailing rights.[30]

Although it is possible to criticize the Court's role as a constitutional adjudicator—and specially within the post-Lisbon AFSJ, where the national choices that will be struck down will often be of a sensitive nature—it is still the case that a federal incomplete bargain such as the Treaties necessitates such an institution to enforce it. It has been pointed out as a common pattern that the constitutional courts of young federal systems tend to favour the centre, rather than the states:[31] this is because the centre is

---

[27] Stone argues convincingly that the countermajoritarian difficulty is not restricted to a constitutional court's role as guarantor of rights: A Stone, ' Judicial Review without Rights: Some Problems for the Democratic Legitimacy of Structural Judicial Review' (2008) 28 OJLS 1.

[28] Waldron, for example, would presumably consider the EU/EC a 'non-core case', meaning that his argument against judicial review may not apply to it: J Waldron, 'The Core of the Case against Judicial Review' (2006) Yale L J 1346. A similar argument is made by M Rosenfeld, 'Constitutional Adjudication in Europe and the United States: Paradoxes and Contrasts' (2004) 2 I-CON 633, 654.

[29] M Poiares Maduro, 'Europe and the Constitution: What if this is as Good as it Gets?' Constitutionalism Web-Papers, University of Bath: www.bath.ac.uk/esml/conWEB/Conweb% 20papers-filestore/conweb5-2000pdf (accessed August 2008) 11. Maduro further argues that giving a voice to foreign actors may even raise the voice of some domestic actors in cases where the national political process has been captured by a national interest group: ibid, 18–19.

[30] But cf Conant, who argues that the Court's bold decisions can (and often are) 'contained' at the national level. A broad mobilization of legal and political pressure is necessary to expand the effects of these controversial judgments. This means that if the Court's decisions have effect it is because of a broader consensus—making them not so counter-democratic after all: L Conant *Justice Contained* (Cornell University Press: Ithaca, 2002).

[31] RD Kelemen, *The Rules of Federalism: Institutions and Regulatory Politics in the EU and Beyond* (Cambridge University Press: Cambridge, 2004) 13–14; D Halberstam, 'Comparative Federalism and the Role of the Judiciary' in KE Wittington, RD Kelemen, and GA Caldeira (eds), *The Oxford Handbook of Law and Politics* (OUP: Oxford, 2008) 151.

necessarily weaker in the initial stages, and a reshuffle of power is necessary to enforce the federal bargain. Equally, it is likely that the Court will engage in this sort of 'centre-building' exercise within the AFSJ, if it acquires full powers as envisaged in the Lisbon Treaty. Yet this seems an unavoidable consequence of the bargain that the Member States have entered into: although it may be justified to criticize the Court for the way in which it chooses to carry out its role in particular instances, the position of the Court as a constitutional adjudicator seems a necessary precondition for the functioning of the—admittedly flawed—system, at least at its present stage.[32]

---

[32] This does not preclude the necessary discussion on the way the judicial system of the Union works, and whether it may be desirable or necessary for the Court to decentralize some of its powers in the future.

BIBLIOGRAPHY

Albors-Llorens, A, *Private Parties in European Community Law: Challenging Community measures* (Clarendon Press: Oxford, 1996)
_____ 'Changes in the Jurisdiction of the European Court of Justice under the Treaty of Amsterdam' (1998) 35 CML Rev 1273
_____ 'The Standing of Private Parties to Challenge Community Measures: Has the European Court Missed the Boat?' (2003) 62 CML Rev 72
Allan, T, *Law, Liberty and Justice: The Legal Foundations of British Constitutionalism* (Clarendon Press: Oxford, 1993)
Arden, LJ, 'Jurisdiction of the New United Kingdom Supreme Court' [2004] Winter PL 699
Arnull, A, 'Does the Court of Justice Have Inherent Jurisdiction?' (1991) 28 CML Rev 669
_____ 'The European Court of Justice and Judicial Objectivity: A Reply to Professor Hartley' (1996) 112 LQR 95
_____ *The European Union and its Court of Justice* (Oxford EC Law Library, OUP: Oxford, 1999)
_____ 'The Rule of Law in the European Union' in A Arnull and D Wincott (eds), *Accountability and Legitimacy in the European Union* (OUP: Oxford, 2003)
_____ 'From Bit Part to Starring Role? The Court of Justice and Europe's Constitutional Treaty' (2005) 24 YEL 1
_____ *The European Union and its Court of Justice* (2nd edn, OUP: Oxford, 2006)
Bartelt, S, and H Zeitler, '"Intelligente Sanktionen" zur Terrorismusbekämpfung in der EU' (2003) 23 Europäische Zeitschrift für Wirtschaftsrecht 712
Beaud, O, 'Reframing a Debate among Americans: Contextualizing a Moral Philosophy of Law' (2009) 7 I-CON 53
Bell, J, S Boyron, and S Whittaker, *Principles of French Law* (OUP: Oxford, 1998)
_____ and L Brown, *French Administrative Law* (Clarendon Press: Oxford, 1998)
Bering Liisberg, J, 'The EU Constitutional Treaty and its Distinction between Legislative and Non-legislative Acts: Oranges into Apples?' Jean Monnet Working Paper 01/06 http://www.jeanmonnetprogram.org/papers/06/060101.html (accessed January 2009)
Besselink, L, 'Curing a "Childhood Sickness"? On Direct Effect, Internal Effect, Primacy and Derogation from Civil Rights. The Netherlands Council of State Judgment in the Metten Case' (1996) 3 Maastricht J of Eur and Comparative L 165
Bickel, A, *The Least Dangerous Branch* (Yale University Press: New Haven, 1962)
Boer, D, 'Justice and Home Affairs Co-operation in the Treaty on European Union: More Complexity Despite Communautarization' (1997) 4 Maastricht J 310

Borgers, MJ, 'Implementing Framework Decisions' (2007) 44 CML Rev 1361

Buergenthal, T, 'Self-executing and Non Self-executing Treaties in National and International Law' 235 1992–IV Hague Recueil des Cours 303

Búrca, G de, 'The European Court of Justice and the International Legal Order after Kadi' Jean Monnet Working Paper 01/09 <http://www.jeanmonnetpro-gram.org/papers/09/090101.html> (accessed March 2009)

Burley, A, and W Mattley, 'Europe before the Court: A Political Theory of Legal Integration' (1993) 47 International Organizations 41

Cameron, I, 'European Union Anti-Terrorist Blacklisting' (2004) 4 HRLRev 225

Canor, I, 'Primus Inter Pares: Who is the Ultimate Guardian of Fundamental Rights in Europe' (2000) 25 ELR 3

Cappelletti, M, *The Judicial Process in Comparative Perspective* (Clarendon Press: Oxford, 1989)

Cassesse, A, 'Modern Constitutions and International Law' 192 1985–III Hague Recueil des Cours 331

Chalmers, D, 'The Court of Justice and the Third Pillar' (2005) 30 ELR 773

____ 'The Secret Delivery of Justice' (2008) 33 ELR 773

Claes, M, *The National Courts' Mandate in the European Constitution* (Hart: Oxford, 2006)

Conant, L, *Justice Contained* (Cornell University Press: Ithaca, 2002)

Constantinesco, V, 'The ECJ as a Law-Maker: Praeter aut Contra Legem?' in D O'Keeffe (ed), *Judicial Review in European Union Law: Liber Amicorum in Honour of Lord Slynn of Hadley* (Kluwer: London, 2000)

Costello, C, 'The Bosphorus Ruling of the ECHR: Fundamental Rights and Blurry Boundaries in Europe' (2006) 6 EHRLRev 87

Craig, P, 'Legality, Standing and Substantive Review in Community Law' (1994) 14 OJLS 507

____ 'Formal and Substantive Conceptions of the Rule of Law: An Analytical Framework' [1997] PL 467

____ *EU Administrative Law* (OUP: Oxford, 2006)

____ and G de Búrca, *EU Law: Text, Cases and Materials* (4th edn, OUP: Oxford, 2003)

Cremona, M, 'A Constitutional Basis for Effective External Action? An Assessment of the Provisions on EU External Action in the Constitutional Treaty' (2006) 30 EUI Working Paper http://cadmus.eui.eu/dspace/handle/1814/6293 (accessed March 2009)

____ 'Case C-403/05, European Parliament v Commission (Philippines Border Management Project), Judgment of the Grand Chamber of 23 October 2007 [2007] ECR I-9045' (2008) 45 CML Rev 1727

____ 'Coherence through Law: What difference will the Treaty of Lisbon make?' (2008) 3 Hamburg Rev of Social Sciences 11

_____ F Francioni, and S Poli, 'Challenging EU Counter-Terrorism Measures through the Courts' EUI Working Paper (forthcoming)

Cullen, H, and A Charlesworth, 'Diplomacy by other Means: The Use of Legal Basis Litigation as a Political Strategy by the European Parliament and Member States' (1999) 36 CML Rev 1234

Dashwood, A, 'The Law and Practice of CFSP Joint Actions' in M Cremona and B de Witte (eds), *EU Foreign Relations Law: Constitutional Fundamentals* (Hart: Oxford, 2008)

_____ and C Hillion (eds), *The General Law of EC External Relations* (Sweet & Maxwell: Oxford, 2000)

_____ and A Johnston, 'Synthesis of the Debate' in A Dashwood and A Johnston (eds), *The Future of the Judicial System of the European Union* (Hart: Oxford, 2001)

Dawes, A, and O Lynskey, 'The Ever-longer Arm of EC Law: The Extension of Community Competence into the Field of Criminal Law' (2008) 45 CML Rev 131

De Hert, P, C Riehle, and V Papakonstantinou, 'Data Protection in the Third Pillar: Cautious Pessimism' in M Martin Crime (ed), *Rights and the EU: The Future of Police and Judicial Cooperation* (Justice: London, 2008)

Denza, E, *The Intergovernmental Pillars of the European Union* (OUP: Oxford, 2002)

_____ 'Common Foreign Policy and Single Foreign Policy' in T Tridimas and P Nebbia (eds), *European Union Law for the Twenty-First Century: Rethinking the New Legal Order* (Hart: Oxford, 2004)

De Witte, B, 'Direct Effect, Supremacy and the Nature of the Legal Order' in P Craig and G De Búrca (eds), *The Evolution of EU Law* (OUP: Oxford, 1999)

Dicey, A, *The Law of the Constitution* (10th edn, Macmillan: London, 1959)

Dickson, B, *Introduction to French Law* (Pitman Publishing: London, 1994)

Dougan, M, 'When Worlds Collide: Relationship between Direct Effect and Supremacy' (2007) 44 CML Rev 931

_____ 'The Treaty of Lisbon 2007: Winning Minds, Not Hearts' (2008) 45 CML Rev 617

Douglas-Scott, S, 'The Rule of Law in the European Union: Putting the Security into the EU's Area of Freedom Security and Justice' (2004) 29 ELR 219

_____ 'A Tale of Two Courts: Luxembourg, Strasbourg and the Growing European Human Rights Acquis' (2006) 43 CML Rev 619

_____ 'Bosphorus Hava Youllari Turizm Ve Ticaret Anonim Sirketi v Ireland' (2006) 43 CML Rev 243

Dworkin, R, *Taking Rights Seriously* (Harvard University Press: Boston, 1977)

_____ *A Matter of Principle* (Clarendon Press: Oxford, 1986)

Eckes, C, 'Annotation to Case T-228/02, Organisation des Modjahedines du Peuple d'Iran v. Council and UK (OMPI), Judgment of the Court of First Instance (Second Chamber) of 12 December 2006' (2007) 44 CML Rev 1117

_____ 'Sanctions against Individuals: Fighting Terrorism within the European Legal Order' (2008) 4 EuConst 205

Editorial, 'The CFSP under the EU Constitutional Treaty: Issues of Depillarization' (2005) 42 CML Rev 325

Editorial, 'The Rule of Law as the Backbone of the EU' (2007) 44 CML Rev 875

Editorial, (2008) 45 CML Rev 1571

Eeckhout, P, 'The European Court of Justice and the "Area of Freedom, Security and Justice": Challenges and Problems' in D O'Keeffe (ed), *Judicial Review in European Union Law: Liber Amicorum in Honour of Lord Slynn of Hadley* (Kluwer: London, 2000)

―――― *External Relations of the European Union: Legal and Constitutional Foundations* (OUP: Oxford, 2004)

――――'Community Terrorism Listings, Fundamental Rights, and UN Security Council Resolutions: In Search of the Right Fit' (2007) 3 EuConst 183

Eleftheriadis, P, 'The Direct Effect of Community Law: Conceptual Issues' (1996) 16 YEL 205

Ely, JH, *Democracy and Distrust: A Theory of Judicial Review* (Harvard University Press: Cambridge, 1981)

Evans, A, 'The Enforcement Procedure of Article 169 EEC: Commission's Discretion' (1979) 4 ELR 442

Everling, U, 'On the Judge-Made Law of the European Community's Courts' in D O'Keeffe (ed), *Judicial Review in European Union Law: Liber Amicorum in Honour of Lord Slynn of Hadley* (Kluwer: London, 2000)

Fallon, R, 'The Core of an Uneasy Case for Judicial Review' (2008) 121 Harvard LR 1693

Favoreu, L, 'Le Droit Constitutionnel, Droit de la Constitution et Constitution du Droit' (1990) 1 Revue Française de Droit Constitutionnel 71

Fennelly, N, 'The "Area of Freedom, Security and Justice" and the European Court of Justice: A Personal View' (2000) 49 ICLQ 1

Ferejohn, J, and P Pasquino, 'Constitutional Adjudication: Lessons from Europe' (2004) 82 Texas L Rev 1671

Ferreres Comella, V, 'The Consequences of Centralizing Constitutional Review in a Special Court: Some Thoughts on Judicial Activism' (2004) 82 Texas L Rev 1705

―――― 'The European Model of Constitutional Review of Legislation: Toward Decentralization?' (2004) 2 I-CON 461

Figueroa Regueiro, P, 'Invocability of Substitution and Invocability of Exclusion: Bringing Legal Realism to the Current Development of the Case-Law of Horizontal Direct Effect of Directives' (2002) Jean Monnet Working Paper 7/02 www.jeanmonnetprogram.org/papers/02/020701.pdf (accessed Jan 2007)

Fijnaut, C, 'Police Co-operation and the Area of Freedom, Security and Justice' in N Walker (ed), *Europe's Area of Freedom, Security and Justice* (OUP: Oxford, 2004)

Fiss, O, 'The Perils of Minimalism' (2008) 9 Theoretical Inquiries 643

Fletcher, M, 'Extending "Indirect Effect" to the Third Pillar: The Significance of Pupino' (2005) 30 ELR 862

Franck, T, *Political Questions/Judicial Answers: Should the Rule of Law Apply to Foreign Affairs?* (Princeton University Press: Princeton, 1992)

Fröwein, J, 'Solange II' (1988) 25 CML Rev 201

Gaja, G, 'Constitutional Court (Italy) Decision No. 170 of 8 June 1984, S.p.a. granital v Amministrazione delle Finanze dello Stato' (1984) 21 CML Rev 756

Garbagnati-Ketvel, MG, 'The Jurisdiction of the European Court of Justice in Respect of the Common Foreign and Security Policy' (2006) 55 ICLQ 77

Garlicki, L, 'Cooperation of Courts: The Role of Supranational Jurisdictions in Europe' (2008) 6 I-CON 509

Gattini, A, 'Annotation: Joined Cases C-402/05 P & 415/05 P, Yassin Abdullah Kadi, Al Barakaat International Foundation v Council and Commission, judgment of the Grand Chamber 2008, nyr' (2009) 46 CML Rev 213

Grief, N, 'EU Law and Security' (2007) 32 ELR 752

Griller, S, 'International Law, Human Rights and the European Community's Autonomous Legal Order: Notes on the European Court of Justice Decision in Kadi' (2008) 4 EuConst 528

Groenendijk, K, 'Reinstatement of Controls at Internal Borders: Why and against Whom?' (2004) 10 ELJ 150

Guild, E, 'The Constitutional Consequences of Lawmaking in the Third Pillar of the European Union' in P Craig and C Harlow (eds), *Lawmaking in the European Union* (Kluwer: London, 1998)

____ and S Peers, 'Deference or Defiance? The Court of Justice's Jurisdiction over Immigration and Asylum' in E Guild and C Harlow (eds), *Implementing Amsterdam* (Hart: Oxford, 2001)

Habermas, J, *Faktizität und Geltung: Beiträge zur Diskurstheorie des Rechts und des demokratischen Rechtsstaates* (Suhrkamp: Frankfurt am Main, 1992)

Hailbronner, K, 'European Immigration and Asylum Law under the Amsterdam Treaty' (1998) 35 CML Rev 1047

Halberstam, D, 'Comparative Federalism and the Role of the Judiciary' in KE Wittington, RD Kelemen, and GA Caldeira (eds), *The Oxford Handbook of Law and Politics* (OUP: Oxford, 2008)

____ and E Stein, 'The United Nations, the European Union, and the King of Sweden: Economic Sanctions and Individual Rights in a Plural World Order' (2009) 46 CML Rev 13

Harpaz, G, 'The European Court of Justice and its Relations with the European Court of Human Rights: The Quest for Enhanced Reliance, Coherence and Legitimacy' (2009) 46 CML Rev 105

Hartley, T, 'The European Court, Judicial Objectivity and the Constitution of the European Union' (1996) 112 LQR 95

Hayes, B, 'The Future of Europol: More Powers, Less Regulation, Precious Little Debate' (Statewatch Analysis 2006) <http://www.statewatch.org/news/2006/oct/future-of-europol-analysis.pdf> (accessed Nov 2006)

Hedemann-Robinson, M, 'Article 173 EC, General Community Measures and Locus Standi for Private Persons: Still a Cause for Individual Concern?' (1996) 2 Eur PL 127

Heliskoski, J, 'Small Arms and Light Weapons within the Union's Pillar Structure: An Analysis of Article 47 of the EU Treaty' (2008) 33 ELR 898

Henkin, L, 'Is there a "Political Question" Doctrine?' (1976) 85 Yale LJ 597
____ *Foreign Affairs and the United States Constitution* (Clarendon: Oxford, 1996)

Herlin-Karnell, E, 'Commission v Council: Some Reflections on Criminal Law in the First Pillar' (2007) 13 Eur PL 69

Hermann, C, 'The Unity of the Legal Order Revisited' in M Cremona and B de Witte (eds), *EU Foreign Relations Law: Constitutional Fundamentals* (Hart: Oxford, 2008)

Herzog, R, and L Gerken, 'Stop the European Court of Justice' <http://www.cep.eu/678.html?&L=1> (accessed Jan 2009)

Hillion, C, and R Wessel, 'Restraining External Competences of EU Member States under CFSP' in M Cremona and B de Witte (eds), *EU Foreign Relations Law: Constitutional Fundamentals* (Hart: Oxford, 2008)
____ and T Downes, 'Making Sense of Rights: Community Rights in EC Law' (2009) 24 ELR 121

Hinarejos, A (2006) 43 CML Rev 583
____ 'Bosphorus v Ireland and the Protection of Fundamental Rights in Europe' (2006) 31 ELR 251
____ 'Judicial Control of CFSP in the Constitution: A Cherry Worth Picking?' (2006) 25 YEL 363
____ 'Recent Human Rights Developments in the EU Courts: The Charter of Fundamental Rights, the European Arrest Warrant and Terror Lists' (2007) 7 HRLRev 793
____ 'On the Legal Effects of Third Pillar Measures: Directly Applicable, Directly Effective, Self-Executing, Supreme?' (2008) 14 ELJ 620
____ 'The Lisbon Treaty versus Standing Still: A View from the Third Pillar' (2009) 5 EuConst 99

Hirschl, R, *Towards Juristocracy: The Origins and Consequences of the New Constitutionalism* (Harvard University Press: Cambridge, 2004)

House of Lords, EU Committee, 'The Future Role of the European Court of Justice: Report with Evidence' (6th Report of Session 2003–4, HL Paper 47)
____ 'Judicial Co-operation in the European Union: The Role of Eurojust. Report with Evidence' (23rd Report of Session 2003–4, HL Paper 138)
____ 'The Constitutional Treaty: Role of the ECJ: Primacy of Union Law—Government Response and Correspondence' (3rd Report of Session 2005–6, HL Paper 15)
____ 'The Criminal Law Competence of the European Community: Report with Evidence' (42nd Report of Session 2005–6, HL Paper 227)

Jacobs, F, 'Is the Court of Justice of the European Communities a Constitutional Court?' in D Curtin and D O'Keeffe (eds), *Constitutional Adjudication in European Community and National Law* (Butterworths: Dublin, 1992)

____ 'Human Rights in the European Union: The Role of the Court of Justice' (2001) 26 ELR 331

____ and S Roberts (eds), *The Effects of Treaties in Domestic Law* (Sweet and Maxwell: London, 1987)

Kelemen, RD, *The Rules of Federalism: Institutions and Regulatory Politics in the EU and Beyond* (Cambridge University Press: Cambridge, 2004)

Kelsen, H, 'Judicial Review of Legislation: A Comparative Study of the Austrian and American Constitution' (1942) 4 The Journal of Politics 183

____ 'La Garantie juridictionnelle de la Constitution' (1928) 44 Revue du Droit Public 197

Komárek, J, 'European Constitutionalism and the European Arrest Warrant: In Search of the Limits of "Contrapunctual Principles" ' (2007) 44 CML Rev 9

Koskenniemi, M, 'International Law Aspects of the Common Foreign and Security Policy' in M Koskenniemi (ed), *International Law Aspects of the European Union* (Kluber Law International: The Hague, 1998)

Koutrakos, P, 'How Far is Far Enough? EC Law and the Organisation of the Armed Forces after Dory' (2003) 66 MLR 759

____ *EU International Relations Law* (Hart: Oxford, 2006)

____ 'Development and Foreign Policy: Where to Draw the Line between the Pillars?' (2008) 33 ELR 289

____ 'Speeding up the Preliminary Reference Procedure: Fast but not too Fast' (2008) 33 ELR 617

____ 'Legal Basis and Delimitation of Competences' in M Cremona and B de Witte (eds), *EU Foreign Relations Law: Constitutional Fundamentals* (Hart: Oxford, 2008)

Kuijper, P, 'The Evolution of the Third Pillar from Maastricht to the European Constitution: Institutional Aspects' (2004) 41 CML Rev 609

Kumm, M, 'Why Europeans Will Not Embrace Constitutional Patriotism' (2008) 6 I-CON 117

Kunoy, B, and A Dawes, 'Plate Tectonics in Luxembourg: The Ménage à Trois between EC Law, International Law and the European Convention on Human Rights Following the UN Sanctions Cases' (2009) 46 CML Rev 73

Laws, J, 'Law and Democracy' [1995] PL 72

Lazowski, A, 'Constitutional Tribunal on the Surrender of Polish Citizens under the European Arrest Warrant: Decision of 27 April 2005' (2005) 1 EuConst 569

____ 'From EU with Trust: The Potential and Limits of the Mutual Recognition in the Third Pillar from the Polish Perspective' in G Vernimmen-Van Tiggelen L Surano, and A Weyembergh (eds), *The Future of Mutual Recognition in Criminal Matters in the European Union/L'Avenir de la reconnaissance mutuelle en matière pénale dans l'Union Européenne* (Éditions de l'Université de Bruxelles: Brussels, 2009)

Leczykiewicz, D, (2006) 43 CML Rev 1181
_____ 'Constitutional Conflicts and the Third Pillar' 33 (2008) ELR 230.
Lenaerts, K, 'The Rule of Law and the Coherence of the Judicial System of the European Union' (2007) 44 CML Rev 1625
_____ and T Corthaut, 'Of Birds and Hedges: The Role of Primacy in Invoking Norms of EU Law' (2006) 31 ELR 287
_____ and P Van Nuffel, *Constitutional Law of the European Union* (2nd edn, Sweet & Maxwell: London, 2005)
Lenz, M, D Sif Tynes, and L Young, 'Horizontal What? Back to Basics' (2000) 25 ELR 509
Maduro - *see* Poiares Maduro.
Mitsilegas, V, 'Border Security in the European Union: Towards Centralized Controls and Maximum Surveillance' in E Guild and F Geyer (eds), *Security versus Justice? Police and Judicial Cooperation in the European Union* (Ashgate: Aldershot, 2008)
Monar, J, 'Justice and Home Affairs in the Treaty of Amsterdam: Reform at the Price of Fragmentation' (1998) 23 ELR 320
_____ 'Alternatives to the Community Method in EU Justice and Home Affairs' (CONNEX 2007) http://www.portedeurope.org/IMG/doc/Jorg_Monar.doc (accessed March 2009).
Mueller, JW, *Constitutional Patriotism* (Princeton University Press: Princeton, 2008)
Neill, P, *The European Court of Justice: A Case Study in Judicial Activism* (European Policy Forum: London, 1995)
Nettesheim, M, 'UN Sanctions against Individuals: A Challenge to the Architecture of European Union Governance' (2007) 44 CML Rev 567
Nihoul, P, 'La Recevabilité des recours en annulation introduits par un particulier à l'encontre d'un acte communautaire de portée générale' (1994) 30 Revue Trimestrielle de Droit Européen 171
O'Keeffe, D, 'Recasting the Third Pillar' (1995) 32 CML Rev 893
Oliveira, A, 'Annotation to Case C170/96, Commission of the European Communities v Council of the European Union, judgment of 12 May 1998, [1998] ECR I-2763' (1999) 99 CML Rev 149
Orakeshevili, A, *Peremptory Norms in International Law* (OUP: Oxford, 2006)
Peers, S, 'National Security and European Law' (1996) 16 YEL 363
_____ 'Who's Judging the Watchmen: The Judicial System of the "Area of Freedom, Security and Justice"' (1998) 17 YEL 337
_____ *EU Justice and Home Affairs Law* (OUP: Oxford, 2006)
_____ 'Transferring the Third Pillar' (Statewatch Analysis 2006) http://www.statewatch.org/news/2006/may/analysis-3rd-pill-transfer-may-2006.pdf (accessed August 2006)
_____ 'Salvation outside the Church: Judicial Protection in the Third Pillar after the Pupino and Segi Judgments' (2007) 44 CML Rev 885

_____ 'The Jurisdiction of the Court of Justice over EC Immigration and Asylum Law: Time for a Change?' in H Toner, E Guild, and A Baldaccini (eds), *Whose Freedom, Security and Justice? EU Immigration and Asylum Law and Policy* (Hart: Oxford, 2007)

_____ 'The European Community's Criminal Law Competence: The Plot Thickens' (2008) 33 ELR 399

Pernice, I, 'Die Dritte Gewalt im europäischen Verfassungsverbund' (1996) 31 Europarecht 27

Peters, A, 'The Bananas Decision 2000 of the German Federal Constitutional Court: Towards Reconciliation with the ECJ as regards Fundamental Rights Protection in Europe' (2000) 43 German Yearbook of International Law 276

Petersmann, E, 'Act of State Doctrine, Political Question Doctrine und gerichtliche Kontrolle der auswärtigen Gewalt' (1976) 25 Jahrbuch des öffentlichen Rechts der Gegenwart NF 587

Poiares Maduro, M, 'Europe and the Constitution: What if this is as Good as it Gets?' Constitutionalism Web-Papers, University of Bath: www.bath.ac.uk/esml/conWEB/Conweb%20papers-filestore/conweb5-2000.pdf (accessed August 2009).

Prechal, S, 'Does Direct Effect Still Matter?' (2000) 37 CML Rev 1047

_____ *Directives in EC Law* (2nd edn, OUP: Oxford, 2005)

_____ 'Direct Effect, Indirect Effect, Supremacy and the Evolving Constitution of the European Union' in C Barnard (ed), *The Fundamentals of EU Law Revisited* (OUP: Oxford, 2007)

Puntscher Riekmann, S, 'Security, Freedom and Accountability: Europol & Frontex' in E Guild and F Geyer (eds), *Security versus Justice? Police and Judicial Cooperation in the European Union* (Ashgate: Aldershot, 2008)

Ragolle, F, 'Access to Justice for Private Applicants in the Community Legal Order: Recent (R)evolutions' (2003) 28 ELR 90

Rasmussen, H, *On Law and Policy in the European Court of Justice* (Martinus Nijhoff: Dordrecht, 1986)

_____ *The European Court of Justice* (GadJura: Copenhagen, 1993)

Raz, J, 'The Rule of Law and its Virtue' (1977) 93 LQR 195

Rosenfeld, M, 'Constitutional Adjudication in Europe and the United States: Paradoxes and Contrasts' (2004) 2 I-CON 633

_____ 'Comparing Constitutional Review by the European Court of Justice and the US Supreme Court' (2006) 4 I-CON 618

Ross, M, 'Effectiveness in the European Legal Order(s): Beyond Supremacy to Constitutional Proportionality' (2006) 31 ELR 476

Sadurski, W, *Rights before Courts: A Study of Constitutional Courts in Postcommunist Countries in Central and Eastern Europe* (Springer: Dordrecht, 2005)

Schermers, H, and C Swaak, 'Official Acts of Community Servants and Article 215(4) EC' in T Heukels and A McDonnell (eds), *The Action for Damages in Community Law* (Kluwer: The Hague, 1997)

Schwarze, J (ed), *The Birth of a European Constitutional Order: The Interaction of National and European Constitutional Law* (Nomos: Baden-Baden, 2000)

Schweitzer, M, *Staatsrecht III* (8th edn, CF Müller Verlag: Heidelberg, 2004)

Shapiro, M, *Courts: A Comparative and Political Analysis* (University of Chicago Press: Chicago, 1981)

____ 'The European Court of Justice' in P Craig and G De Búrca (eds), *The Evolution of EU Law* (OUP: Oxford, 1999)

____ and A Stone, 'Introduction: The New Constitutional Politics' (1994) 26 Comparative Political Studies 397

Simpson, G, 'Asylum and Immigration in the European Union after the Treaty of Amsterdam' (1999) 5 Eur PL 91

Skouris, V, 'The Position of the European Court of Justice in the EU Legal Order and its Relationship with National Constitutional Courts' (2005) 60 Zeitschrift für Öffentliches Recht 323

Slaughter, A-M, AS Sweet, and JHH Weiler (eds), *The European Courts and National Courts: Doctrine and Jurisprudence* (Hart: Oxford, 1998)

Spaventa, E, 'Remembrance of Principles Lost: On Fundamental Rights, the Third Pillar and the Scope of Union Law' (2006) 25 YEL 153

____ 'Opening Pandora's Box: Some Reflections on the Constitutional Effects of the Decision in Pupino' (2007) 3 EuConst 5

____ 'Fundamental What? The Difficult Relationship between Foreign Policy and Fundamental Rights' in M Cremona and B de Witte (eds), *EU Foreign Relations Law: Constitutional Fundamentals* (Hart: Oxford, 2008)

Spencer, J, 'The European Arrest Warrant' (2004) 6 Cambridge Ybk of European Legal Studies 201

____ 'Child Witnesses and the European Union' (2005) 64 CLJ 569

Spencer, M, *States of Injustice: A Guide to Human Rights and Civil Liberties in the European Union* (Pluto: London, 1995)

Sternberger, D, *Verfassungspatriotismus* (Insel: Frankfurt am Main, 1990)

Stone, A, 'Judicial Review without Rights: Some Problems for the Democratic Legitimacy of Structural Judicial Review' (2008) 28 OJLS 1

Stone-Sweet, A, *Governing with Judges* (OUP: Oxford, 2000)

Sunstein, C, 'Incompletely Theorized Agreements' (1995) 108 Harvard LR 1733

____ *One Case at a Time: Judicial Minimalism on the Supreme Court* (Harvard University Press: Cambridge, 1999)

Thym, D, 'The Schengen Law: A Challenge for Legal Accountability in the European Union' (2002) 8 ELJ 218

Timmermans, C, 'The Constitutionalisation of the European Union' (2002) 21 YEL 1

Tobler, C, 'Annotation to Case C-176/03, Commission v Council, judgment of the Grand Chamber of 13 September 2005, nyr' (2006) 43 CML Rev 835

Tomuschat, C, 'Annotation to Yusuf and Kadi' (2007) 43 CML Rev 537

Treanor, WM, 'Judicial Review before Marbury' (2005) 58 Stanford L Rev 455

Tridimas, T, 'The Court of Justice and Judicial Activism' (1997) 2 ELR 199

_____ 'Black, White and Shades of Grey: Horizontality of Directives Revisited' (2002) 21 YEL 327

_____ 'The European Court of Justice and the Draft Constitution: A Supreme Court for the Union?' in T Tridimas and P Nebbia (eds), *European Union Law for the Twenty-First Century: Rethinking the New Legal Order* (Hart: Oxford, 2004)

_____ *The General Principles of EU Law* (2nd edn, OUP: Oxford, 2006)

_____ and JA Gutierrez-Fons, 'EU Law, International Law, and Economic Sanctions against Terrorism: The Judiciary in Distress?' (2009) 32 Fordham Int LJ 660

Tushnet, M, *Taking the Constitution away from the Courts* (Princeton University Press: Princeton, 1999)

Ukrow, J, *Richterliche Rechstfortbildung durch den EuGH* (Nomos: Baden-Baden, 1995)

Unger, R, *Law in Modern Society: Toward a Criticism of Social Theory* (Free Press: New York, 1976)

Usher, JA, 'Direct and Individual Concern: An Effective Remedy or a Conventional Solution?' (2003) 28 ELR 575

Van den Wyngaert, C, 'Eurojust and the European Public Prosecutor' in N Walker (ed), *Europe's Area of Freedom, Security and Justice* (OUP: Oxford, 2004)

Van Ooik, R, 'Cross-Pillar Litigation before the ECJ: Demarcation of Community and Union Competences' (2008) 4 EuConst 399

Von Mehren, AT, and PL Murray, *Law in the United States* (2nd edn, Cambridge University Press: Cambridge, 2007)

Waldron, J, 'The Core of the Case against Judicial Review' (2006) Yale L J 1346

Ward, A, 'Access to Justice' in S Peers and A Ward (eds), *The EU Charter of Fundamental Rights* (Hart: Oxford, 2004)

_____ *Judicial Review and the Rights of Private Parties in EU Law* (OUP: Oxford, 2007)

Weatherill, S, 'Activism and Restraint in the European Court of Justice' in P Capps, M Evans, and S Konstadinidis (eds), *Asserting Jurisdiction: International and European Legal Perspectives* (Hart: Oxford, 2003)

_____ *Cases and Materials on EU Law* (8th edn, OUP: Oxford, 2007)

Weiler, JHH, 'Fundamental Rights and Fundamental Boundaries: On Standards and Values in the Protection of Human Rights' in N Neuwahl and A Rosas (eds), *The European Union and Human Rights* (Martinus Nijhoff Publishers: The Hague, 1995)

_____ and UR Haltern, 'Constitutional or International? The Foundations of the Community Legal Order and the Question of Judicial Kompetenz-Kompetenz' in A-M Slaughter, A Sweet, and JHH Weiler (eds), *The European Courts and National Courts: Doctrine and Jurisprudence* (Hart: Oxford, 1998)

Winter, J, 'Direct Applicability and Direct Effect: Two Distinct and Different Concepts in Community Law' (1972) 9 CML Rev 425

Wolfrum, R, 'Kontrolle der auswärtigen Gewalt' (1997) 56 Veröffentlichungen der Vereinigung der Deutschen Staatsrechtslehrer 38

Wyatt, D, and A Dashwood (eds), *European Union Law* (5th edn, Sweet & Maxwell: London, 2006)

Zeitler, FC, 'Judicial Review und Judicial Restraint gegenüber der auswärtigen Gewalt' (1976) 25 Jahrbuch des öffentlichen Rechts der Gegenwart NF 621

Ziegler, K, 'Strengthening the Rule of Law, but Fragmenting International Law: The Kadi Decision of the ECJ from the Perspective of Human Rights' (2009) HRLRev 288.

INDEX